Decide, Now

A Guide to Mastering Abundance and Fulfillment

By: Julia Young Sandrock

Decide, Now: A Guide to Mastering Abundance and Fulfillment

ISBN's
eBook - 978-1-960346-89-6
Paperback - 978-1-960346-90-2
Hardback - 978-1-960346-91-9

Table of Contents

Dedication

To all the courageous souls entering a journey of introspection, self-growth and evolution, this guidebook is your trusted companion. Dedicated to the brave hearts determined to unearth the profound beauty, purity and authenticity that our Universe holds. Your pursuit of self-discovery, commitment to honoring your essence and resolve to stay true to yourself amidst external influences are testaments to your extraordinary courage and resilience. May this guide shine as a light, gently leading your every step and uplifting your spirit as you explore the depths of your true self. Thank you for your steadfast dedication to the transformative and gorgeous journey ahead.

♥ Julia

Epigraph

Abundance is not something you chase; it is something you choose.

-Julia Young Sandrock

Foreword

Many of us move through life on autopilot, reacting to circumstances instead of shaping them. We live in an age where stress, uncertainty and burnout feel almost universal. At the same time, many of us feel a pull toward something deeper: a search for meaning and for purpose. More than ever before, we are asking ourselves: *Why am I here? Who am I? What is my purpose? How can I create a life filled with abundance?* These questions, timeless and universal, transcend age, culture and history. Yet, in today's world, saturated with information, endless perspectives on social media and knowledge always at our fingertips, it is easy to forget the most important voice: our own. We search for answers outside ourselves. When seeking truth, clarity begins from within.

Decide, Now takes you on an incredible journey of deep insight, introspection, integration and evolution. While Julia shares her wisdom, she guides you toward the most important step of all: turning inward. Through *Decide, Now,* it feels as if Julia takes your hand, holds it, and walks with you through a transformational process, helping you break free from limitations and create your most abundant life. Julia Sandrock, a life and wellness coach, expert on the mind-body-soul connection, and advocate of holistic wellness, has a passion for supporting others in reaching their fullest potential. She has empowered people worldwide through her writings, workshops and one-on-one coaching, teaching mindfulness, guiding individuals to harness their thoughts, beliefs and intentions, and leading them toward a genuinely fulfilling life. Her frameworks have helped many step into abundance, a theme that is reflected throughout *Decide, Now.*

When Julia first reached out to me to read her manuscript, I was honored. I already had some understanding of these topics through my own spiritual journey, but Julia's words and insights lifted me to an entirely new level. Once again, I was confronted with questions and concepts I had not yet asked myself. Revealing to me a much deeper way of being and thinking. From the very beginning, I was struck by Julia's curiosity and the depth of her thinking. Our conversations often wandered through life, choices and our personal journeys. I always came away inspired. Something I truly admired was when she told me that, before and during the writing of *Decide, Now*, she had asked herself and those around her, deep, soul-stirring questions about abundance, fulfillment, joy and universal values. She took those reflections and wove them together to create the core principles that are discussed throughout this book.

The central concept of *Decide, Now* is abundance, which can be a difficult concept to grasp. A common misconception is that it is something we must search for, but thinking this way assumes abundance exists outside of us, when in truth, it comes from within. In *Decide, Now*, Julia reminds us that creating your most abundant life begins with a choice. Every day, we make countless decisions, yet most of them are automatic and subconscious. From the small, *What will I wear today?* to the life-defining, *What is my next step?* or *Who do I choose as my life partner?* our lives are shaped by the choices we make, both big and small. Yet, too often, we forget the choices that matter most. We chase, we work, we follow expectations, overlooking that abundance, creating our dream life, and knowing ourselves more deeply are all choices too. By simply picking up this book, you have already begun to make that choice, so congratulations! In *Decide, Now*, Julia takes you even further, helping you reflect, ask new questions and make the decisions that lead to a truly intentional, fulfilling and abundant life.

To Julia, I extend my deepest gratitude for your dedication to writing this book; it has transformed my life in many ways. To the readers, you are stepping into a transformative journey of self-discovery. My hope is that you approach these pages with an open mind, honesty about where you are on your journey, and curiosity about where you want to go. Most importantly, I hope you remember that life is not merely something that happens to you—it is something you shape, something you *create.*

-Isabelle Marguerite, Founder of The Mindful Journal, Writer, Speaker

Prelude

Every abundant life begins with a *powerful decision*: to embrace insights, introspection, integration and evolution as your greatest allies. Imagine stepping into a life where abundance is not merely material wealth, but a deep, lasting sense of purpose and joy. Within these pages lies a roadmap to transform your life from ordinary to extraordinary, a guide to breaking free from limitations and tapping into an endless source of abundance and fulfillment like never before. By deeply understanding your true self and your place within the greater collective, you reveal the path to genuine fulfillment. The question is: *Are you ready to make the life-changing commitment to* ***decide, now*** *and leap into a new reality?*

PREFACE

To My Precious Readers – Many of us have navigated periods of uncertainty and disconnection, grappling with external pressures that silence our inner voice. For countless souls, life's journey has been sidetracked by pursuits dictated by society's outdated values, leading us away from our authentic selves and core beliefs. The challenge lies in discerning our essence amidst the loud noise of external influences. It is all too common to become entangled in societal definitions of success, fulfillment and purpose. Our inner voices often get overshadowed, leaving us feeling adrift, unfulfilled and detached from genuine self-awareness and consciousness. Many of us have experienced moments when we felt trapped by unrecognized constraints, leading to a sense of displacement from our purest identity. Yet, within these shared experiences lies a profound realization: *the journey toward reclaiming authenticity, abundance and fulfillment often requires confronting vulnerabilities, transcending societal norms and conditioning and pursuing a transformative path of self-discovery.*

As you step boldly into this journey, may the insights you discover lead the way to rediscover, realign and embrace the essence of your authentic self, empowering you to navigate life's complexities with clarity, purpose and resilience. *Yearning for personal enlightenment?* This book holds the wisdom you need. Within its pages, you will discover powerful insights, invitations for deep introspection and practical tools to help you integrate the knowledge you gather along the way, offering a unique opportunity to explore your essence and cultivate a profound sense of abundance and fulfillment. Each chapter fosters a deeper connection with yourself, offering self-awareness and self-empowerment. Indeed, *there is no gift more invaluable than strengthening the bond between yourself and your soul.*

This guidebook is a heartfelt testament, a literary offering crafted expressly for you, the resilient, audacious soul traveling the realms of inner awakening, consciousness and transformation. May the words within these pages resonate deeply with you, offering the freedom to extract wisdom from a single passage, a fleeting paragraph or the intricate network of principles interwoven throughout. With each page, may you be invigorated with the conviction to clearly define and pursue a life rich with purpose, seizing the destiny that speaks to your inner spirit and honoring your sacred mission and calling. *May you realize, today and always, that you have everything within you to* ***decide, now*** *to live a life of unadulterated abundance and fulfillment.*

How to Navigate This Guidebook

This guidebook is designed to be a sacred companion on your journey of awakening, transformation and evolution. It is a living invitation, an offering to yourself, to engage deeply, tenderly and without judgment. While it follows a natural progression, there is no single "correct" way to move through its pages. Trust your intuition and let this guide meet you where you are.

There Is No Set Order

Although it is recommended to begin at the start and move through the journey in sequence, you are welcome to begin with any chapter or concept that speaks to you. If something resonates with where you are now, start there. You can always return to the beginning later. Each chapter is a doorway; open the one that feels ready for you.

You Can Bounce Around

Each section contains insights and tools that stand on their own. You are encouraged to explore the guidebook in a way that suits your current needs, energy or questions. Let it adapt to you rather than forcing yourself to adapt to it.

Introspection Can Wait

The introspection prompts are designed to deepen your understanding and growth. You do not need to complete them in a single sitting. Sometimes reflection happens in the moment, and other times it emerges days, weeks or months later. Give yourself grace to absorb the reflections and return when you are ready.

Integration Is Ongoing

The Integration sections offer practices and tools to support lasting transformation. They are not a checklist but a living resource, one to revisit repeatedly as your path unfolds. Integration is a continuous process, and your relationship with these tools will deepen over time.

Take Your Time

The concepts within these pages are rich and layered. This is not a guidebook to be rushed; it is meant to be savored. Let your reading be like sipping a fine tea. Move at your own pace, linger over passages that speak to your heart, and allow the wisdom to settle in its own time.

Engage as a Gift to Yourself

Approach *Decide, Now* as a sacred gift, to yourself, your growth and your truth. This is your space to explore who you were, who you are and who you wish to become. You are invited to engage in the work of self-discovery with openness, compassion and curiosity.

Curate Your Own Journey

This book is your safe space to curate, cultivate and become. Think of it as your private laboratory for transformation. Here you are free to experiment, reflect and expand, without fear or expectation.

Practices for Extra Support

At the end of this guidebook, you will find a dedicated section of powerful practices. These practices are here for you whenever you need additional support, whether you are moving through a challenging moment, seeking grounding or simply wishing to reconnect with yourself. Use them as your personal toolkit for alignment and balance.

Remember: This Is Yours

Decide, Now is a living relationship between you and your inner self. There is no "right" way to engage with it. Whether you approach it with deliberate intention or gentle curiosity, let it serve as a mirror, a teacher and a companion on your path.

...Above all, trust your intuition as you navigate these pages. This is your journey, and it will unfold exactly as it is meant to.

Abundance and Fulfillment: The Connection

Abundance and **fulfillment** are deeply connected themes, each nurturing the other to create a life rich with meaning and joy.

Abundance is more than material wealth; it is a state of being, a mindset rooted in the knowing that *there is always enough*: enough love, opportunity, growth and possibility. It begins with recognizing and appreciating what already exists in your life. From that place of gratitude, joy and openness, more naturally flows your way.

Fulfillment, on the other hand, is the deep contentment that comes from living in alignment with your values, beliefs, purpose and passions. It is the quiet peace of knowing you are aligned with what truly matters to you, when your outer world begins to reflect your inner truth.

These two states are inseparable.

Abundance fuels fulfillment. When you move through life with a sense of plenty, you feel free to follow your passions, take inspired risks and welcome new opportunities. This alignment with your core values and truth opens the door to genuine fulfillment.

Fulfillment expands abundance. When you live in alignment with your truth, you radiate joy, excitement and positive energy and that energy draws even more abundance into your life.

Together, abundance and fulfillment create a beautiful, virtuous cycle: abundance provides the resources and opportunities, while fulfillment ensures those resources are used in ways that bring real joy and meaning.

Consider the example of an artist.

They embody a state of abundance and hold a mindset that sees endless creative possibilities instead of competition or scarcity. Because of this openness, opportunities naturally come their way: gallery invitations, collaborations, commissions and access to the materials and connections that help them expand.

But what truly sustains them is fulfillment, the joy of creating art that feels authentic to their soul. They are not chasing trends; they are expressing truth. Each piece brings a sense of purpose and peace, and that inner joy continues to attract new opportunities for growth and connection.

When abundance and fulfillment work hand in hand, success becomes more than achievement; it becomes harmony. The artist's outer prosperity (abundance) and inner joy (fulfillment) reflect one another, forming a continuous flow of creativity, purpose and peace.

Ahead lies **The Fulfillment Framework™**, a practical yet soulful guide designed to support and empower you on your path toward deep, lasting abundance and fulfillment.

The Fulfillment Framework™

The Fulfillment Framework™

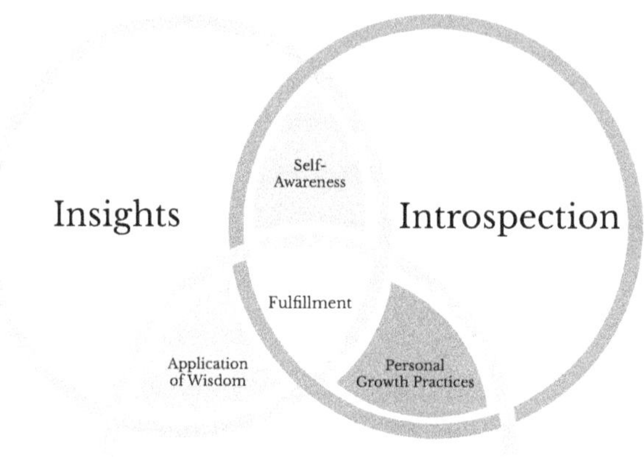

The Fulfillment Framework™ is a transformative and structured methodology designed to guide you toward intentional living, deep alignment and lasting abundance. It functions as a repeatable system designed to lead you from awareness to alignment to action, thereby transforming personal insight into meaningful and sustainable life outcomes.

The framework is organized into three interconnected and sequential stages, **Insights, Introspection** and **Integration**, which together form a cohesive system for growth and transformation. Each stage plays a critical role: **Insights** establish foundational knowledge and cognitive orientation, **Introspection** cultivates self-awareness, self-connection and alignment, and **Integration** translates awareness into sustainable action and embodiment.

Insights

Objective: To gather the wisdom and knowledge necessary for personal growth and transformation.

Purpose: Insights provide the foundational awareness needed to recognize core beliefs, values, purpose and goals. This stage expands perspective and creates clarity around direction and possibility.

Key Concepts:

> **Wisdom Acquisition**: Exploring core principles and concepts that inform intentional living and personal development.
>
> **Self-Awareness**: Strengthening awareness of internal patterns, external influences and behavioral tendencies.
>
> **Perspective Shift**: Challenging limiting beliefs and expanding perception to open pathways for growth.

Outcome: A strong and informed foundation that supports deeper reflection and intentional progression.

Introspection

Objective: To deeply examine how acquired insights apply to your identity, values and life circumstances.

Purpose: Introspection transforms knowledge into personal meaning through structured self-reflection and evaluation.

Key Concepts:

- **Self-Discovery**: Identifying core values, strengths, passions, talents, purpose and mission.
- **Personal Alignment**: Evaluating whether goals, decisions and behaviors reflect authentic identity and long-term vision.
- **Reflection**: Pausing intentionally to examine thoughts, emotions and patterns to gain clarity on necessary adjustments.

Outcome: A clear understanding of identity and purpose that establishes intentional alignment between internal awareness and external action.

Integration

Objective: To implement practical systems, habits and routines that sustain alignment and fulfillment.

Purpose: Integration ensures that insights and self-discoveries are translated into consistent behavior and lived experience.

Key Concepts:

- **Habit Formation**: Establishing daily practices that reinforce aligned values and goals.
- **Tools and Practices**: Applying structured exercises that support mental, emotional, physical and spiritual well-being.
- **Sustainability**: Building adaptable systems that support continuous growth and resilience through life changes.

Outcome: A balanced and fulfilling life characterized by intentional action, stability and ongoing development.

Framework Structure

The Fulfillment Framework™ is **not linear but cyclical.** You are encouraged to revisit **Insights**, refine **Introspection** and strengthen **Integration** over time.

This iterative design creates a built-in feedback loop that reinforces continuous learning, realignment and behavioral reinforcement. Through repeated engagement with its stages and ongoing refinement, the framework embeds alignment at a structural level, ensuring transformation becomes integrated and sustained over time.

In the spirit of *Decide, Now*, this guidebook invites you to make the powerful decision to embrace these components as the foundation of your journey. By engaging with this framework, you will first acquire the knowledge and **Insights** necessary for profound **Introspection** and learn to apply **Integration** practices that foster lasting abundance and fulfillment. By doing so, you will be postured to align your beliefs, values, goals and purpose with your daily actions. Your decision to fully commit to this process will be the key to elevating your life and realizing your fullest potential.

Introduction

Imagine a life pulsating with boundless abundance, unbridled joy and profound fulfillment. A gorgeous blend of prosperity, effortless grace and unmatched freedom, where the possibilities are endless, inviting limitless possibilities. Envision a realm where every aspiration and dream feels tantalizingly within grasp. What if this dimension, this exalted state of existence, was not a mere distant mirage but a tangible reality ripe for the taking, *here, now, today*? I challenge you to entertain this idea, to grasp the profound truth that such a life awaits your embrace: *Believe it, feel it, know it*. This is no unattainable fantasy. It is a tangible destiny awaiting your deliberate choice. *The gateway?* A life-changing decision to awaken your transformative power of abundance, integrating a clear, intentional approach that empowers you to master your mind, essence and energy and ultimately align your life with the flow of collective consciousness. This path demands more than mere aspiration. It calls for unwavering discipline, commitment and intentionality. If this tantalizing prospect stirs a flicker of intrigue within you, a whisper of possibility, then I strongly encourage you: ***surrender to an experience that can revolutionize your reality.***

In crafting this guidebook, the intent was neither lofty nor pretentious. I harbor no illusions of presenting an antidote to mend all tribulations or unveil a miraculous elixir for life's complexities. Rather, imagine these pages as a guide, revealing new paths to navigate life with renewed energy and perspective. Your journey transcends conventional paradigms, daring to challenge entrenched notions of what constitutes a life brimming with abundance and fulfillment. Whether you embrace or challenge the insights herein, my desire is to simply awaken the curiosity within you, to invite you toward unexplored horizons of possibility. Above all, my hope is for you to recognize this fundamental truth: *the pathway to abundance and fulfillment unfolds from a conscious decision, a deliberate choice echoing with immediacy*. As you walk your own path of self-discovery, growth and evolution, let this guidebook be a gift, an open invitation to nurture self-love, explore new layers of who you are and welcome the abundance that unfolds along the way.

Before moving forward, I want to share one more important note about how this guidebook is designed to support your journey. Throughout these pages, each chapter is structured around **The Fulfillment Framework™** of three elements: Insights, Introspection and Integration. Insights will provide cognitive orientation as we introduce core concepts and perspectives to expand your awareness. Introspection will invite you into reflective inquiry and self-connection, guiding you inward through prompts and questions. Integration will offer practical tools, practices and rituals to help you embody what you are learning in your daily life. **This rhythm will carry you through each of the four chapters.**

In the pages ahead, you will begin with the foundational insights of scarcity and abundance, two forces that shape perception, belief and experience. Understanding your relationship with these concepts will serve as a fundamental basis for everything that follows, empowering you to *consciously choose the reality you are cultivating.*

INSIGHTS — SCARCITY

Many concepts exist in duality: to truly understand one, we must also explore its counterpart. A deep exploration of abundance therefore begins with a clear view of its counterpart: **Scarcity**. At its essence, abundance is a state of boundless possibility, a flow of resources, opportunities and well-being unbound by the notion of lack. Scarcity, in contrast, describes both a condition and a mindset, a way of seeing the world shaped by the belief that resources are limited and opportunities are finite. Consider precious commodities like gold, silver and oil: as demand rises, accessibility often declines, casting scarcity in shades of limitation and inadequacy, language that carries low-vibrational energy, a theme we will explore more deeply later. This scarcity mindset quietly shapes perception, guiding thoughts, choices and actions. Its ripple extends far beyond the individual, influencing social behaviors and shaping how communities structure themselves.

More than a way of thinking, a scarcity mindset is a deeply ingrained pattern of perception that shapes how we experience the world. It is the belief that resources, opportunities and success are limited, where benefit for one means loss for another. This mindset casts life through a lens of competition and fear, narrowing vision and anchoring us in a sense of lack. It influences our choices, driving us to protect rather than expand and to cling rather than trust. Over time, scarcity thinking becomes a self-reinforcing cycle, shaping not only individual decisions but also collective behaviors, and ultimately limiting the possibility of true growth and shared prosperity. When we view resources as limited, our vision contracts and fear quietly steers our decisions. This leads to protective actions such as hoarding, competing, withdrawing, each reinforcing the belief that there is never enough. Left unexamined, this pattern becomes a self-perpetuating cycle, deepening the sense of lack and clouding the possibility of recognizing, creating and living in true abundance.

Stephen Covey (1989), in *The 7 Habits of Highly Effective People*, explores this dichotomy of scarcity versus abundance. He describes a scarcity mindset as seeing life as a finite pie, where gain for one comes at the expense of another. In such a worldview, a job promotion is not only an individual accomplishment but feels like a blockade that limits others' opportunities. That perception fosters cutthroat competition, rivalry and an exaggerated individualism. Rather than recognizing a world rich with potential, scarcity trains us to view prosperity as a zero-sum game, a restrictive narrative that stands in direct opposition to the liberating principles of abundance we will unpack in the next section.

Have you ever met someone so consumed by discontent that they cannot celebrate another's success? Take Bob. Frustrated with his day job, he is wrapped in a persistent bitterness that spills into his relationships and decisions. When a colleague courageously leaves the company to launch a startup aligned with their passion, Bob feels not inspired but resentful, angry and increasingly isolated. *Is Bob operating from scarcity or abundance?* Pause here and reflect on that question before moving forward.

Understanding and naming scarcity is only the first step. The deeper shift, from scarcity to abundance, happens through the conduit of our inner life: the thoughts we rehearse, the words we speak to ourselves and others and the energy we carry into each situation. Habitual scarcity thinking narrows focus, shapes decisions toward self-protection and solidifies into patterns that perpetuate lack. Conversely, when we intentionally alter our inner narrative and the language we use, practicing curiosity instead of judgment, generosity instead of hoarding, gratitude instead of grievance, we change what we notice, how we act and the signals we send to others. This is not mere optimism; it is practical work: repeated thought and speech shape neural pathways, influence physiology and transform social dynamics. In short, shifting to abundance begins with shifting the energy you radiate and the stories you tell.

Recognizing scarcity is essential to grasping abundance and fulfillment because it reveals the core obstacle: the perception of lack and limitation. When that perception shifts, we begin to recognize true abundance as an ever-present flow of resources, opportunities and well-being, available to all. Scarcity and abundance are enduring themes embedded within larger cultural frameworks, such as individualism and collectivism, which we will explore later in this guidebook. In many modern Western societies, competition and personal achievement are prized, often at the expense of collective unity and shared prosperity. While the polarity of scarcity and abundance appears across cultures, this guidebook will show you how to cultivate an abundant state of being that not only transforms your personal future but also radiates outward, reshaping the world around you.

INTROSPECTION — SCARCITY

Being genuinely joyful for someone else's success may not come naturally to most of us, particularly when we are challenged and not fulfilled. This is a skill and acumen that one can develop. Recall a moment when you felt genuine joy for someone's happiness or success. What emotions did you experience? How did it shape your perspective on abundance versus scarcity?

____

____

____

____

____

____

____

____

Consider Bob's character. What underlying beliefs or fears might be driving his scarcity mindset? How would you approach helping him shift towards abundance?

____

____

____

Identify instances in your life where you have felt scarcity-driven emotions like resentment, envy or frustration. What triggered these feelings and how did they impact your mindset?

Insights — Abundance

He said to them, "Take care, and be on your guard against all covetousness, for one's life does not consist in the abundance of his possessions" (The Holy Bible: English Standard Version, 2001, Luke 12:15). This verse reminds us that a meaningful life is not measured by the quantity of what we own, but by the depth of how we live. It calls us to move from accumulation toward alignment, cultivating purpose, joy, gratitude and connection. True **Abundance** is found not in possessions, but in a life lived in harmony with values, spirit and the flow of the Universe. This timeless truth, rooted in ancient scripture, is affirmed throughout countless sacred texts that show abundance transcends material wealth. At its core, abundance is a life overflowing with joy, gratitude and the alignment of mind, body and spirit, a state that emerges from within, beyond the fleeting pull of materialism.

Echoing these divine tenets, the broader spiritual community perceives abundance as a profound state of consciousness, an enduring embrace of gratitude and a tangible sense of plenitude. It transcends mere mindset, becoming a state where you fully embody and resonate with the essence of plenty. Abundance champions the liberating belief in life's boundless offerings, embodying a Universe brimming with inexhaustible opportunities. Within this paradigm, abundance signifies a limitless reservoir of well-being devoid of scarcity's stifling grip. It honors the complex interplay of unseen universal forces working in our favor, urging us to let go of futile efforts to control. Embracing a state of abundance frees the spirit, granting a profound serenity and self-empowerment to navigate life's unfolding mysteries gracefully. This powerful connection between abundance and freedom, a cornerstone principle explored later in this guidebook, invites you on a transformative journey toward profound liberation and enlightenment.

While religious and spiritual perspectives often view abundance as an internal or divine state, modern capitalist philosophy tends to equate it with external accomplishments such as career success, power, prestige, financial wealth and material possessions. This prevailing belief asserts that the higher your professional and social standing in society, coupled with an accumulation of wealth and possessions, the happier and more fulfilled you will be. In today's world, an excess of material wealth has been crowned as the ultimate path to abundance and fulfillment. *But what if this contemporary notion of abundance is fundamentally flawed? What if the relentless pursuit of things and societal and career advancements is not the true path to fulfillment but merely a diversion from vital aspects of the human experience?* These questions, perhaps mirroring your inner questions, will be thoughtfully considered as we continue our journey.

This guidebook offers guidance on discovering your own path to abundance. It is an invitation to embrace self-love, self-discovery and joy in your everyday life. Engage fully with critical insights by examining the *Core Principles of Abundance* and the *Abundance Pillars*, both of which will be introduced next, and begin integrating them into your life. Apply the introspection exercises and practices offered throughout this guidebook to nurture and sustain a continual state of abundance. This guidebook leaves no stone unturned in revealing an authentic guide to living a life full of intrinsic joy and prosperity. Be open to the idea that these concepts and approaches have the potential to become the awakening force for profound and enduring transformations in your life. As you enter this journey of self-discovery, evolution and fulfillment, poised on the precipice of boundless potential, I extend a heartfelt invitation: *Are you ready to* ***decide, now*** *and embrace the abundant life that awaits?*

INTROSPECTION — ABUNDANCE

Reflect on your current understanding of abundance. Do you perceive it more in alignment with the spiritual perspective of gratitude and plenitude or do you find yourself leaning towards the materialistic definition dictated by societal norms? Explain why.

Explore the idea of a state of abundance as a source of profound serenity and self-empowerment. Can you recall a time when adopting such a state of being and mindset helped you navigate life's challenges more gracefully? How did it influence your overall well-being?

Contemplate the societal definition of abundance as synonymous with external achievements and material possessions. Have you ever felt pressured to conform to this definition? How has it affected your sense of fulfillment and joy?

CHAPTER RECAP: INTRODUCTION

In this chapter, we journeyed through the contrasting concepts of scarcity and abundance.

Scarcity

Key Insights: We begin our journey to abundance and fulfillment by understanding scarcity, a mindset of limitation and competition, where success is perceived as a zero-sum game. This perspective can shape thoughts, emotions, behaviors and social structures, often hindering both personal growth and collective prosperity.

Integration: Challenge and shift your scarcity mindset by focusing on the potential for growth and collaboration. Embrace opportunities for abundance in both personal and professional areas. Cultivate generosity and a spirit of shared success to promote collective well-being and enrich your own life.

Abundance

Key Insights: We explore the essence of abundance, which transcends material accumulation and is rooted in inner fulfillment, gratitude and a profound sense of plenitude. Abundance is not merely a mindset, but a state of being that empowers and liberates.

Integration: Cultivate a sense of abundance by practicing gratitude and focusing on inner fulfillment rather than external achievements. Align your actions with a vision of plenitude and seek to enhance your well-being by embracing and sharing your sense of abundance with others.

Introspection Exercises: Use the introspection exercises from each section to apply the principles of abundance to your life. Embrace these exercises as a transformative tool to challenge and reshape your state of being, transitioning from a state of scarcity to one of limitless possibility: abundance.

Conclusion: By integrating these insights and introspective exercises, you are invited to shift from a scarcity-based perspective to an abundant way of life. This transformation promises personal growth and a more fulfilling existence. As you move forward, remember that embracing this abundant state is both a conscious decision and a journey towards a richer, more vibrant life.

CHAPTER 1:

THE CORE PRINCIPLES OF ABUNDANCE

Now that we have uncovered the energies of scarcity and abundance, we are ready to awaken to the heart of fulfillment: the *Core Principles of Abundance.* In this chapter, we will explore a unique perspective on the true essence of abundance. These pages hold insights designed to encourage thoughtful contemplation and inner discovery. While this guidebook offers no rigid guidelines or fixed rules, it simply invites you to approach each page with **curiosity**. Feel free to inquire relentlessly: *What resonates with you? What challenges you? What do you want to learn more about?* It is recommended that you take deliberate pauses after each chapter, engaging fully with the introspective exercises interwoven throughout to capture any epiphanies, questions or insights that emerge. GET READY. We are about to plunge into what makes up the core structure and foundation of abundance and fulfillment.

Someone once asked, "*How can you even begin to define principles for something as abstract and intangible as abundance?*" That question stayed with me. It stirred something deep within, prompting me to withdraw into a period of solitude and deep reflection. I needed to understand abundance on a personal level before I could even begin to speak to it outwardly. What followed was an immersive journey, first inward, then outward. After gaining clarity within myself, I stepped into the world, seeking connection with others who were also chasing abundance, fulfillment and deeper meaning. I engaged with people from every walk of life, each offering their own perspective. And though their stories were unique, there was something striking: recurring themes and shared truths interlaced throughout their definitions of abundance. Despite the variety in how they expressed abundance, the core elements remained astonishingly aligned.

Born from personal reflection and grounded in real-world insight, the principles we are about to discuss were crafted to honor the essence of abundance and resonate deeply with the hearts of others. Before creating this guidebook, and the framework you are about to explore, a series of intentional, soul-stirring questions were asked both of myself and of those around me: *What do abundance and fulfillment truly mean within the human experience? What are the universal values and desires that connect us all? What truly makes life joyful, meaningful and whole? And how can we sustain a state of abundance not just momentarily, but for a lifetime?* These questions led me on a path of deep introspection, inner excavation and meaningful conversations with others. From quiet reflection and collective wisdom arose the core principles you are about to encounter, a distillation of what it truly means to live in abundance.

Refining the essence of abundance into seven foundational elements was both a profound challenge and a deeply enlightening experience. This process became a distillation of years of lived insight drawn from deeply human conversations and interviews with people across every walk of life: strangers and lifelong friends, peers and mentors, elders and children, colleagues and family members, the prosperous and those navigating difficult seasons, the young and the old, and all those in between. From this breadth of real human experience, a shared truth emerged with striking clarity: abundance is not accidental. It consistently expresses itself through seven core principles: **Your Essence (Self) – Mind, Body**

and Soul Alignment – Joy and Peace – Love and Connection – Growth and Evolution – Freedom and finally, Gratitude.

Each core principle has layers of profound substance and significance that we will meticulously unravel in the pages ahead. While distinct and remarkable in their own right, you will soon discover their intricate interconnectedness. Each principle fortifies the others. Upon completing this guidebook, you will realize that abundance transcends religious doctrines and contemporary perceptions. *Abundance lives within you, waiting to be awakened and gracefully infused into your life the moment you decide to align with it.* By mastering and applying these principles, you will be exceptionally equipped to create the abundant life you have always envisioned and desired.

I invite you to explore these seven core principles in the pages that follow, discovering how each one lives within you and shapes your experience of abundance.

Insights — Your Essence (Self)

A truly abundant life is built on self-connection. When you know who you are at your core, you act in alignment with your values and create a life that reflects your deepest truth. Embracing authenticity involves deliberating tuning into your **Essence**, which guides you toward experiences, conversations and environments that deeply resonate with your innermost desires. This alignment propels you toward fulfillment by immersing yourself in relationships and spaces that invigorate your spirit and support your aspirations. While this insight honors the beauty of living authentically, it invites us to ask deeper questions: *What does it mean to discover and embrace our essence? How do these concepts intertwine with pursuing a deeply fulfilling and abundant life?* Exploring these questions will reveal how authenticity contributes to a richer, more meaningful existence. Pause now and reflect deeply on these questions before moving forward.

The textbook definition of authenticity merely scratches the surface, portraying it as being genuine or real. However, authenticity runs deeper. It embodies the essence of your true self and higher self, a concept we explore in greater depth in a subsequent chapter. It is the unfiltered, unadulterated version of you, devoid of external influences or societal expectations. Your essence resonates as the inner voice aligned with your core values and belief systems. We will explore both values and belief systems in a later segment. They serve as your compass of the soul in navigating life's complexities. Operating from this authentic core means living life on your terms, *guided solely by what feels right to you*, unaffected by external opinions or influences. It shapes how you show up in the world, driving your behavior, the connections you nurture and the choices you make. This deep alignment with your true self echoes through every aspect of your life, powerfully impacting the depth of your relationships and the inner fulfillment you feel.

Two distinct aspects of the self dwell within each of us: one flowing from the authentic self, the other arising from the false self: a constructed identity shaped by conditioning and embodied in the persona, or "mask," we present to the world. We will begin by exploring the nature of the false self. The false self refers to a socially constructed self that a person adopts to protect themselves or gain approval from others. It is typically a façade that hides one's true feelings, desires and essence. It can manifest as a defense mechanism that arises from insecurity, fear or societal pressure, and can ultimately lead to a disconnection from one's authentic self. The false self emerges from external influences such as cultural conditioning, societal standards, achievements, failures and the judgments of others. It builds a carefully crafted image designed to adapt to different situations and relationships, assembled gradually over time. This false self can lead us astray, driving us towards pursuits that leave our spirits unfulfilled. In extreme cases, our false selves can estrange us from our very essence, leaving us strangers to ourselves.

An example of the false self is a person who outwardly presents a façade of success and happiness to the external world despite feeling insecure and unfulfilled in their personal life. This individual might carefully present an image of a flawless life free from challenges to gain approval and validation from others. In truth, they may struggle with self-doubt, depression, anxiety or dissatisfaction but choose to maintain this false self to meet societal expectations and mask their true feelings. This disconnection between their public guise and private reality can lead to internal conflict and a diminished sense of authenticity.

Similarly, a persona, according to Carl Jung (1968), represents the social mask or role adopted to align with societal expectations. A common example of a persona is the professional mask someone may wear at work. Consider an introverted individual who prefers deep, reflective conversations but adopts an extroverted, sociable persona to fit in and advance their career. They engage actively in meetings, casual conversations, and project enthusiasm and confidence, despite these behaviors conflicting with their true feelings and comfortability. While this persona facilitates their professional interactions, excessive identification can overshadow their authentic self, leading to stress and a sense of disconnection from their true identity.

In essence, the false self is the underlying construct (the root), and the persona is the external expression (the mask). The persona and false self involve aspects of identity that may not fully reflect one's essence. *Consider if you have ever shown up as your false self in social or professional situations. How did you feel? How could operating from your authentic self help you express your truth and vulnerability, leading to more meaningful connections?* Pause now and consider these questions before moving forward.

It is important to note that adapting to different situations or roles does not necessarily mean you are being false. Human beings are naturally fluid and adaptable, and much of this adaptability is healthy and normal. For instance, you might be more animated and outgoing at work, more playful with your children or more reflective and analytical with a close friend or partner. These shifts in expression are not a betrayal of your true self but rather reflections of your versatility. What remains constant, even as your outward personality adjusts, are your core values, moral compass and inner integrity. The distinction lies here: when adaptation is rooted in clarity and alignment with your essence, it enhances connection and growth. But when adaptation hardens into a mask that suppresses your real feelings, denies your needs or seeks only to gain approval, it can drift into the territory of the false self. This guidebook does not suggest that being adaptable is inauthentic. Rather, authenticity is about knowing when you are expressing a flexible version of yourself that still honors your essence, and when you are hiding behind a façade that disconnects you from it.

Many of us have found ourselves in situations where we compromised our core self, leading us to feel fraudulent and, at times, spiritually empty. These compromises often stem from a lack of self-awareness regarding our values, beliefs, purpose and authentic identity. Consider this scenario: *Have you ever found yourself in a relationship, career or situation where you felt unfulfilled, directionless or detached?* Perhaps it was not a specific circumstance, but a period marked by a lack of passion or purpose in life. Regardless of outward success, there is often an underlying sense of unfulfillment and dissatisfaction. In those moments, *were you operating from your authentic self or were you succumbing to the direction of your false self?* Pause now and reflect deeply on this question before moving forward.

Envision your authentic self as the master navigator of your life's vessel. It guides you towards interactions and relationships that resonate with your essence. Living authentically sends a clear message to the Universe: you are receptive to people, opportunities and circumstances that align with your true identity and aspirations. Like a magnetic force, you draw towards you the very essence of how you think, how you feel, what you desire and what you embody. Additionally, when you possess a deep self-awareness and remain rooted in your values and beliefs, you navigate through life unshaken by external opinions, judgments or criticisms, fostering a profound sense of peace and tranquility. Embracing your values and belief systems, concepts explored more thoroughly in a later section, amplifies this gravitational pull, drawing you closer to the people, experiences and opportunities that authentically reflect who you are. As you will discover later in this guidebook, embracing and mastering your essence sets the foundation for a deeply fulfilling journey aligned with your true nature.

Living authentically and abundantly necessitates a deep understanding of your values and belief systems and continual evaluation of whether they align with your evolving self. At the core of a fulfilling existence lies the process of discovering, defining and refining your values and beliefs, at times, over and over again. *Why is this crucial?* Your values and beliefs guide every action you take, serving as the driving force in how you interact with the world. Developing a value and belief system that reflects your core identity profoundly impacts the direction of your life and shapes your interactions with both yourself and your external environment.

You might be wondering, *what exactly are values?* Put simply, they represent what matters most to us, elements of life we truly respect and strive to live by. Aspects of life that are the most sacred to us, both internally and externally. Our value system encompasses all our individual values, shaping our perceptions and interactions with the world. At its core, our value system directs us toward what we genuinely consider meaningful in life. When we live in alignment with our values, we generate a powerful magnetic energy that draws in people and experiences aligned with our true essence, inviting deep joy and fulfillment into our lives. At the same time, honoring our values creates an inner resistance to anything misaligned with our authentic self. Our values are the silent force that shapes our inner world and steers the course of our lives. Living by our values profoundly influences our alignment with our essence and the choices we make in life. Our value system acts as a filter, bonding us with individuals and circumstances that resonate with our core beliefs. By establishing and adhering to our values, we transition from reactive living to conscious, intentional living, a concept we explore in more depth later.

Now, what about beliefs? Our beliefs consist of deeply ingrained convictions and principles that fundamentally shape how we perceive and interpret the world. These convictions may relate to ethics, morality, life's purpose and our view of reality. Like values, our belief systems provide the internal framework through which we perceive and engage with life. These beliefs, deeply ingrained within the fabric of our consciousness, serve as guiding principles that dictate our attitudes, behaviors and decision-making process. Recognizing that values and belief systems evolve is vital, as they continually shift and refine throughout our journey of self-discovery. Our values and beliefs can be tested and shaped by new experiences, insights and personal growth. A deeper exploration of both values and beliefs will follow in an upcoming chapter. Achieving clarity on our values and beliefs enables us to align with relationships and situations that resonate with our essence. This deep alignment fosters true abundance and fulfillment, empowering us to live with clarity, authenticity and purpose.

Introspection — Your Essence (Self)

Reflect on a time when you felt deeply aligned with your essence. How did it impact your decisions, relationships and overall sense of fulfillment?

____

____

____

____

____

____

____

____

Consider the concept of the false self and persona. Their influence on your life experiences. Reflect on moments when you compromised your authenticity for external validation or approval. How did it affect your sense of fulfillment and well-being?

____

____

____

____

Consider your current relationships and circumstances. Do they align with your values, beliefs and authentic self? If not, what steps can you take to realign them?

Insights — Mind, Body and Soul Alignment

The concept that we are spirits inhabiting a body, rather than bodies containing a spirit, is gaining acceptance in contemporary society. Within this understanding, living abundantly becomes rooted in recognizing the alignment and interconnection between our mind, body and soul, and how they support and nurture each other to cultivate a life of vitality and prosperity. Thriving abundantly means caring for every aspect of our being, recognizing that all parts are deeply connected. When one area of our being, mental, physical or spiritual, is supported, the others naturally strengthen. When these dimensions operate in equilibrium, energy flows freely, resilience strengthens and clarity of purpose emerges. Conversely, when one dimension falls out of alignment, it can influence the others, reducing coherence and creating tension, fatigue or a sense of disconnection. **Flourishing arises when mind, body and soul function together in balance.**

Mind, Body and Soul Alignment emphasizes the profound interconnectedness between our mental, physical and spiritual dimensions. Our thoughts and emotions (mind and psyche) influence our physical health (body) and spiritual well-being (soul). In turn, our physical state affects our mental and spiritual balance, and our spiritual wellness shapes both our mind and body. **The well-being of one component profoundly influences the health of every other aspect of our being.** Holistic wellness practices aim to nurture alignment between the mind, body and soul by integrating routines and habits that enhance and nourish their interconnectedness. Understanding how these elements work together becomes natural when you support your overall well-being and build a strong foundation for abundance.

True alignment of mind, body and soul is not merely a state to aspire to. It is a dynamic process of listening, responding and consciously deepening balance within oneself. It calls for attunement to the inner dialogues of the mind, the subtle signals of the body and the quiet wisdom of the soul, recognizing that each communicates vital information about our overall well-being. By intentionally fostering alignment, we nurture a powerful foundation for abundance to manifest, not as material prosperity, but as vitality, joy, meaningful relationships and a profound sense of inner peace. This principle invites us to become conscious stewards of our own wellness, embracing practices that honor the whole self while uniting mind, body and soul into a cohesive, flourishing life.

As healing and inner work deepens, alignment becomes something you experience rather than simply understand. For instance, as you begin to regulate and heal your nervous system (topics we explore later in this guidebook), your mind-body connection naturally strengthens. You become more attuned to bodily sensations, internal cues and emotional signals, allowing the body to inform the mind with greater clarity and safety. Similarly, when you engage in inner work to gain mastery over your essence, one of the central themes of *Chapter 3: The Abundance Pillars – Mastering Your Essence (Self) and Energy*, your self expression begins to align more authentically with your inner authority, reinforcing the powerful mind-soul connection. Communication becomes clearer, boundaries more embodied and actions more congruent with your beliefs and values. When your essence, mind and body enter inner coherence and alignment, operating on the same energetic frequency, vitality expands, resistance softens and forward momentum becomes effortless. In this state of alignment, growth feels natural rather than forced, and abundance becomes a byproduct of internal integration.

Embodying the alignment of mind, body and soul invites us to recognize their sacred oneness and to live with intention, balance and mindful awareness, opening the path to true abundance. Although the journey to mind, body and soul alignment is deeply personal and unique to everyone, there are universally effective practices, such as yoga, mindfulness meditation, breathwork, mindful movement, journaling and nurturing meaningful relationships, that support this balance. These approaches will be explored in greater depth in the chapters ahead. These practices help integrate your mind, body and soul, supporting the development of sustained vitality, meaningful fulfillment and a fully abundant life.

In a world rich with writings on yoga, mindfulness and holistic well-being, this guidebook offers a renewed lens, one that moves beyond the familiar to uncover deeper, less explored dimensions of wellness. Its focus lies in awakening to the innate unity of mind, body and soul, the essential integration that forms the foundation of true abundance and enduring fulfillment. Embracing a mindful and intentional existence, wherein every aspect of your being is nurtured and nourished, will transform your life. The second principle of abundance, mind, body and soul alignment, opens the door to transformative wellness practices and meaningful expansion. These practices are intended to effortlessly fit into your everyday routine, hoping to fill your life with strength, vitality, prosperity and richness.

Introspection — Mind, Body and Soul Alignment

Take a moment to deeply recognize the powerful connection between your mind, body and soul. How does this concept resonate with your own experiences and observations in life?

Mind-Body-Soul Connection: Consider how your thoughts and emotions influence your physical and spiritual health. Reflect on instances where you have noticed this connection in your own life.

___

___

___

Explore the various holistic wellness practices mentioned, such as yoga, mindfulness meditation, breathwork and journaling. Which of these resonate with you the most, and how do you envision incorporating them into your daily routine?

___

___

___

___

___

___

___

___

Insights — Joy and Peace

To embody lasting **Joy and Peace** is to touch the very core of abundance itself. These states transcend emotion; they are living energies, sacred forces that flow through the essence of our being and form the very foundation of a deeply fulfilling life. Joy, the radiant energy of feeling alive and aligned with purpose, fuels creativity and magnetizes abundance. Peace, the stabilizing energy of inner harmony and acceptance, anchors the soul, allowing joy to flourish without being overshadowed by stress or discord. United, they form an enduring sanctuary within, joy awakening the moment and peace holding it in stillness. This divine alignment gives rise to a life of true abundance, one that attracts experiences and opportunities resonant with fulfillment rather than mere material gain.

Joy and peace transcend fleeting emotional highs; they embody a profound state of being characterized by wholeness, contentment and self-nourished serenity. To consciously cultivate and sustain these energies each day is to live in alignment with your highest self, to embody the essence of a purposeful, abundant and deeply meaningful life. Though modern culture often glorifies the pursuit of happiness, through media, coaching and self-help rhetoric, the deeper path to genuine fulfillment lies not in the chase for temporary pleasure, but in the intentional cultivation of joy and peace as your natural energetic state.

While happiness and joy are often used interchangeably, it is important to understand the clear distinction between them. Happiness, often shaped by external circumstances, such as receiving praise or achieving a goal, tends to be fragile and fleeting. Conversely, joy and peace transcend circumstance. They are the steady, unwavering states that endure through challenge, loss and uncertainty, manifesting as inner calm in difficult seasons or gratitude amidst hardship. While happiness is transient, joy and peace are more akin to an existential state, a profound experience rather than a momentary feeling. It is the capacity to embrace life's wonders and savor its essence, irrespective of emotional turbulence or external situations. They represent enduring states of being, virtues similar to hope, faith and love. These virtues can evoke emotions and serve as the foundation of our thought processes, shaping our behaviors. Just as the interconnectedness of the mind, body and soul influences our well-being, the integration of sacred virtues into our lives directs our thoughts, which govern our emotions and actions. Joy and peace emanate from the profound realization that every facet of our being requires tender nurturing, and that our virtues must remain steadfast and uncompromised.

When this understanding deepens, it invites an essential question: *How valuable are material possessions or professional achievements if, despite having them, we feel empty, unfulfilled and hollow inside?* The profound emptiness within is a clear signal of the absence of joy, peace and fulfillment, acting as a poignant call from the depths of our souls, indicating that a crucial element may be absent from our lives. It prompts us to question whether we are truly aligning with our values and living mindfully or if we have strayed from our authentic path. The absence of joy and peace is a potent sign that our current investments of time, energy and attention may not align with our essence. Conversely, experiencing joy and peace affirms that we are living in alignment with our authentic self, values, mission and purpose. Joy and peace serve as powerful indicators that our life is aligned with the true intentions of our higher self, a concept that will be explored in *Chapter 3: The Abundance Pillars – Mastering Your Essence (Self) and Energy*.

Joy and peace are foundational states of being, living energies that embody our deepest values and form the essence of abundance. Attaining a sustained state of joy and peace represents the pinnacle of achievement and resilience, a true testament to one's mastery of life. Even amidst life's trials and tribulations or when energy levels wane, an innate sense of joy and peace persists, underscoring the profound significance of the human experience, regardless of circumstances. Joy and peace are unmistakable frequencies emanating from the depths of the soul, ever-present forces in our lives. While some moments effortlessly evoke joy and peace, others require vigilance and mindfulness to access its depths. The empowering truth is that we possess the agency to steer our focus and tune into joy and peace each day. Choosing joy and peace catalyzes abundance, acting as a magnetic force that draws us toward experiences and connections that amplify our inner sense of fulfillment. Doing so lays the vital groundwork for our next principle: **Love and Connection**.

Introspection — Joy and Peace

What does joy and peace mean to you on a personal level? How would you describe the experience of joy and peace in your own life?

Reflect on the interconnectedness of joy and peace with the principles of abundance and fulfillment. How does prioritizing joy and peace contribute to your own purpose-driven existence?

____

____

____

Think about the concept of choosing joy and peace as described in the text. How do you actively choose joy and peace in your daily life? Are there specific practices or habits you engage in to cultivate joy and peace?

____

____

____

____

____

____

____

____

Insights — Love and Connection

When you have achieved the pinnacle of sustained joy and peace, signifying that you are living authentically aligned with your true self and core values, you have laid the groundwork for our next principle: **Love and Connection**. Undoubtedly, nothing is more significant in this world than love and meaningful human connections. For countless individuals, it represents the highest ambition, often seen as the peak of achievement in life. *Everything else seems to pale in comparison when weighed against the worth and value of genuine love and connection.* Ultimately, *when our lives draw to a close, the true measure of success will be the love we have given and received in our lifetime.*

Love stands as one of the deepest and most transformative forces in the human experience, both an emotion we feel and a state of being we embody. This powerful and essential energy has driven people to remarkable lengths, ignited wars and conflicts and inspired countless individuals to devote their entire lives to seeking it. Yet, many remain unaware that love is not something to be sought externally but a force already existing within and around them. As humans, we have an inherent longing for love, deeply rooted in our biological wiring and nurtured from childhood. Though often experienced as an emotion, love in its purest form is a state of being, an ever-present energy that arises from within rather than something to be pursued outside of ourselves. Love is not only our core nature; it is our birthright. Embracing this truth allows us to navigate life intentionally, with love as the guiding force behind our behaviors and actions. When this profound energy fills your being, acting from a place of love should feel natural, bringing you an abundance of joy, peace and fulfillment.

Although love is our birthright, it does not always come easily. Just as we are biologically hardwired to seek companionship and community for survival, we are also deeply driven to pursue love and connection. This impulse, genetically encoded and fundamental to our existence, can feel challenging, vulnerable or even uncomfortable for many, especially when past wounds, fear or mistrust influence the way we connect. This too is part of the human journey. Loving is not always instinctive; it is a practice that unfolds and deepens over time. Be gentle and patient with yourself if expressing or receiving love feels difficult or unfamiliar. Like a muscle, the art of loving strengthens with consistent care and intention. The more you nurture it, the more effortless it feels, unfolding into a quiet ease that nourishes your life and the lives of those around you. When you embody and express love in every facet of your life, you naturally radiate an aura of abundant energy. Moving with love as your guiding force cultivates a profound sense of joy and inner tranquility that cannot be matched.

When love is cultivated and expressed fully, toward others and ourselves, it becomes the truest reflection of our nature. While giving and receiving love through acts like spending time with loved ones or showing affection is undeniably fulfilling, the highest form of love, the foundation for all other expressions of love, is the love you nurture for yourself: self-love. Without self-love, different expressions of love can be fragile and unsustainable. Loving yourself completely establishes the benchmark for the love you extend outwardly and the love you accept from others. Because abundance is rooted in alignment with your true self, embracing your essence and honoring your values are key steps in cultivating deep self-love. Later in this guidebook, we explore specific approaches for nurturing and adhering to your values and belief systems to reinforce ways to cultivate self-discovery and self-love.

As you grow ever more attuned to your true essence, and live in alignment with it, your self-love deepens beyond measure. Just as you would invest time and care in truly knowing a partner or friend, so too must you journey inward in the art of self-discovery. Before opening your heart to another, it is essential to first love, embrace and cherish yourself deeply and completely. *Without this foundational self-love, how can you expect others to love and appreciate you fully?* Embracing deep, unconditional self-love, paired with intentional actions rooted in this love, lays the foundation for building more nourishing and enduring relationships with others. When you genuinely love yourself and let that love drive your interactions and decisions, you establish a stronger, more authentic connection with those around you. This practice enhances the quality of your relationships and ensures they are built on a solid, lasting foundation of mutual respect, understanding and genuine affection.

Now what are ways we can nurture self-love? It begins in the quiet moments, in the whispers of your own heart and the tenderness of your thoughts. Speak to yourself with kindness, for your words are spells that shape the landscape of your inner world. Care for yourself as you would a sacred garden, tending to your mind, body and spirit with gentleness and devotion. Honor your boundaries as acts of love, not resistance. Each time you say "no" to what depletes your energy, you say "yes" to what nourishes your soul. Rest without guilt, knowing that stillness is not the absence of progress but the soil where renewal takes root. And treat yourself as someone worthy of reverence, gifting yourself moments of joy, softness and care simply because you exist. Through these simple yet profound practices, self-love ceases to be a concept and becomes communion, a living relationship with your own essence. From this sacred alignment, love flows effortlessly outward, touching every life you encounter with grace, compassion and abundance.

In this flow, love naturally seeks connection for love and connection are inseparable, each giving life to the other. *But what does connection truly mean in the context of abundance and fulfillment?* At its essence, connection is a sacred resonance, a deep sense of belonging and attunement with someone or something that transcends words or understanding. It is a magnetic pull that feels both comforting and exhilarating, a deep inner knowing that you are in alignment with your true self and purpose. When you experience a connection with a person or an aspect of life, you feel compelled to follow its pull, guided by an invisible force that transcends rational understanding. It is a profound and unspoken recognition that what you are drawn to resonates deeply with your core spirit. In human connections, you may at times embody what the other person needs, and vice versa, while in other cases, you are drawn to qualities that reflect your authentic self. Connections often serve as mirrors, reflecting back the virtues of your own essence and the intentions you carry. What naturally draws you in reveals the alignment of your inner energy, offering subtle but essential feedback about who you are becoming. This idea resonates closely with the principles of the Law of Attraction, which remind us that like attracts like: the vibrations you emit shape the people, opportunities and experiences you welcome into your life. We will explore these concepts in greater depth later.

Love and connection, inseparable and mutually sustaining, stand as the fourth principle of abundance. They are essential not only for their transformative role in the human experience but also because each amplifies and nourishes the other. Without love, cultivating meaningful connections feels hollow and incomplete; without deep connection, love struggles to flourish fully. Together, they form a living testament to what it means to experience a life of profound richness and purpose. For in truth, no achievement, no pleasure and no sensation compares to the sublime fulfillment that flows from love shared and connection felt.

It is important to recognize that love and connection extend far beyond our relationships with others. They can also be expressed deeply toward personal causes, passions or missions, revealing a broader, more profound resonance that shapes not only our lives but the world around us. *Falling in love with your life's purpose can be an unparalleled union, especially if you navigate it with love, intentionality and dedication.* Some suggest that aligning with your personal mission or sacred calling can provide a sense of fulfillment that rivals, or even surpasses, the satisfaction gained from human connections. Embracing your sacred mission or life's calling, with an awareness of collective consciousness, concepts discussed in *Insights and Integration — Embody Your Purpose-Driven Life* segment of *Chapter 4: The Abundance Pillars – Mastering Your Life and Collective Consciousness,* ensures enduring fulfillment and satisfaction. Ultimately, the choice of how to prioritize love and connection in your life is entirely yours. As we journey through these enlightening principles of abundance, the hope is that you feel open, curious and excited about the profound insights unfolding. We will now turn our attention to our next principle: **Growth and Evolution**.

Introspection — Love and Connection

Reflect on a time when you experienced profound love or connection in your life. What was the situation, and how did it make you feel?

Reflect on how love and connection intersect with the other principles of abundance we have explored, such as joy and peace. How can you harness love and connection to create a more abundant and meaningful life for both yourself and others?

___

___

___

Identify one practical step you can take today to cultivate more love and connection in your life, whether towards yourself, others or a meaningful cause.

___

___

___

___

___

___

___

___

Insights — Growth and Evolution

Recognizing your innate capacity to grow and evolve is among the most liberating realizations on the path to abundance. True empowerment arises when you embrace openness, a willingness to learn, unlearn and receive new perspectives with humility and curiosity. Your intuitive insights and deepest wisdom do not come from external sources but from lived experience, self-reflection and the lessons life continually offers. When you listen closely, you discover that life itself is a mirror, and you are both the student and the teacher. To remain open-minded is to remain fluid, allowing space for inquiry, introspection and transformation. **Growth and Evolution** are not abstract ideals but living processes, both a mindset and a form of energy that invites expansion at every level of your being. They are the conscious choice to remain open, curious and receptive, as well as the inner force that propels transformation from within. The question, then, is not whether you can evolve, but how embracing this mindset and channeling this energy can guide you toward greater abundance, fulfillment and alignment with your truest self.

When envisioning someone with a growth mindset, we see an individual who firmly believes in their capacity for continuous improvement and self-exploration. They approach their inner work with curiosity, patience and accountability, recognizing these as gateways to new possibilities, insights and personal maturation. They understand that transformation is not a single event but an ongoing process, a continual unfolding that refines and expands their being from the inside out. This mindset frees them from stagnation or confinement, allowing life itself to become a dynamic, evolving journey of development and awakening.

In many ways, evolution mirrors this inner journey, a gradual unfolding from simplicity into greater depth, complexity and refinement. It is the movement from the basic to the beautifully intricate, from instinct to awareness. To truly understand evolution, however, one must also acknowledge its biological foundation, for the very principles that govern life's physical development also reveal the pathways of our personal and spiritual growth. From its inception, life blossomed from single-celled origins into the vast diversity of forms that inhabit the Earth today. Evolution reminds us that stagnation stands in opposition to existence itself; all of life is in motion, continuously refining, adapting and ascending toward greater expression and wholeness.

Growth and evolution serve as fundamental principles of abundance, enabling individuals to embrace the unfamiliar without preconceived judgments but instead with excitement and anticipation. Those with a growth and evolution mindset continuously seek to expand their understanding across various realms of knowledge and thought. Conversely, those who cling tightly to rigid beliefs may struggle to embrace perspectives that differ from their own, making it difficult to form deep and meaningful connections. Such inflexibility narrows the lens through which life is perceived, validating only familiar viewpoints while dismissing or distorting others. This rigidity becomes a quiet barrier to authentic communication and understanding, constraining one's ability to recognize the richness and nuance within other people's experiences and, ultimately, within life itself.

Consider John, for instance. John is a public figure who thrives on engaging in contentious debates within his field, holding steadfast to his opinions while rarely exploring alternative perspectives. This tendency can create division and hinder deeper dialogue. Pause and reflect for a moment. *Does John embody a mindset of growth and evolution? How might his relationships and connections deepen if he approached conversations with openness, curiosity and a willingness to expand beyond his own perspective?*

A growth and evolution mindset is the ability to hold a broader perspective, staying open and curious about the intricacies of the world.

With this mindset, and energy, you become more receptive and resilient to life's unexpected wonders and mysteries. The more you nurture and embody this inner force, the more your capacity to evolve expands, a skill that will serve you well as you engage with the insights and practices in this guidebook. As humans, our understanding of the world is naturally limited, calling for an openness to new perspectives and evolving approaches to deepen our experience of abundance and fulfillment. Those with a growth and evolution mindset embody a spirit of receptivity, refusing to confine themselves to restrictive, narrow modes of thinking. These individuals are the ones who have the potential to transform in ways that break conventional boundaries, achieving unprecedented levels of personal and professional success. *Think of growth and evolution as a dove, soaring high into the sky, reaching destinations beyond the naked eye, uncaged and liberated*: the perfect segue to our following principle of abundance: **Freedom**.

Introspection — Growth and Evolution

Think about an aspect of your life where you have experienced growth or evolution over time. What factors contributed to this growth, and how did it impact your overall well-being?

____

____

____

____

____

____

____

____

Consider the role of biology in the evolutionary process. How does the diversity of life on Earth reflect the principles of growth and evolution we have explored?

____

____

____

____

____

Imagine yourself as the dove mentioned in the passage, soaring into the unknown. What destinations do you envision for yourself on your journey of growth and evolution?

Insights — Freedom

Freedom stands as a cornerstone in the pursuit of abundance and fulfillment. Alongside love and connection, it is a deep, innate longing within the human spirit, a desire to live fully, authentically and unrestrained. *Yet what does it truly mean to be free? Is freedom merely the absence of limitation or is it the presence of alignment with your highest self, the liberation of your thoughts, choices and energy?* To understand freedom in its fullest sense is to uncover the inner space where your essence can soar, unbounded by fear, expectation or self-imposed constraints and limitations. It is the ability to act, think and express oneself without doubt or consequence. True freedom, though subjective, is the ability to live a life filled with genuine joy and peace, where your creative vision is fully expressed while honoring your authentic self and deepest desires.

It is important to acknowledge that the definition and experience of freedom can vary greatly, shaped by each individual's unique circumstances and perspectives. For instance, when examining freedom from the standpoint of someone living under strict cultural or societal restrictions, it might translate to the ability to express their true self without fear of judgment or persecution. For them, freedom could mean having the choice to pursue a passion, speak openly about their values and belief systems or make life decisions without constraint. It might be as simple as choosing their daily routine, selecting the work they wish to do or deciding how they spend their personal time. Freedom might revolve around financial stability for a single parent juggling multiple jobs to support their family. It could involve the ability to avoid the necessity of balancing several jobs simply to cover basic living expenses. In this scenario, achieving financial freedom becomes the primary focus. Using these examples as a foundation, reflect on what freedom means to you in your present situation. Pause now and reflect deeply on this question before moving forward.

Many yearn for a life where they have the autonomy to shape their daily schedules, waking up at their leisure and relishing in the ability to allocate their time as they see fit. At its core, this longing reflects a wish to direct the course of their everyday experiences without restriction or limitations. For many, particularly those in corporate roles, daily life often involves bartering personal resources, such as time, energy and focus, in exchange for the financial means to sustain their basic needs. This sets up a careful balancing act, where the demands of earning a living can at times constrain the pursuit of a life aligned with one's true values and aspirations. For many, work is not just a part of life, it is a fundamental necessity. The freedom to step away from this reality is often a luxury reserved for those with substantial financial independence. Yet even within the constraints of a structured and demanding lifestyle, one can cultivate a profound sense of inner freedom. The question becomes: *how can individuals awaken and sustain this inner freedom while navigating the obligations and routines that daily life requires?* Pause now and reflect deeply on this question before moving forward.

Freedom is not always found by changing external circumstances. More often, it is discovered through the quiet release of the inner forces that bind us, including resistance, attachment and unconscious emotional weight. Psychiatrist and consciousness researcher David R. Hawkins, M.D., Ph.D., describes this process as *letting go* through what he calls the *Pathway of Surrender*, as detailed in his book *Letting Go*. In his work, Hawkins teaches that much of human suffering stems not from life itself, but from our emotional resistance to it. The desire to control outcomes, avoid discomfort or cling to specific identities can subtly imprison the mind, even when external freedom appears attainable. According to Hawkins, true liberation arises not through force or effort, but through **surrender**, not as passive resignation, but as a conscious willingness to release inner resistance and emotional attachment. When we stop resisting what is, we reclaim our power. In releasing the need to control, justify or suppress our emotions, we create space for clarity, peace and inner sovereignty to emerge naturally. Surrender becomes an act of strength rather than weakness, allowing life to move through us without contraction.

Hawkins emphasizes that letting go is a process of awareness rather than analysis. It begins by noticing emotional reactions as they arise, such as fear, frustration, guilt, anger or longing, without judgment or narrative. Rather than feeding these emotions with stories or attempting to push them away, we allow them to be fully felt and then released. As the emotional charge dissolves, so too does the grip it holds over our thoughts, behaviors and sense of limitation. What remains is presence, neutrality and a deep inner freedom that no longer depends on external conditions.

As layers of emotional attachment fall away, freedom becomes less about what we are able to do and more about *how we are able to be*. We no longer require life to unfold a certain way in order to feel at peace. We are no longer ruled by the illusion that fulfillment exists somewhere in the future or beyond our present circumstances. Freedom reveals itself as an **internal state** that is stable, accessible and resilient, available in every moment, regardless of obligation, routine or responsibility. This inner liberation, as Hawkins teaches, is the natural byproduct of surrendering what no longer serves our highest good. Pause here and reflect: *Where in your life are you gripping, resisting or striving? What might shift if, instead of forcing change, you allowed yourself to release the emotional weight you are carrying?* As Hawkins reminds us, freedom often enters not when we acquire more, but when we **let go**.

True freedom can manifest in the small, cherished moments between life demands and daily routines. It resides within the routine of your everyday responsibilities, where intentional choices can infuse joy and delight into mundane tasks. Freedom can look like embracing the opportunity to derive pleasure amidst your obligations, whether it is dancing to music while folding laundry, sharing a joke with a colleague before a meeting or engaging in a playful tickle fight with your children before preparing dinner for the family. Freedom, in its essence, resides within the deep well of gratitude, the last of our core principles, for the many everyday pleasures that color our existence.

You achieve freedom through a delicate dance of balance and finesse, navigating life with both responsibility and liberty. It is about maximizing every moment and extracting joy and peace, whether life is moving at full speed or at a standstill. Hawkins teaches that true freedom is not dependent on changing external circumstances but emerges as we release resistance, attachment and the emotional weight that subtly binds us. By consciously letting go of the need to control outcomes, justify our feelings or cling to specific identities, we create space for clarity, presence and inner sovereignty to arise naturally. Most importantly, freedom lies in the awareness that you are never bound by your circumstances. You possess full agency over your life and reality, and this realization serves as potent medicine, granting you the freedom to embrace each day with hope, appreciation and excitement, regardless of what life presents. Exploring the concept of freedom is both fascinating and essential on the journey toward abundance and fulfillment, as it helps us break free from limiting constraints, surrender what no longer serves us, and align more deeply with our true desires and potential.

Introspection — Freedom

Have you ever experienced a moment where you felt truly liberated despite external constraints or limitations? Describe this experience and how it made you feel.

____

____

____

____

____

____

____

____

Imagine your ideal vision of freedom. What does this vision look like for you, and what actions can you take in your daily life to get closer to it?

____

____

____

____

____

Identify areas where you are holding onto resistance, attachment or the need to control outcomes. How might letting go of these inner weights, as David R. Hawkins teaches in *Letting Go*, bring more clarity, presence and freedom? Write about what surrender could look like for you and how it might shift your experience of freedom.

Insights — Gratitude

Gratitude, the final yet foundational principle of abundance, is a transformative state and energy that profoundly shifts our focus from scarcity to *deep appreciation* for the blessings we already possess. Embracing gratitude recalibrates the mind, serving as a guiding force for reshaping our neural pathways and shifting us from cycles of negativity toward a more positive and abundant state of being. By focusing on what we have rather than what we lack, we begin to create new neural pathways that reinforce feelings of joy, appreciation and fulfillment. This practice aligns our thoughts, emotions and beliefs to foster abundance and fulfillment, creating a profound sense of coherence and alignment.

Spiritually, embodying gratitude for what we wish to experience draws our vibration into resonance with the creative intelligence of the Universe. This alignment works like a magnetic force, attracting the people, circumstances and resources we need to manifest our goals and dreams. When we embody gratitude in this way, we signal to the Universe that we are open and ready to receive, cultivating a state of abundance rather than scarcity. Regularly practicing gratitude shifts our perspective, helping us to see opportunities where others might see obstacles. This simple but profound action can greatly enrich our lives, activating a stream of energy that invites abundant opportunities, meaningful connections and life-changing experiences. By embracing gratitude as a way of being, we attune ourselves to the Universe's natural flow, opening the door to a life filled with possibility and fulfillment.

At its core, gratitude transcends mere appreciation; it is about embracing the intricate experience of life with deep gratification. It is finding joy in the present moment, recognizing that our fulfillment persists even if circumstances remain unchanged. Gratitude is embracing the richness of our current blessings and lived experience without craving more. While ambition propels us forward, gratitude anchors us in delight and pleasure, resonating deep within our essence. When practiced consistently, gratitude and appreciation infuse everyday experiences with profound depth, transforming even the simplest moments into rich opportunities for reflection, connection and presence. It allows us to notice subtleties we might otherwise overlook such as the warmth of sunlight, the quiet generosity of a friend, the rhythm of our own breath, revealing layers of meaning that elevate ordinary life into extraordinary awareness. Gratitude, like abundance, is not merely a fleeting feeling; it is a conscious way of living that permeates every facet of our existence, shaping our perceptions, actions and relationships. By embracing gratitude as a guiding principle, we cultivate an inner richness that anchors us, enhances resilience and opens us to the fullness of life's offerings, creating a profound sense of fulfillment that transcends external circumstances.

The force of gratitude is both potent and magnetic. In alignment with the Law of Attraction, gratitude reveals that our inner energy molds the outer world. The vibrations we radiate attract corresponding relationships, opportunities and experiences, inviting more positivity and fulfillment into our lives. When you nurture gratitude and attune yourself to the energies of joy and appreciation for the Universe's blessings, you effortlessly draw even more gifts and moments worthy of gratitude into your life. Simply, the more you embody gratitude, the more you attract circumstances and blessings that further fuel your gratitude. Conversely, focusing on complaints and cultivating a mindset of ingratitude tends to attract situations and experiences that amplify your dissatisfaction. What you focus on manifests in your life.

In addition to its neurological and spiritual effects, gratitude fosters greater physical vitality and mental clarity, enriching overall well-being. Adopting an attitude of gratitude has been associated with a broad range of positive impacts including improved sleep quality, elevated mood, reinforced immunity and reduced instances of depression, anxiety, chronic pain and illness. Pausing to express gratitude can trigger physiological changes in the body, activating the parasympathetic nervous system, which promotes relaxation, calm and restorative functions like digestion. This response can lower blood pressure, heart rate and respiration, fostering an overall sense of ease. Additionally, practicing gratitude has been shown to enhance social bonds and deepen feelings of connection, in part by stimulating the release of oxytocin, sometimes called the "love hormone," which supports nurturing and intimate relationships.

Incorporating gratitude into your daily life is simple in practice yet profoundly powerful in nurturing peace and balance within mind, body and spirit. This practice can take various forms, such as maintaining a gratitude journal on a regular basis, whether daily, weekly or monthly, expressing words of thanks aloud either to yourself or to a cherished individual, or engaging in a mindful gratitude walk. Consider affirming statements like, *I appreciate the strength and health of my body for providing me the ability to take a walk today*, *I am grateful for this simple cup of water that quenches my thirst*, *I am thankful for the unwavering love and support of my partner*, or *I am grateful for my job, which affords me financial stability*. Consistency is the cornerstone of this practice. The more you intentionally cultivate gratitude, the more it becomes an ingrained way of being, naturally flowing into your thoughts, actions and perception of everyday life.

Beyond simply vocalizing or writing down your gratitude, it is essential to truly *feel* the sense of gratitude within yourself on a deep emotional level. This practice requires intentional moments of solitude, coupled with conscious engagement in mindfulness meditation, breathwork and visualization. Mindfulness meditation trains your attention, allowing you to observe thoughts without judgment and deepen self-awareness. Breathwork helps regulate your body's energy, oxygenates your cells and brings immediate clarity to your mind. Visualization engages your imagination to mentally rehearse goals, cultivate positive outcomes and strengthen focus and intention. We will continue to deepen and strengthen these practices in the chapters ahead. For now, let us begin with a simple integration practice that combines these techniques.

To start, close your eyes and bring to mind the person, place or object you are grateful for. Visualize it in vivid detail, immersing yourself in the mental image of your gratitude's subject. As you do so, take a deep breath, inhaling the positive energy and joy that this visualization evokes. Slowly exhale, allowing the gratitude to radiate from your core, embodying the sensation of thankfulness fully. Let this feeling permeate every part of your being. Engage in this process by incorporating both breathwork and visualization, while grounding yourself in the present moment through mindfulness meditation. Take a moment to bask in these feelings of gratitude before moving forward, fully embracing the connection between your mind, body and spirit.

Gratitude holds paramount significance due to its profound vibrational and magnetic energy, which has the power to manifest our deepest desires. Its impact extends beyond the physical, emotional and mental realms, encompassing profound spiritual benefits and contributing to overall well-being. Through gratitude, we affirm to ourselves and the Universe that we can find joy and appreciation in life's offerings despite adversity. Even in the face of life's unavoidable challenges, we can still find solace in the beauty of our human experience. Gratitude reveals life's complexity and polarity; joy can still flourish amidst suffering. Serving as both practice and instrument, gratitude lays the groundwork and pathway for authentic abundance and fulfillment. It is worth emphasizing that merely speaking, writing, or reading words of appreciation pales in comparison to fully experiencing and embodying gratitude. The true power of transformation emerges when gratitude is expressed, *genuinely felt* and *lived authentically*. Gratitude will serve as a foundational practice throughout our journey together, playing a vital role in nurturing and sustaining the life we aspire to create.

Introspection — Gratitude

Write about three things you are grateful for and explore why each holds significance for you.

Think about a challenging situation you are currently facing. How might cultivating gratitude influence your approach to this challenge?

Take a gratitude walk in a natural setting. As you stroll, jot down or record your observations of the beauty around you and reflect on how it inspires gratitude.

Chapter Recap: The Core Principles of Abundance

Chapter 1 explores the core principles that form the foundation of an abundant and fulfilling life:

1. **Your Essence (Self)**
2. **Mind, Body and Soul Alignment**
3. **Joy and Peace**
4. **Love and Connection**
5. **Growth and Evolution**
6. **Freedom**
7. **Gratitude**

Principle 1: Your Essence (Self)

Key Insights: Alignment with your authentic self is essential for living in truth and integrity. Take time to discern between your genuine essence and the conditioned identities you may have unconsciously assumed.

Integration: Strive for authenticity in your decisions and relationships to create a more meaningful and fulfilling life.

Principle 2: Mind, Body and Soul Alignment

Key Insights: Your mind, body and soul are interconnected, and achieving holistic wellness requires attention to all three aspects.

Integration: Integrate grounding practices such as yoga, mindfulness meditation and reflective journaling to bring these aspects of self into alignment and cultivate greater balance and vitality.

Principle 3: Joy and Peace

Key Insights: Joy and peace are deeper, more enduring states than happiness, which is often fleeting and dependent on external circumstances.

Integration: Nurture an enduring sense of joy and peace that arises from within, independent of life's fluctuations, to embody true and lasting abundance.

Principle 4: Love and Connection

Key Insights: Love and meaningful connections are transformative forces that should flow both ways: given and received. They extend beyond human relationships to include the deep bond we share with our mission, passions and life's calling.

Integration: Let self-love serve as the root from which all relationships grow, while you deepen your connection to others and your life's calling, allowing your purpose and passion to enrich every aspect of your life.

Principle 5: Growth and Evolution

Key Insights: Embrace your capacity for personal growth and evolution, as stagnancy is contrary to your nature; a growth mindset opens doors to new possibilities.

Integration: Stay open-minded and receptive to new experiences and lessons, continuously evolving from within to foster a dynamic life.

Principle 6: Freedom

Key Insights: True freedom comes from releasing inner resistance, attachment, and the need to control outcomes. Surrendering what no longer serves you allows clarity, presence and a deep sense of inner sovereignty, while helping you find joy and gratitude in each moment and balance responsibilities with personal liberty.

Integration: Build a life that allows freedom of expression and joy in the ordinary. Notice where you are holding on and practice letting go. Recognize your ability to influence your experiences and embrace freedom as an internal, resilient state available at any moment.

Principle 7: Gratitude

Key Insights: Gratitude shifts your focus from scarcity to abundance, enhancing your overall well-being.

Integration: Regularly embodying and expressing gratitude as though your desires have already been met will attract the resources and people necessary for achieving your goals.

Introspection Exercises: Use the introspection exercises in each section to integrate these principles into your life, deepening your connection with your essence, aligning mind, body and soul, cultivating joy, peace, love, gratitude and freedom, nurturing deeper connections, and supporting your ongoing growth and evolution.

Conclusion: Mastering these core principles is essential for manifesting abundance in your life. Let these insights serve as a foundation for deeper exploration, integrating them into your daily routine to enhance both understanding and practical application.

CHAPTER 2:

THE ABUNDANCE PILLARS – MASTERING YOUR MIND (THOUGHTS)

We have come to understand that abundance goes beyond traditional and societal definitions, transcending religious and capitalistic constructs. Abundance encompasses embodying your essence, achieving mind, body and soul alignment, experiencing joy and peace (distinct from mere happiness), fostering love and connection, embracing growth and evolution, cherishing freedom and practicing gratitude. These core, high-vibrational principles form the foundation of a life rich in true fulfillment. In a later section, we will explore the contrasts between high and low vibrations and how they shape your experience of abundance.

At the heart of it all lies a powerful truth: achieving abundance and fulfillment ultimately rests on a conscious decision, an individual commitment to embodying prosperity and gratitude each day, irrespective of life's circumstances. It is not about waiting for everything to align perfectly or for external conditions to improve, but about choosing to show up every day with intention, embracing joy, appreciation and purpose in the present moment. This intentional decision becomes the basis upon which lasting transformation is built.

Now that we have explored the core principles of abundance, we transition into the next phase of our journey, bringing these insights into everyday life and cultivating mastery over each vital dimension of the self. We do this through **The Fulfillment Framework™**, which guides us through three essential stages: gaining insight and wisdom, engaging in meaningful introspection, and integrating practical tools, rituals and daily practices that sustain lasting abundance and fulfillment.

This process unfolds through three transformative pillars:

- **Mastering Your Mind (Thoughts)**
- **Mastering Your Essence (Self) and Energy**
- **Mastering Your Life and Collective Consciousness**

Each pillar introduces powerful concepts, reflective inquiry and embodied practices designed to cultivate joy, prosperity, high-vibrational energy and fulfillment. Whether your intention is to elevate your mindset, reconnect with your inner essence or consciously design a life of meaning and purpose, these pillars offer essential guidance for expansion.

Chapter 2 begins with the first pillar: **Mastering Your Mind (Thoughts)**.

Your thoughts shape how you perceive reality, relate to yourself and others and interpret your experiences. Long before abundance or scarcity manifests in the external world, it takes form internally through perception, belief systems and inner dialogue. Mastering your mind is not about controlling thoughts, but about understanding them, becoming aware of their origins and learning how to consciously choose those that align with growth, clarity and abundance. Throughout this chapter, we explore consciousness and self-awareness as the gateways to inner mastery. You will examine where your thoughts come from, how they are shaped by personal experience, language, environment and the larger collective mind, and how these influences impact your beliefs and behaviors. As awareness deepens, so does your capacity to respond to life intentionally rather than reactively.

It is also important to acknowledge that thoughts are often byproducts of your internal state, particularly your nervous system. When the nervous system is in stress, protection or dysregulation, the mind frequently mirrors that state through fear-based thinking, scarcity narratives or self-doubt. When the nervous system feels safe and regulated, the mind naturally becomes more spacious, creative and resilient. While this guidebook does not explore the nervous system in depth, we briefly introduce it in *Chapter 3: The Abundance Pillars – Mastering Your Essence (Self) and Energy*, within *Insights and Integration — Healing and Releasing*. It is strongly encouraged to further explore nervous system healing and regulation, as it is fundamental to expansion and to building the capacity required to carry the life you are creating.

This chapter also examines the relationship between thoughts and spoken language. Words are powerful. They reinforce beliefs, influence emotional states and shape lived experience. When thoughts and language are aligned, they become tools for clarity, confidence and creation. When they are misaligned, they often perpetuate inner conflict and limitation. You will learn how to work intentionally with language, affirmations and reframing to support a healthy, empowered mindset. We will also bring awareness to mental blockages and limiting beliefs, patterns often rooted in past experiences or unconscious conditioning. By identifying and gently challenging these narratives, you open space for new possibilities to emerge.

Finally, this chapter introduces **The Art of Manifesting Abundance** as an embodied practice of alignment. Manifestation is not wishful thinking; it is the integration of thoughts (beliefs), words (language) and actions, all rooted in a state of abundance. Through intentional decision-making, visualization, creative imagination and embodiment, you learn to live *from* abundance rather than striving endlessly *for* it.

As you move through this chapter, you will explore a series of foundational insights designed to deepen your understanding of the mind and its role in shaping abundance. These include **Understanding Consciousness, Achieving Self-Awareness, Where Are My Thoughts Coming From?, Thoughts and Spoken Language (Words), Why Are Words So Powerful?, Mental Blockages and Limiting Beliefs, Cultivating A Healthy Mind,** and **The Art of Manifesting Abundance.**

Alongside these insights, you are invited to engage deeply with the introspection exercises and integration practices embedded throughout. These practices are not meant to be rushed, but *lived.* Mastering your mind and your thoughts is an ongoing relationship, one that, when nurtured with *awareness* and *compassion*, becomes a powerful foundation for personal growth, fulfillment and a life of authentic, sustainable abundance.

Insights — Understanding Consciousness

History is filled with spiritual visionaries who recognized the extraordinary influence of the human mind. Take Buddha's timeless wisdom, for instance: "*The mind is everything; what you think, you become.*" These powerful words suggest that our thoughts possess extraordinary power, shaping the very fabric of our realities. Our thoughts are more than fleeting ideas; they are the architects of our lived experience. Our internal dialogue influences not only our perceptions but also the emotions and actions that define who we are and who we are evolving into. We can transform our realities by consciously reshaping our mindset, altering thought patterns, feelings and behaviors. When we embrace this truth, we open the door to transformative growth, shaping lives radiant with fulfillment and meaning. With deep self-awareness and intention, we can leverage the power of our thoughts to manifest a more meaningful and abundant life. *Now, how do we begin this journey?* By making small, conscious shifts in our daily thinking, we lay the foundation for a life aligned with our deepest desires and values.

To expand this discussion meaningfully, we must begin by examining the nature of **Consciousness**. At the heart of human inquiry lies consciousness, a concept bridging philosophy, psychology and spirituality. Despite centuries of reflection, its true nature remains open to interpretation, inviting continued exploration and contemplation. Yet, as society enters a new era of awakening, marked by a growing recognition of conscious awareness, the possibility of defining consciousness with clarity draws nearer, awaiting the alignment of collective insight.

As we have seen in exploring abundance versus scarcity, clarity often emerges through the lens of contrast: light against dark, sound against silence, awareness against unawareness. In the same way, the depths of consciousness are most clearly revealed when contrasted with its counterpart: unconsciousness. To truly comprehend what it means to be conscious, we must first examine the unconscious forces that quietly shape our thoughts, behaviors and perceptions. This differentiation provides the foundation for a more complete and embodied understanding of consciousness as a dynamic, ever-evolving state.

We begin by exploring how unconsciousness, unawareness, is understood across both medical and spiritual realms. From a medical perspective, unconsciousness is characterized by a deep lack of responsiveness, leaving an individual disconnected from the world around them. This condition can arise from a variety of causes, including traumatic injuries or specific medical conditions, which lead to a significant decline in cognitive functions such as awareness, self-recognition and responsiveness. In the most severe cases, unconsciousness can result in a comatose state, where an individual becomes nearly impervious to external stimuli and detached from the passage of time. Similarly, from a spiritual perspective, unconsciousness signifies a lack of profound self-awareness, where individuals are unaware of the motivations behind their actions and are disconnected from their conscious thoughts, feelings and memories.

It mirrors a state of sleepwalking through life, functioning without deliberate intention and mindfulness, unaware of the underlying forces that shape behaviors. Unconscious behaviors can manifest in various ways, such as self-sabotage, habitual negative thinking or the avoidance of meaningful opportunities due to fear of failure or rejection. For example, a person may subconsciously, without full conscious awareness, avoid career advancements or fulfilling relationships due to unresolved childhood traumas or deeply ingrained beliefs of unworthiness. These behaviors often operate below the level of conscious awareness, subtly shaping actions, decisions and patterns in life. This unawareness can lead to a life distant from true abundance and fulfillment, as individuals become trapped in unconscious patterns that obscure their potential. Living on autopilot, disconnected from authentic desires and purpose, they may unknowingly erect barriers to personal growth, joy and well-being.

To grasp why unconsciousness, unawareness, can limit fulfillment, it is essential to explore the mind's hidden layers; how the subconscious and unconscious silently guide thoughts, emotions and actions, often outside our conscious control. The subconscious holds memories and information just beyond immediate awareness, influencing thoughts, feelings and behaviors when accessed. The unconscious, however, lies deeper. It is a hidden domain containing repressed memories, desires and drives that remain largely beyond awareness, quietly shaping the patterns of our mind and life. When left unexamined, these hidden terrains can confine us to habitual patterns, preventing the conscious pursuit of our true desires and potential.

Accessing the hidden terrains of the mind requires intention, patience and self-awareness. Practices such as mindfulness meditation, reflective journaling and introspection create a safe space to observe thoughts, emotions and recurring patterns without judgment. Exploring dreams and visualization, tools we explore later, can also offer insights into repressed desires or unresolved experiences, gently revealing what lies beneath conscious awareness. By cultivating presence and consistently turning inward, you begin to uncover these unseen layers, gradually understanding the influences that shape your behaviors and decisions. This process allows you to reclaim autonomy over your inner world, transforming unconscious patterns into conscious choices aligned with your deepest values, desires and potential.

While the subconscious and unconscious quietly shape our inner world, consciousness represents active awareness, allowing us to step into clarity and deliberate choice, engaging fully with our thoughts, experiences and surroundings. For example, as you read this text, you might simultaneously recall past events or imagine future possibilities, all while maintaining awareness of the present moment. Consciousness encompasses the full spectrum of experience, shifting fluidly between thoughts and moments while sustaining a continuous and inherent sense of self-awareness. It reveals itself through various distinct states, such as your awake state, sleep and dreaming. Certain practices and techniques, such as deep mindfulness meditation and breathwork, can lead to heightened states of consciousness, often associated with profound spiritual or esoteric experiences that may be challenging to articulate or comprehend fully.

These experiences represent an advanced level of awareness, allowing you to gain deeper insights into yourself, your purpose and the Universe. Attaining consciousness at any level is regarded as a crucial milestone in accessing a life of profound abundance. To ascend to the highest degree of prosperity and fulfillment, one must embrace consciousness, mindfulness, intentionality and purpose as guiding principles. With a firm understanding of consciousness established, consider this question: *How will you initiate the path toward self-awareness and heightened consciousness today?* Pause now and reflect deeply on this question before moving forward. Further introspective questions on consciousness follow in the next section.

Introspection — Understanding Consciousness

How do you interpret Buddha's quote, "*The mind is everything, what you think, you become*," in the context of your own life? Can you identify instances where your thoughts or beliefs have shaped your reality?

How do you define consciousness? Reflect on the complexities of this concept and consider how your understanding of consciousness has evolved over time.

____

____

____

____

Explore the notion of unconsciousness and its impact on daily life. Have you ever experienced moments of unconscious behavior or a lack of self-awareness? How did these moments influence your decisions and experiences?

____

____

____

____

____

____

____

____

Insights — Achieving Self-Awareness

Building on our exploration of consciousness and unconsciousness, we now delve into a vital dimension of inner growth: **Self-awareness**. Self-awareness is a specific facet of consciousness that focuses on understanding oneself within the broader spectrum of awareness. While consciousness encompasses all levels of awareness, including self-awareness, external awareness and the ability to reflect on these experiences, self-awareness specifically involves recognizing and examining one's thoughts and emotions. Think of consciousness as the ocean's expansive surface, encompassing everything from the gentle waves of everyday awareness to the deep currents of complex thoughts and feelings. It represents the full spectrum of awareness and perception. Self-awareness is the lighthouse, focusing on the immediate surroundings: the shoreline, the rocks and the light it casts. It provides a clear, focused understanding of oneself amidst the vastness of the ocean (consciousness), helping to navigate personal experiences and emotions.

Equally essential to this exploration is understanding the cognitive forces that sustain consciousness and self-awareness, bridging the inner workings of the mind with the essence of being. Among these cognitive processes, metacognition stands out, uncovering the intricate workings of the mind and offering profound insight into how our thoughts are shaped, not as fixed truths, but as dynamic constructs influenced by countless factors and perceptions. It involves becoming aware of and actively managing your own thinking processes, essentially *thinking about your own thinking*. For instance, when studying for an exam, you might notice that a particular concept is not sticking. Instead of simply continuing to read, you pause and reflect on your approach: *Perhaps rereading this section and taking notes will help solidify my understanding*. You may also observe that your focus wanes after a few pages, prompting you to take short breaks to maintain mental clarity. After studying, you assess your progress by quizzing yourself and identifying areas that need further review. This awareness of how you think and how to adjust your methods is a practical example of metacognition in action. It is about consciously guiding your mental processes to enhance learning and growth.

Despite our innate tendency to ascribe absolute truth to our thoughts, metacognition invites us to challenge this assumption, inviting us to recognize that *our minds function as conduits for the flow of thoughts rather than authoritative judges of reality*. This understanding nurtures self-empowerment, allowing clarity and purpose to emerge more naturally. By embracing the notion that our thoughts are malleable and subject to interpretation, we have the potential to reshape our realities for the better. Through the cultivation of self-awareness, the ability to recognize and understand our own thoughts, feelings and behaviors, we gain the capacity to discern the nuances of our thought patterns, freeing ourselves from the constraints of unconscious conditioning and societal expectations.

Consider this following example to reinforce these concepts. Suppose you have a challenging work project that initially seems impossible and overwhelming. By accepting that you can reshape your thoughts, you choose to change your perspective. Instead of dwelling on the difficulties, you start viewing the project as an opportunity for growth and learning. You approach it with curiosity and optimism, setting small, manageable goals and celebrating each success. This change in mindset shifts you from a state of stress and anxiety to one of engagement and enthusiasm. Consequently, your performance on the project improves, and you experience greater job satisfaction and confidence. By deliberately altering your perception of the task, you have transformed your experience and reality, leading to better results and a more profound sense of fulfillment.

Just as metacognition highlights our ability to observe and question our thoughts, the brain itself contains a network that reflects this inner activity: The Default Mode Network (DMN).The Default Mode Network

(DMN) is a network of brain regions that activates when the mind is at rest, disengaged from external tasks. Often described as the brain's "idle" mode, it comes online during daydreaming, self-reflection and contemplation of personal memories or experiences. When attention shifts to goal-directed tasks or external engagement, DMN activity generally diminishes. This network plays a pivotal role in self-referential thinking and internal cognitive processes, including memory recall, envisioning the future and introspective thought, serving as a central hub for understanding the mind's inner workings.

Imagine that you are sitting in your bedroom, gazing out the window on a lazy Sunday afternoon. You are not actively involved in any specific task while your thoughts begin to drift freely. As you observe the world outside, you reflect on past experiences, contemplating plans and pondering various ideas and memories. In this default mode state, your mind effortlessly shifts from one thought to another, without any conscious effort to direct your thinking. Perhaps you find yourself lost in daydreams, recalling pleasant moments from the past or contemplating profound questions about life. In this state, your mind is free to explore a range of thoughts, emotions and memories, allowing for creative insights, problem-solving and self-awareness. While some may view this state as a form of idleness or distraction, it plays a crucial role in cognitive processes and can lead to valuable revelations and self-reflections. Embracing moments of mind wandering and allowing your thoughts to flow freely can foster creativity, enhance self-understanding and promote overall mental well-being.

Concepts like consciousness, self-awareness and cognitive mechanisms such as metacognition and the Default Mode Network form the foundation of a fulfilling and abundant life as they support and enhance our understanding of ourselves and the world. Consciousness and self-awareness enable us to understand our thoughts and emotions allowing us to live more authentically and intentionally. Metacognition helps us explore the true nature of our thoughts, while the Default Mode

Network fosters creativity and self-reflection. Together, these concepts enable us to live mindfully, leading to a life of authenticity, fulfillment and purpose. Integrating these principles into your life empowers you to begin a meaningful journey of self-discovery, navigate challenges with clarity and create a life aligned with your deepest values and aspirations. By peeling back the layers of our cognitive processes, we unearth the transformative power inherent within our minds, paving the way for the manifestation of our deepest desires.

Imagine a scenario where we dwell on past mistakes, allowing them to create feelings of inadequacy or unworthiness. These misleading narratives, rooted in the subconscious or unconscious mind, shape our inner dialogue, erode self-esteem and influence the energy we project into the world. Yet, when we perceive negative thoughts as transient shadows rather than reflections of our true selves, we regain authority over our inner world. By consciously reframing experiences through a lens of possibility and nurturing empowering thoughts, a practice we will explore in greater depth later, we transform not only our emotions but also our actions. Aligning our mental focus with our deepest desires and aspirations allows us to cultivate a life rich in authentic joy, abundance and fulfillment.

A pervasive tendency among people worldwide is to view their inner dialogue and thoughts as inconsequential, which may be a hidden driver behind the widespread mental health issues we see in modern society. Take, for instance, the case of Steven. Following a reprimand at work for an error on a client deliverable, Steven finds himself trapped in a spiral of self-critical thoughts, triggering doubts about his competence and prompting contemplations of quitting his job entirely. *Is Steven allowing his thoughts to take control over his reality, shaping his perceptions and actions, or is he exercising agency over his mindset, actively choosing how to interpret and respond to the situation at hand?* Pause now and reflect deeply on this question before moving forward.

Steven's experience illustrates how deeply our thoughts, both conscious and those rooted in the subconscious and unconscious mind, shape our reality and well-being. His response to the reprimand reveals the impact of unchecked negative self-talk, emphasizing the importance of mindfulness and self-awareness in confronting life's challenges with resilience. By cultivating self-awareness and intentionally examining our thought patterns, we can disrupt harmful mental loops and foster a more empowering inner dialogue, ultimately strengthening our emotional and mental health.

Chronic negative thinking can take a significant toll on the mind, body and spirit, exacerbating anxiety, depression and even physical issues like high blood pressure and a compromised immune system. Yet, despite this understanding, many rely solely on medication, often providing short-term relief without addressing the underlying causes of their distress. A more sustainable approach lies in mastering your mind through self-awareness, the intentional cultivation of healthier thought patterns, and consistent holistic wellness practices. By understanding the inner workings of your mind and actively applying the practical tools presented throughout this guidebook to navigate emotions and beliefs, you will be positioned to experience deeper, more enduring transformations in your mental, emotional and physical well-being.

On the journey toward living full, abundant lives, mastering our minds is the pivotal first step, laying the groundwork for all we attract. Echoing the timeless wisdom of Buddha, who taught, "*The mind is everything; what you think, you become*," we are reminded to let these words guide our awareness and mastery of our own thoughts. Our thoughts hold the power to shape our emotions, drive our behaviors, and ultimately determine the quality of our lives. To access the full potential of our minds, we can cultivate discipline by integrating specific tools, techniques and practices into our daily routines. These tools will be explored in greater depth in the *Integration* section of this segment.

Introspection — Achieving Self-Awareness

Reflect on a recent situation where you were caught in negative thought patterns. What triggered these thoughts, and how did they influence your emotions and actions? What strategies could you employ to reframe these thoughts and cultivate a more positive mindset?

____

____

____

____

____

____

____

____

Consider a time when you experienced a significant life event, such as the end of a relationship or a career setback. How did you initially perceive this situation, and how did your thoughts shape your response? Looking back, can you identify any positive aspects or lessons learned from this experience? How might reframing your perspective have impacted your emotional well-being?

____

____

Reflect on the interconnectedness of thoughts, emotions and actions in shaping your reality. How do your thoughts influence your emotional state, and vice versa? Can you identify any recurring thought-emotion-behavior patterns in your life? What steps can you take to interrupt negative cycles and create more positive and fulfilling outcomes?

Integration — Achieving Self-Awareness

Cultivating mastery over your mind, along with developing consciousness and self-awareness, is not merely attainable with the right practices, it is a vital gateway to experiencing genuine abundance and fulfillment. Fostering awareness and mastering your thoughts, an essential practice that shapes your emotions and behaviors, begins with **intentional stillness**, deep **introspection** and courageous **self-inquiry**. Ask yourself: *Where do my thoughts originate? Are they anchored in past wounds or fears of the future? Do any patterns repeat themselves, and what truths do they reveal?* Especially when confronted with a pattern of negativity, applying metacognitive principles and recognizing our thoughts as mere thoughts can significantly reduce their impact and influence on our psyche. Through this reflective practice, we develop the capacity to acknowledge our thoughts and consciously choose whether to embrace, **reframe** or **release** them, thereby reclaiming agency over our mental landscape and fostering a greater sense of inner peace and autonomy.

When you embrace and welcome a thought, you access the ability not only to accept it but also to reframe its narrative or observe it with clarity, detachment and **objective awareness**. Let us start by exploring the concept of reframing in the context of a profound ending: the close of a significant relationship. It is natural to feel grief, loss and even inadequacy in such moments; these emotions are valid and a testament to the depth of your heart. At the same time, you have the ability to shift your perspective toward a more empowering view. You might see the ending as a driver for personal evolution, embracing the understanding that every challenge carries valuable lessons and opportunities for learning and growth. Reframing involves recognizing the silver linings within adversity and using them to cultivate a mindset rooted in gratitude, resilience and optimism.

Embracing a thought creates space for reframing and empowers you to step into a state of objective awareness. From this perspective, you rise above emotional entanglement, gaining the clarity needed to see the situation for what it truly is, free from bias, distortion or reactive patterns. For example, let us consider the same example as earlier: the aftermath of a breakup. Rather than spiraling into self-blame or resentment, you might observe the thought, "*I wasn't good enough*," and, from a place of objective awareness, reframe it as, "*This ending is creating space for a relationship that aligns with who I'm becoming.*"

Renowned spiritual leader, Eckhart Tolle, celebrated for his profound insights in *The Power of Now: A Guide to Spiritual Enlightenment*, extensively elaborates on this transformative practice. He implores individuals to relinquish the clutches of the ego-mind and transition into the role of the detached "watcher." This shift in consciousness enables one to transcend the constant chatter of thoughts and the mayhem of emotions, ushering in a profound state of heightened awareness and inner tranquility. Through deliberate cultivation of this practice, individuals can free themselves from the constraints of the ego, accessing a realm of profound clarity and peace (Tolle, 1999). We explore the concept of freeing yourself from the constraints of the ego in *Chapter 4: The Abundance Pillars – Mastering Your Life and Collective Consciousness* in the *Insights and Integration* segment of *Transcending the Ego*.

To achieve success in this practice, we might initiate a process of introspection by asking: *What insights would an impartial observer bring to this scenario? How would my perspective shift if I encountered this situation as an outsider?* By cultivating curiosity, you open the door to exploring the origins of your thoughts, along with the beliefs and expectations that shape them, concepts we introduced earlier when discussing metacognition. By reflecting on your own thinking, you can question why you hold certain convictions and belief systems, uncover their underlying motivations and assess their alignment with your authentic self. This intentional process of self-inquiry allows you to distinguish between beliefs rooted in personal experience and those grounded in objective truth. Developing this awareness enables you to make more informed decisions, cultivate a mindset aligned with reality and intentionally direct your thoughts and beliefs toward your deepest desires, enhancing self-awareness, clarity and purpose.

While accepting a thought offers a valuable opportunity to reframe it and adopt a stance of objective awareness, releasing a thought provides a powerful opportunity to ground yourself in the present moment, freeing you from the hold of past regrets or future anxieties. Imagine you are immersed in a project when an unsettling thought about a past mistake surfaces. This thought begins to distract you, stirring feelings of anxiety and frustration. To release it, start by acknowledging its presence without judgment. Simply recognize, *I am thinking about that past event.* This act of mindful awareness creates a space between you and the thought, allowing it to pass without keeping you hostage. By observing the thought without attachment, you anchor yourself in the present moment, fostering clarity and focus. To initiate this practice, begin by pausing and taking a few slow, deep breaths, allowing each inhale and exhale to gently ground you in the present moment. As you settle into this awareness, observe the thought that has arisen and consider: *Is this thought serving a constructive purpose right now?* If it is not, acknowledge its presence without judgment, and gently redirect your attention back to your current task. By consciously shifting your focus, you can release the thought's hold, reduce its emotional impact, and restore your concentration and inner calm.

The most effective approach to accomplish this involves centering your attention firmly on the here and now. Techniques such as **mindfulness meditation** and **breathwork** are powerful and effective practices for fostering present-moment awareness. Both methods ground your attention to the present by immersing the mind in current experiences and sensations, minimizing distractions and enhancing awareness. With just a few simple steps, you can engage in both mindfulness meditation and breathwork to cultivate present-moment awareness. Let us participate in a simple mindfulness practice now:

Begin by creating a dedicated space free from distractions, allowing yourself to fully immerse in the present moment. Sit comfortably with your back straight and hands resting gently in your lap. Close your eyes and bring your awareness to the natural rhythm of your breath. Feel the coolness of the air as it enters your nostrils and the warmth as it exits. Notice the gentle rise and fall of your chest and abdomen with each breath. As thoughts arise, acknowledge them without judgment and gently return your focus to your breath. If distractions occur, observe them with curiosity and compassion, then redirect your attention back to the soothing rhythm of your breathing. Remain in this mindful state for as long as you wish. Before proceeding, reflect deeply on how this mindfulness practice has made you feel.

It is important to remember that the more you practice and integrate practices such as mindfulness meditation and breathwork into your life, two mutually reinforcing methods that combine for greater present-moment awareness, the more effective the results will be. Consistent and dedicated practice of the tools and techniques presented in this segment offers a profound opportunity for self-discovery and inner transformation, guiding you toward a state of greater presence, clarity and inner peace. These self-awareness tools are just a sampling of practices designed to help you steer your mind, deepen your self-awareness, and channel your thoughts toward personal growth and evolution, without allowing them to dominate or derail you. By intentionally focusing on positive thoughts and emotions, you can shape your daily experiences, filling them with joy, peace, resilience, and a deep sense of fulfillment. By consistently practicing mindfulness and maintaining a vigilant awareness of your mental landscape, you equip yourself with the capacity to navigate life's challenges with greater clarity and purpose. This heightened state of self-awareness enables you to discern the nature of your thoughts, distinguishing between those that uplift and empower you and those that inhibit and constrain you.

Moreover, by consciously generating positive thoughts and emotions, you leverage the transformative power of your mindset to shape your reality. Instead of allowing negative thought patterns to dictate your experiences, you actively choose to focus on optimism, gratitude and joy, thereby infusing each moment with a renewed sense of energy and purpose. These self-awareness tools serve as agents of change for personal evolution, empowering you to transcend limitations, cultivate resilience and embrace a life of abundance and fulfillment. By nurturing self-awareness, positive thoughts and emotions, you activate the potential to shape a reality that resonates with your deepest aspirations, desires and values, thereby enriching your life and the lives of those around you.

Insights — Where Are My Thoughts Coming From?

The profound journey into consciousness and self-awareness begins with these questions: ***Where Are My Thoughts Coming From?*** *And what shapes them?* These inquiries bridge both spiritual wisdom and scientific understanding. Spiritually, we can turn inward, viewing thought as an expression of the soul and the greater collective consciousness. As Eckhart Tolle teaches, our thoughts are not entirely our own but often arise from the collective mind and the subtle energetic fields that surround us. He explains that we can absorb thoughts from this universal field, especially those that align with our current emotional state. As we experience heightened self-awareness, we often come to realize that our thoughts, insights and inner shifts are not occurring in isolation; they are part of a much larger, interconnected field of collective consciousness. This shared energetic and informational space subtly influences our perceptions and inspirations, suggesting that our personal awakenings are inextricably linked to the evolution of human consciousness through a comprehensive network of interconnected experiences. Tolle notes that our emotions operate in much the same way, linking our individual experiences to the broader field of collective consciousness.

Tolle's view that our thoughts emerge from the collective consciousness of the Universe invites us to take mindful ownership of them, reminding us of the importance of intentional thought management and guiding our focus toward positivity and constructive expression, both within ourselves and in our interactions with others. Some spiritual thinkers believe that negative thoughts directed at individuals can attach themselves to them, strengthening and prolonging their current state, nature and attitude. Consider a workplace scenario where one team member consistently harbors criticism or resentment toward a colleague. Over time, the targeted individual may begin to feel demoralized or anxious, even if they are unaware of the specific negative focus. This example highlights how thought energy can subtly influence others. Therefore, it becomes imperative that we cultivate thought processes geared toward nurturing positive outcomes, with a collective consciousness in mind, to foster balance and cohesion within the broader community.

Having explored the spiritual origins of thought, we can now turn to the insights that science provides on where our thoughts arise. Neuroscience shows that our thoughts are closely linked to brain activity, influenced by our personal identity, social environment and the wider collective of humanity. In essence, our thoughts emerge as a response to how our brain functions, our personal experiences and the social and relational context in which we exist. Though the biological definition of thoughts and the processes by which neural activity generates them are still not completely understood, overwhelming evidence supports the brain's fundamental role in both the creation and storage of thoughts. It serves as the central conduit from which thoughts spring forth, shaping our perceptions, actions, and, ultimately, our reality. External stimuli such as cultural norms or societal expectations you encounter daily, intertwined with our personal history, memories and the wealth of knowledge we accumulate over time, plays a key role in the complex process of thought formation. By creating neural connections, these diverse inputs coalesce to give rise to the complex range of our thoughts, manifesting as streams of consciousness that guide and influence every perception and decision.

It is essential to note that thoughts possess the potential to gradually transform into belief systems and deeply held convictions over time. Repeated thoughts, shaped by personal experiences and reinforced by social and cultural influences, take root in our consciousness. Over time, these patterns solidify into core beliefs that guide how we perceive the world, make decisions and interact with others, subtly directing the course of our lives. The cumulative impact of this shift (thoughts to beliefs) is powerful, highlighting the crucial role our thoughts play in forming the foundation of our reality and guiding how we move through life. Beliefs and belief systems will be explored in greater detail in a forthcoming section.

Regardless of one's stance on the origin of thoughts, whether they are perceived as personal creations derived from our history, memories and life experiences or as manifestations of the collective conscious mind, it is crucial to explore their origins and impact in our journey toward greater self-awareness. By exploring these powerful ideas, we embrace an evolutionary journey to cultivate deeper consciousness, empowering ourselves with the insights needed to master our minds and navigate the complexities of our inner worlds. Through this process, we deepen our understanding of the elaborate relationship between our consciousness and the broader network of universal consciousness, fostering a heightened sense of awareness and agency in shaping our realities. Thus, by embracing this deliberate exploration of thought origins, we lay the foundation for profound personal growth and evolution.

Introspection — Where Are My Thoughts Coming From?

Reflect on Eckhart Tolle's perspective that our thoughts may arise from a collective consciousness rather than solely from within ourselves. How does this idea influence your understanding of your thoughts and emotions? Consider a recent thought or emotion you experienced and explore how it might connect with broader, collective influences.

____

____

____

____

____

____

____

____

Explore how your personal history, memories and external stimuli contribute to your thought patterns according to neuroscience. What specific experiences or knowledge have shaped your current way of thinking? Consider how these elements intertwine to shape your current perceptions and behaviors.

____

____

Contemplate the impact of nurturing positive thoughts versus harboring negativity, as suggested by spiritual leaders. How might your thought patterns affect not only your well-being but also the broader community? Reflect on a situation where you had a negative thought about someone and consider how changing your perspective could foster more alignment and growth in your interactions.

Insights — Thoughts and Spoken Language (Words)

Mastering your mind demands a deliberate and mindful exploration of your thoughts, unraveling their origins, understanding their pathways and leveraging their transformative power to create a life brimming with fulfillment, prosperity and joy. As human beings, we are born with the extraordinary capacity for thought formation, a fundamental aspect of our cognitive architecture and abilities. While the capacity for thought is innate to us, the evolution of spoken (and written) language results from environmental factors and societal influences. At its core, thinking is a cognitive process fueled by the pursuit for the construction of meaning and connections within the world we inhabit and interact with every day. Yet, through the medium of spoken language, our thoughts find structure, expression and coherence, providing the framework for our ideas, values, belief systems and the articulation of both conscious and unconscious thoughts. While thinking is the foundation for our mental landscape, language acts as the conduit through which our innermost thoughts are expressed and conveyed to the outside world.

The intricate relationship between **Thoughts and Spoken Language (Words)** highlights a fundamental aspect of human cognition. Our thoughts (and the feelings and emotions they generate) shape the words we choose, the tone we use and even the structure and patterns of our spoken language. Simultaneously, spoken language profoundly influences how we perceive and interact with the world. Many theorists argue that the language we speak can significantly impact our cognitive processes and worldview. For instance, the vocabulary we possess, the associations we attach to specific words and the patterns of spoken language we use, all play a pivotal role in influencing our perceptions. The Sapir-Whorf Hypothesis, also known as linguistic relativity, suggests that the structure and vocabulary of a language can subtly shape how its speakers perceive and interpret the world. Instead of constraining thought, language guides attention, frames perception and highlights certain aspects of our environment, subtly shaping how we experience and interpret reality.

Consider two people: one who speaks English and another who speaks Pirahã, an Amazonian language. In English, we have precise words for numbers like "one," "two," and "three." In contrast, Pirahã lacks specific words for exact numbers, using only terms like "few" and "many." This linguistic difference profoundly impacts how speakers of each language perceive and interact with the world. An English speaker, accustomed to precise numerical terms, can accurately count and match exact quantities. In contrast, a Pirahã speaker, without words for exact numbers, relies on an approximate sense of quantity. When asked to match a group of objects, the Pirahã speaker would group them based on an overall impression of "few" or "many" rather than counting each item individually.

By comparing English and Pirahã speakers, we gain compelling insight into how linguistic structures shape not only thought but the very lens through which individuals experience the world. While spoken language (and words) profoundly influences how we perceive and interpret reality, it does not inherently constrain the breadth or complexity of human thought. Instead, individuals possess the remarkable capacity to transcend linguistic boundaries and engage in abstract conceptualization that surpasses the confines of linguistic expression. Personal experiences, cultural influences and imaginative faculties fuel this capacity, animating human cognition.

Consider the concept of love, which is expressed in many languages but often described in unique ways. For instance, in English, we might use the word "love" to describe romantic affection, deep friendship or familial bonds. In Greek, however, there are distinct words for different types of love: "eros" for romantic love, "philia" for friendship, "storge" for familial love, and "agape" for unconditional or selfless love, often associated with spiritual or altruistic feelings. Despite these linguistic differences, people across cultures experience and understand love similarly. For example, a person speaking Greek might express their feelings of deep friendship using the word "philia," while an English speaker uses the term "love." Both individuals are experiencing and understanding a profound emotional connection, showing that the essence of their experience transcends the limitations of their specific language. This illustrates how, although language shapes how we discuss our feelings, it does not limit our ability to experience and understand complex emotions and energies like love. Language shapes our cognitive landscape, but it is not a prison. Rather, it functions as a dynamic instrument that works in concert with our innate cognitive abilities.

Beyond shaping thought, language also serves as a conduit for expression and connection, allowing us to translate internal experiences into shared understanding. It allows us to share our experiences, convey ideas and cultivate understanding, naturally nurturing connections with others. Through spoken language, we have a powerful way to express our inner thoughts and feelings, engage with those around us and build aligned perspectives within our communities. For instance, a friend describing the challenges of a difficult week not only conveys their emotions but also invites empathy and support, deepening the connection between speaker and listener. The intricate connection between thought and spoken language is multifaceted and ever-evolving, influenced by a myriad of individual, societal and environmental variables. Spoken language serves not only as a channel for expression but also as a powerful shaper of our experiences and interpretations of reality.

The words we choose, whether in our inner dialogue or in conversation with others, deeply influence our conscious and subconscious thought patterns. In turn, these thoughts shape our emotions, reactions and behaviors, both within and beyond us. While language undoubtedly shapes how we perceive and express our thoughts, it represents only one facet of a deeper process. Our internal mental activity is the true engine of understanding and engagement with the world. Language may guide how we articulate ideas, but it is our core cognitive processes that ultimately define how we interpret and interact with reality.

Understanding the relationship between thoughts and spoken language profoundly shapes our reality and quality of life. Just as we apply self-awareness tools to manage our thoughts, we must approach our spoken words with the same mindfulness and deliberate intention. Spoken words serve as the channel through which we connect with others and perceive the world around us, making it a crucial tool in our pursuit of abundance and fulfillment. By aligning our thoughts and spoken words with intentional actions, as we will explore in subsequent segments, we empower ourselves to create the life we desire. It is important to highlight that for our intentions to actualize effectively, all three elements: thoughts, spoken words and intentional actions, must operate in alignment.

Introspection — Thoughts and Spoken Language (Words)

Consider how the language you use affects your perception of the world. Think of a recent situation where your choice of words influenced your interpretation or reaction. Write about how language serves as a lens through which you view and interact with your surroundings and how adjusting your language might shift your perspective or outcomes.

____

____

____

____

____

____

____

____

Explore a situation where your internal thoughts and external language were not aligned. How did this misalignment impact your communication or relationships? Reflect on how aligning your thoughts with your spoken words could enhance your interactions and create a more fulfilling and prosperous life.

____

____

Examine the impact of language on your ability to manifest your goals and intentions. How does the way you speak about your desires and aspirations either support or hinder your progress? Reflect on a recent goal-setting experience and write about how changing the language you use in your declarations and affirmations could lead to greater alignment and success.

Integration — Thoughts and Spoken Language (Words)

Using spoken language effectively is not merely about articulating words accurately, but about engaging in conscious, intentional communication rooted in love, gratitude, positivity and conviction. The potency of our words lies not only in their literal meaning but also in the emotions they evoke and the meaning (and feelings) we infuse into them. Hollow utterances lacking genuine emotion and conviction lack the resonance necessary to effect meaningful change. Harnessing the transformative power of our words requires a profound sense of **mindfulness**, a deliberate awareness of the thoughts and emotions behind our speech. Just as mindfulness serves as a vehicle for self-awareness and grounding oneself in the present moment, it also proves indispensable in cultivating the conscious awareness necessary to channel the potential utility of both our internal and external dialogue.

Mastering mindfulness with spoken words entails deliberating aligning our thoughts and emotions with our intentions, both in our inner monologues and external interactions. By examining our choice of words, communication habits and styles, we can activate transformative shifts in our lives, exerting greater control over the impact our words wield on ourselves and those around us. Incorporating simple yet powerful practices into our daily routine, such as integrating intentionality through **pausing and introspection**, can facilitate mindful speaking. For instance, adopting the habit of posing check-in questions to ourselves during self-talk or conversations with others serves as a powerful technique for utilizing our spoken words effectively.

Let us say you are engaging in self-talk or conversing with a friend. You have made it a habit to ask yourself check-in questions such as, *"Is what I'm saying coming from a place of authenticity and kindness?"* or *"Am I truly expressing my authentic self?"* These questions serve as powerful tools to help you use your spoken words in a way that authentically represents who you are and how you want to show up in the world. They prompt you to reflect on the underlying message you want to convey and whether it reflects values like love, kindness, positivity and authenticity. If discrepancies arise, we have the opportunity to consciously reshape our words to ensure they align with our intentions and desired outcomes. By engaging with spoken language mindfully, we open the door to deeper connections, genuine self-expression and transformative shifts in both our lives and relationships.

Acknowledging the profound role of **silence** in both our external communication and inner reflection reveals another powerful tool for activating the transformative power of language. Embracing moments of silence grants us invaluable space to discern the essence of the message we wish to convey, affording us the precious opportunity to align our words with our deepest intentions and desires. Though often seen as uncomfortable, silence and pauses in conversation can be reimagined as valuable opportunities for introspection, fostering more intentional and mindful communication. Rather than hastily filling the void with idle chatter, embracing silence allows us to attune to the subtle nuances of our thoughts and their origins. In moments of quiet reflection, we can gain clarity and authenticity in our expressions, making sure our words truly reflect our deepest intentions and goals. Honoring the power of silence allows us to nurture more intentional, meaningful and impactful communication, both within ourselves and in our relationships with others.

As integration deepens, **affirmations** serve as a powerful practice for mastering the mind and reinforcing conscious communication. They allow us to leverage the transformative power of our words, supporting personal growth and inner transformation. Through consistent use, affirmations help reprogram limiting thought patterns, foster self-belief and protect us from discouragement, negative self-talk and self-sabotage. These uplifting statements of truth offer more than just positive reinforcement; they act as a driver for powerful changes in our mindset, emotions and behavior. By consistently affirming our inherent worth, capabilities and potential, we imbue ourselves with confidence and self-empowerment that propels us towards our aspirations and deepest desires. Moreover, affirmations possess the remarkable ability to recalibrate our thought patterns, transmuting negativity into positivity and fostering a mindset of joy, abundance and opportunity.

Through the deliberate practice of affirmations, we can cultivate empowering belief systems that anchor us in resilience and optimism, paving the way for transformative growth and fulfillment. For instance, reframing self-limiting beliefs such as "*I am inexperienced*" into affirmations like "*I am continuously learning and growing*" empowers us to embrace challenges with courage and determination. Affirmations serve as a powerful tool for aligning our words with the vision of our desired outcomes, stimulating profound shifts in consciousness and guiding us towards manifesting our highest potential.

For affirmations to truly transform, consistency and genuine belief are essential. Much like the emotions behind gratitude, the true power of our affirmations lies not just in the words we say, but in the depth of emotion and conviction we pour into them. Utterances devoid of genuine feeling lack the vibrational resonance required to instigate profound shifts in consciousness. Consider the affirmation "*I will engage in loving and kind thoughts about myself and to myself.*" While this declaration holds the promise of bolstering self-confidence, its impact is contingent upon your unwavering belief in its validity and the steadfast repetition of this affirmation in your daily practice. By infusing this statement with unshakable certainty and repeating it regularly, you access its transformative potential to foster a mindset devoid of self-limiting beliefs and negative thought patterns. The strength of affirmations lies not merely in their verbal articulation but in the depth of faith and consistency with which they are embraced, serving as effective triggers for personal growth and self-empowerment.

Engaging in "*I AM*" affirmations can significantly amplify the power of your self-talk, reinforcing your self-worth and self-esteem by reshaping your self-perception. These affirmations, whether spoken out loud or written down, have a significant way of building a positive self-image and boosting your confidence in your abilities and potential. To begin working with these empowering affirmations, start by choosing a quality, trait or achievement and focusing on its positive aspects. For instance, you might declare, "*I am poised to accomplish all of my goals because I possess strength, capability and discipline.*" This affirmation not only serves as a potent reminder of your inherent worth and value but also instills a sense of accountability towards your aspirations. Integrating positive affirmations into your daily routine can lead to reduced stress levels, heightened well-being and a more optimistic worldview, laying the groundwork for a life brimming with abundance and fulfillment.

Take a moment to create positive and empowering affirmations for yourself right now. Choose a quality, trait or accomplishment you are proud of, and emphasize its most uplifting and powerful attributes. Use the previous example as a guide if needed. Once you have created your affirmations and spoken them aloud (with full conviction), pause and reflect on how they made you feel. Notice any shifts in your energy or mindset. Keep in mind that speaking affirmations out loud can feel awkward or unnatural at first, especially if they challenge long-held beliefs, but this discomfort is part of the growth process. Over time, it becomes a powerful tool for rewiring the mind and embracing life's flux. Remember, the more consistently you engage in this practice, the stronger and more impactful it becomes. As you continually reinforce these affirmations, you will begin to internalize them, allowing them to become a natural and empowering part of your daily self-talk and routine.

Insights — Why Are Words So Powerful?

Have you ever experienced the phenomenon where something you spoke about materialized in real life, seemingly out of thin air, almost as if you were casting a spell? Many might dismiss these occurrences as mere coincidences, but let us entertain another possibility. *What if everything we express outwardly, stemming from the thoughts we cultivate, has the potential to manifest into reality?* Imagine the impact this realization could have on how we communicate, both with ourselves and with others. These ideas may diverge from mainstream discourse, yet they prompt profound questions about the nature of reality and the power of our thoughts and language. As we journey toward abundance and fulfillment, we ask: ***Why Are Words So Powerful?*** Embracing unconventional ideas and cultivating an *open, curious mindset* allows us to recognize and channel the transformative energy embedded in our spoken words, shaping both our experiences and the reality we create.

Spoken words are remarkable; they resonate with a unique vibrational energy that reverberates in the space around us. When we give voice to our thoughts, we release powerful vibrational frequencies, sound waves that ripple through space, imprinting our intentions upon the energy field of the Universe. Each word we speak and every statement we form carries with it a distinct vibrational pattern, capable of shaping the world around us in profound ways. Reflect on the Law of Attraction, a powerful principle asserting that like energies inevitably draw each other in. This principle becomes even more potent when applied to the spoken word and its inherent energetic force. The energy we send out through our thoughts, emotions and words has a powerful effect on attracting similar experiences into our lives. If we consistently align our thoughts, words, emotions and actions with abundance, fulfillment, love, joy and peace, we are likely to attract more of these positive experiences into our lives. Conversely, if our thoughts, words, emotions and actions are steeped in negativity, scarcity, worry and problems, we may find ourselves drawing more of these experiences toward us.

Fundamentally, **words infused with higher vibrational frequencies, such as those imbued with gratitude, prosperity and positivity, possess the inherent ability to resonate at elevated levels of energy**. Conversely, **words marked by negativity, anger and fear tend to vibrate at lower frequencies, emanating a less potent energetic resonance**. This distinction in vibrational frequencies emphasizes the profound impact of our choice of words on the energetic landscape of our existence. In a later segment, we will explore in greater detail the intricacies of energy, the contrast between high and low vibrations and the notion of vibrational frequencies. Through this exploration, we aim to highlight how these vibrational frequencies intricately shape our experiences, perceptions, and, ultimately, our realities. By understanding the energetic dynamics at play, we can leverage the power of language to consciously cultivate the vibrational frequencies that align with our desires and aspirations, thereby charting a path toward greater abundance, fulfillment and joy.

Spoken words transcend their conventional function as tools of communication. They become powerful carriers of energy and drivers for transformation and manifestation. Through this process, they become instrumental in forming the reality we envision. Grounded in the principles of the Law of Attraction, this perspective holds that the frequency and vibrations emanating from our thoughts, words, emotions and actions dynamically interact with the powers of the Universe, exerting a profound influence on our lived experiences. When we engage in spoken communication, we are not merely articulating thoughts but actively shaping the energetic environment surrounding us. This recognition highlights the pivotal role we play as co-creators of our reality, actively participating in the ongoing process of manifestation in collaboration with the Universe. Far from being passive observers, we are empowered agents endowed with the capacity to channel this inherent power to manifest our deepest desires and aspirations into tangible existence.

This empowering realization acts as a gateway, inviting us to explore the depths of our being and embrace transformative change. It encourages us to understand the intricate workings of our minds, recognizing the immense power inherent in our words and thought formations. By cultivating mindfulness and intentionality in both our external speech and inner dialogue, we position ourselves as active participants in the creation of our reality. Through conscious awareness and deliberate thought, we align ourselves with vibrational frequencies that resonate with our deepest desires, aspirations and values. In doing so, we not only direct the course of our own lives but also shape the unfolding narrative of our shared human experience. By influencing the energy, values and actions we bring into our communities, we create ripple effects that inspire, uplift and shift collective consciousness and social dynamics. In essence, we become architects of our destiny, co-creators of the beautiful story that unfolds before us, and stewards of our shared reality, fostering growth, fulfillment and well-being for ourselves and the collective.

The impact of our spoken words extends beyond audible communication. It encompasses the silent dialogue we engage in within the depths of our minds. This internal discussion, often overlooked yet profoundly influential, possesses the inherent ability to shape our realities in much the same way as our vocalized expressions. Much like spoken words, which carry energy that influences our thoughts, emotions and actions, the stories we tell ourselves hold a similar power. These personal conversations, cultivated from our innermost thoughts and beliefs, resonate with energy vibrations that reverberate throughout our consciousness, subtly molding our perceptions and shaping our lives. It is therefore imperative that we approach our internal dialogue with the same mindfulness and intentionality as we do our outward expressions, recognizing its potential to either uplift and empower us or undermine and disempower us.

When we infuse our internal dialogue with positivity and encouragement, it becomes a powerful force for manifestation, aligning our thoughts and emotions with the vibrational frequencies that help realize our dreams and aspirations. Conversely, when negativity infiltrates our inner narrative, it generates discordant vibrations that manifest a reality at odds with our deepest desires and intentions. In essence, the alignment of our thoughts and spoken words with our intentions and desires must be mirrored in the silent conversations we have with ourselves. It is through this harmonization of internal and external dialogue that we wield the transformative power of manifestation, consciously steering the trajectory of our lives toward abundance and fulfillment.

Introspection — Why Are Words So Powerful?

Reflect on a time when something you spoke about or repeatedly thought of seemingly materialized in your life. Describe the situation in detail. What words did you use, and how did they align with your thoughts and emotions at that time?

____

____

____

____

____

____

____

____

Choose a current goal or desire in your life. What words and phrases do you typically use when thinking or speaking about this goal? Do these words carry a high vibrational energy (e.g., optimism, confidence) or a low vibrational energy (e.g., doubt, fear)?

____

____

____

____

____

____

____

____

Reflect on your internal dialogue, especially in moments of stress or decision-making. How do your inner thoughts support or hinder your goals? Are they empowering, or do they generate conflict within you?

____

____

____

____

____

____

____

____

Insights — Mental Blockages and Limiting Beliefs

We have explored the depths of consciousness, delved into self-awareness and the origin of our thoughts, and examined the transformative power of spoken language and words. Now, we step into a phase of intentional mental mastery: cultivating a resilient, empowered and flourishing inner world. The following sections unfold through a variety of intentional practices and pathways, each serving the broader goal of nurturing a mind that is not only strong and resilient, but also deeply attuned to clarity, purpose and well-being. This journey may unfold in diverse ways, with each path contributing to the cultivation of an empowered mind. Building on the foundational tools we have explored, we have established a firm platform for nurturing lasting mental well-being. These tools plant the seeds for a mind that stands strong, clear and unshaken amidst life's storms. This segment aims to support you in creating a radiant internal landscape, one that powerfully influences how you perceive and engage with the world around you.

In our journey to master our mind, we face both intricate challenges and profound opportunities for growth. Confronting and releasing the limiting thoughts and beliefs that hinder self-empowerment, inner peace and genuine fulfillment is essential to revealing your highest potential. By addressing these obstacles directly, we clear the path for deep transformation and personal evolution. We will explore the art of training the mind and refining your thoughts through consistent, purposeful practices and unwavering commitment, fostering sharpened focus, heightened mental acuity and resilient strength in the face of life's challenges. Through mastering our thoughts, we regain control over our inner world, unleashing limitless potential for personal growth and self-discovery. Furthermore, by cultivating a mindset consistently rooted in abundance, gratitude and possibility, we transcend the confines of scarcity and limitation, embracing a reality exploding with opportunity and prosperity. The pursuit of a healthy mind is an ongoing process, one that demands steadfast patience, dedication and self-reflection.

Just as recognizing the essence of scarcity is key to embracing abundance, understanding the true nature of **Mental Blockages and Limiting Beliefs** is crucial for effectively cultivating a strong and thriving mind. *Now, what are mental blockages and limiting beliefs?* Mental blockages and limiting beliefs are deeply ingrained thought patterns that hinder personal growth and success. Common mental barriers such as perfectionism, self-doubt, fear of rejection and overthinking can paralyze action and stall progress. Deep-seated limiting beliefs, such as "*I'm not worthy*," "*I don't deserve success*," or "*It's too late to change*," trap individuals in cycles of self-sabotage, keeping them from fully realizing their potential.

Mental blockages and limiting beliefs are major obstacles to our inner well-being, casting a shadow over our daily lives and leaving us feeling overwhelmed and stuck. They serve as the antithesis of mental health, obstructing our path to growth and evolution, cornerstones of abundance. Furthermore, they can trigger cognitive distortions, alter our perceptions of reality and divert us from the truth. Often shaped by past experiences or societal conditioning, these blockages and limiting beliefs can quietly sabotage our growth, eroding our potential for personal and professional fulfillment. To overcome these blockages, it is vital that we cultivate self-awareness, engage in self-reflection and commit to replacing negative thought patterns with empowering beliefs. It is essential to acknowledge these blockages and their origins while arming ourselves with the tools and practices needed to overcome them, cultivate healthier thought patterns and nurture a more positive mindset.

Understanding the roots of mental blocks and limiting beliefs is crucial as it enables us to identify the underlying causes of our self-imposed limitations. By uncovering the sources of these patterns, whether from past experiences, societal influences or personal fears, we gain the clarity needed to challenge them. Whether in our careers, relationships or self-perception, understanding the origins of our challenges is essential. Many of these struggles stem from unresolved trauma or the beliefs and values we have internalized from the world around us. Let us begin by examining the profound influence of trauma. Unresolved trauma can silently shape our core beliefs about ourselves and the world, erecting mental barriers intended to protect us from perceived threats, yet simultaneously limiting our growth, potential and capacity for fulfillment.

For example, consider someone who experienced emotional neglect during childhood. This unresolved trauma might lead them to develop the belief that they are unworthy of love or success. As a result, they may subconsciously avoid opportunities for connection or career advancement, fearing rejection or failure. This fear of failure becomes a mental block, preventing them from fully pursuing their goals and reaching their potential. The belief that they are not good enough may also trigger self-doubt, causing them to second-guess their decisions and abilities, even when opportunities arise. Healing this past trauma through therapy, self-reflection or other healing methods can help them confront these limiting beliefs and transform their mindset, ultimately freeing them to embrace growth and fully engage with life's possibilities. We will explore the topic of healing in greater detail in a later segment.

In addition to trauma, our upbringing, particularly the manner in which our parents imparted their values, cultural norms and belief systems upon us during our formative years, plays a pivotal role in shaping our mental and psychological landscape. When childhood is marked by unrealistic expectations or overly critical parenting, we may internalize feelings of inadequacy and unworthiness. These ingrained beliefs can persist into adulthood, quietly shaping our choices and creating invisible barriers to new opportunities. As our inner dialogue repeats messages of limitation and incapacity, these convictions can subtly erode our confidence, curtail our ambitions and inhibit the full expression of our potential.

Understanding the roots of our limiting beliefs is paramount to our growth and self-realization. By acknowledging that these beliefs may stem from childhood conditioning and past experiences, we can disentangle them from our sense of self-worth and value. By bringing these unconscious patterns to light, we can question their validity and reassess our beliefs based on where we are now and what we hope to achieve. In doing so, we cultivate a more profound sense of grace, self-compassion and acceptance, recognizing that our worth extends far beyond the limitations imposed by our past experiences. By embracing our inherent worthiness and ability to evolve, we empower ourselves to transcend the constraints of our limiting beliefs and live authentically aligned with our essence.

Beyond trauma and our early upbringing, the people and environments we interact with daily, both socially and professionally, play a major role in shaping our personal beliefs and values, particularly if we have not yet solidified our own set of beliefs and values. Our interactions within these circles can shape our perceptions of ourselves and the world around us in profound ways. For instance, if our social circle is rife with individuals with conflicting values, harboring limiting beliefs or engaged in unhealthy, competitive or ill-intentioned behavior, it can seep into our own psyche, affecting our self-perception and outlook on life. The pervasive presence of their limiting beliefs, destructive habits and negative attitudes may act as deterrents, steering us away from our journey towards growth and evolution, undermining our confidence and hindering our progress towards achieving our goals. It is widely believed that we become the average of the people we spend the most time with. Consequently, it is vital to select your social circle deliberately, ensuring that those closest to you align with your values and actively champion your growth and success, while offering the same in return.

Imagine being immersed in a community of individuals who embody your values, inspire expansive thought and engage in authentic, collaborative and compassionate action. Their presence becomes a mirror of possibility, elevating your mindset, refining your self-perception and nurturing a more empowered outlook on life. Surrounded by their optimism and aligned energy, you naturally rise, propelled toward greater growth, fulfillment and purpose. This supportive environment could bolster your confidence and expedite your journey toward realizing your aspirations and ambitions. The relationships and environments you immerse yourself in can become either gateways to growth or barriers to evolution. Since your surroundings shape your thoughts, attitudes and beliefs, being discerning about who you keep close is an act of both self-awareness and self-respect.

By choosing our social connections with care and intention, we can surround ourselves with people who truly align with our values and support our growth. Through mindful observation, we become attuned to the undercurrents within our relationships, sensing which ones expand us and which ones restrict us. This conscious awareness empowers us to nurture bonds that elevate our spirit and align with our deeper purpose. Introspection invites us to thoughtfully explore our relationships and the subtle ways they shape our mental, emotional and spiritual well-being. It asks us to consider whether our connections are grounded in authenticity, mutual respect and genuine reciprocity, qualities that foster a supportive environment where growth and fulfillment can flourish.

Beyond trauma, upbringing and external influences, our personal experiences also play an important role in shaping our mental blockages and limiting beliefs. Consider, for instance, the moments in our lives where we may have faced failure or embarrassment. Such experiences can etch themselves into our subconscious, breeding self-doubt and internal criticism that sustain limiting narratives about who we are and what we are capable of achieving. When we encounter setbacks or missteps, our internal critic often seizes the opportunity to amplify its voice, inundating our mental landscape with self-criticism. This internal dialogue can create a distorted perception of ourselves, leading us to internalize these negative experiences and interpret them as reflections of our inherent inadequacies.

It is during these experiences that it is imperative to recognize and confront this internal noise, challenging the false narratives that it seeks to impose upon us. By actively cultivating self-awareness, employing reframing techniques, practicing gratitude and embracing self-compassion, tools we will explore in more detail, we can weaken the influence of our inner critic and develop a more resilient and empowered mindset. Adopting a growth and evolution mindset helps us see setbacks as chances to learn and grow, giving us the confidence and determination to overcome obstacles and chase our goals with boldness and trust.

INTROSPECTION — MENTAL BLOCKAGES AND LIMITING BELIEFS

Reflect on a recent mental blockage or limiting belief you have encountered. Explore its possible origins, such as unresolved trauma or past experiences, and consider how these influences have shaped your current mindset. Adopt new, empowering beliefs or strategies to help you transcend these barriers.

____

____

____

____

____

____

____

____

Evaluate the impact of your closest social and professional connections on your mindset. Examine how their values and behaviors shape your beliefs and aspirations. Consider making intentional shifts in your social circle to better reflect your values and support your personal development.

____

____

Revisit a past failure or moment of embarrassment that still affects you. Reinterpret this experience as a valuable lesson or growth opportunity. Reflect on how this reframing enhances your self-confidence and prepares you for future challenges with renewed resilience.

Insights — Cultivating A Healthy Mind

Now that we have explored the roots of mental blockages and limiting beliefs, our attention turns toward **Cultivating A Healthy Mind**, one centered in clarity, resilience and empowered thought. This next stage invites us to consciously nurture the qualities that sustain mental and emotional vitality. In the *Integration* section, we will uncover practical tools and daily practices that transform these insights into lived experience, helping you embody balance and strength in everyday life. As you begin to envision your ideal state of mind, you may identify qualities such as stability, confidence, self-empowerment, grace, compassion and continuous growth. Conceptualizing and embodying these traits lays the foundation for a thriving inner world, fostering a mindset that supports sustained well-being and fulfillment.

Think of these qualities as your armor on the battlefield of life. They serve as powerful shields, protecting you from adversity and negative thought patterns and equipping you to face challenges with trust, faith and steadfast determination. By cultivating such a mindset, you create a foundation for a life rich with purpose, joy and well-being. Pause and turn inward: *What does your ideal mindset look like? What qualities do you aspire to embody as you pursue mental wellness and personal growth?* Reflect deeply on these questions before moving forward.

There are many indicators of a healthy mind, but one of the most powerful is a genuine and consistent sense of well-being. When you regularly find yourself *feeling good*: calm, clear and aligned, it reflects a thriving, resilient mindset. You are able to experience a pervasive sense of inner joy and peace, internally and externally. You readily embrace feelings of love, compassion and positivity, both within yourself and in your interactions with the world. Consequently, you approach life's varied experiences with optimism, easily noticing the light within challenges and embracing each moment as a chance to learn and evolve. Additionally, you avoid situations that elicit negative emotions or foster pessimism, effortlessly bypassing harmful thought patterns as they seem unfamiliar and incongruent with your mindset. *Feeling good, really good,* is a clear sign that you possess a healthy mind.

Another reflection of a healthy mind is the ability to honor the natural ebb and flow of your thoughts and emotions. While a clear sign of mental well-being is embracing life's unpredictability with positivity, it is equally important to recognize that you will not always respond perfectly. Granting yourself patience and grace during moments of less positivity or when circumstances feel challenging, is a vital part of self-compassion and sustaining a resilient, balanced mindset. Understanding that not every day will be perfect allows for self-love and acknowledgment of the complexities of our human experience. *It is also healthy to recognize that encountering lower mental health days, including periods of anxiety or depression, does not indicate an unhealthy mind. Instead, it highlights our common humanity and the intricacies of navigating life's journey. Cultivating resilience and embracing the transient nature of life's ups and downs are emblematic of a healthy and adaptive response to our ever-changing circumstances.*

In addition to embracing life's natural fluctuations, another key sign of a thriving mind is maintaining positive self-talk and inner dialogue. Engaging in supportive and uplifting inner dialogue is a crucial, though often neglected, practice for nurturing healthy thoughts and sustaining a balanced mind. As discussed earlier, the conversations we hold with ourselves profoundly shape our perceptions and, ultimately, the reality we experience. The stories we tell ourselves, rooted in our deepest thoughts, emotions and beliefs, carry energetic vibrations that ripple through our consciousness, quietly influencing how we perceive the world and guiding the direction of our lives. Therefore, we must approach our internal dialogue with mindfulness and intentionality, acknowledging its potential to either empower or disempower us. The way we talk to ourselves, grounded in love, self-compassion and empowerment, reflects the strength and resilience of our minds.

Building on the importance of inner dialogue, the quality and health of the relationships in your life also reflect the state of your mind. If you treat yourself and your mind with patience, grace and compassion, you are more inclined to offer the same treatment to others, fostering healthy connections and dynamics in your life. Moreover, a healthy mind is reflected in your ability to assess your relationships with clarity and intention, discerning which connections nurture your soul and align with your core values, and which do not. Consistently fostering and sustaining these supportive relationships serves as a powerful indicator of a resilient, thriving mind and heart.

Experiencing a consistent sense of well-being, honoring the natural ebb and flow of your thoughts and emotions, engaging in positive self-talk, and cultivating meaningful relationships are key indicators of a healthy mind. While these are among the most visible signs of mental wellness, they represent just a few facets of a resilient and thriving mindset. In the *Integration* segment, we will explore practical tools and practices designed not only to overcome mental blockages and limiting beliefs but also to consciously strengthen your mind, fostering and sustaining long-term mental vitality.

Introspection — Cultivating A Healthy Mind

Imagine your ideal mental state. What qualities do you want to embody? How can you incorporate these traits into your daily life, and what steps can you immediately take to align with this mindset?

Recall a recent moment when you genuinely *felt good*. What conditions led to this feeling, and how did it affect your actions? How can you create more of these positive experiences in your life?

Think about a recent challenge or negative emotion. How did you handle it, and what did you learn? How can accepting these fluctuations as natural help you approach future challenges with more resilience and self-compassion?

Integration — Cultivating A Healthy Mind

The quote, often attributed to Buddha, "*Nothing can harm you as much as your own thoughts unguarded,*" succinctly captures the immense influence of our mental landscape on our overall well-being. Indeed, few endeavors match the importance of cultivating a healthy mind. With humans generating up to 60,000 thoughts each day, the unmanaged or unguarded nature of these mental currents can profoundly shape our experiences, for better or worse. Amidst this constant influx, learning to work with our thoughts as allies rather than adversaries becomes essential. Developing mastery over thought management, employing intentional tools and practices to steer our thoughts toward constructive outcomes, forms the backbone of this journey.

A resilient and optimistic mindset establishes the foundation for an abundant and fulfilling life and acts as the driving force behind more deliberate and impactful actions. This is due to our thoughts having a profound impact on our emotional well-being, which, in turn, shapes our behaviors and, ultimately, the quality of our lives. When we infuse our thoughts with resilience and positivity, they generate empowering emotions that drive us to take purposeful and intentional actions aligned with our goals and aspirations. With a strong and thriving inner world, we gain the resilience to find joy, peace and gratitude, core principles of abundance, no matter what life brings our way. Cultivating a healthy mind thus positions us to manifest the life we have long envisioned.

Having explored how mental blockages and limiting beliefs can hinder growth, alongside the transformative potential of a well-nurtured mind, we now turn to practical strategies for mastering and disciplining our mental landscape. Our goal is to steer clear of negative thought patterns, mental blockages and limiting beliefs, while nurturing healthier cognitive habits. Central to this pursuit is the cultivation of **self-awareness**, a concept we have explored that empowers us to observe and understand our thoughts and the language we use, both internally and externally.

By honing self-awareness, we can discern the subtle nuances of our thought patterns and how they shape our lives. With this awareness, we can identify and address any negative or limiting patterns that might be hindering our progress. Moreover, self-awareness allows us to recondition these patterns, aligning them more closely with our aspirations and ideal life trajectories. By practicing mindful introspection and intentional self-reflection, we lay the foundation for a mindset that is resilient, fostering growth and abundance.

To effectively apply self-awareness in overcoming negative thought patterns, it is important to attentively observe recurring thoughts that provoke negative reactions. For example, consider your response when encountering a mistake at work. *Do you tend to engage in self-criticism and doubt your capabilities, or do you seize the opportunity to utilize **reframing** to pull valuable lessons from the situation?* Pause now and reflect deeply on this question before moving forward.

Reframing, as we discussed, provides a chance to identify the positive aspects within challenges, enabling the development of a mindset enriched with gratitude, resilience and optimism. If you notice that your initial reactions tend to be negative, consistently practicing reframing can transform and recondition your habitual thought patterns, ultimately cultivating a healthier mindset. When faced with setbacks, it is easy to think, "*I failed at this task, so I must not be good at it.*" However, by reframing this thought, we can shift our perspective to something more constructive: "*This task did not go as planned, but it provides me with an opportunity to learn and improve for next time.*" This reframing allows us to move away from self-criticism and instead focus on growth and development, turning challenges into valuable learning experiences.

Gratitude, a core principle of abundance, exerts a similarly powerful influence on our mindset. By shifting our attention to the blessings and joys present in our lives, gratitude helps rewire our thinking, nurturing a mindset rooted in positivity and abundance. Regularly practicing gratitude plays a vital role in cultivating a healthy mindset. One simple yet powerful approach is keeping a gratitude journal, where you write down or speak aloud the things in your life that inspire thankfulness. As mentioned earlier in this guidebook, thoughts and words gain power when paired with genuine emotion and belief. Simply recording or voicing gratitude can be helpful, but its impact deepens when we truly feel and embrace the emotion. By fully engaging with the sense of appreciation and embodying the sentiments we express, we enhance gratitude's positive influence on our mental and emotional well-being.

Take a moment to engage in a simple yet powerful gratitude practice now. Reflect on three specific aspects of your life that you are genuinely thankful for at this very moment. Allow yourself to deeply immerse in the sensations of gratitude, letting these positive feelings wash over you and envelop your entire being. Pause and deeply reflect to observe the emotions and shifts you experience after this practice of appreciation. Notice how simply acknowledging what you are grateful for can lift your mood, shift your perspective and bring a deeper sense of fulfillment and contentment.

Additionally, embracing **grace and self-compassion** is essential to nurturing our mental well-being. It means embracing our humanity and recognizing that we are all imperfect beings doing our best to navigate life's complexities. Yet in the midst of life's daily demands, we frequently neglect to offer ourselves patience and kindness, practices that are essential for shaping a mind that supports, rather than obstructs, the pursuit of our goals and aspirations. By embracing grace and self-compassion, we affirm our humanity and inherent worthiness, recognizing that making mistakes and facing challenges are innate aspects of the human experience.

Putting this into practice means replacing harsh self-judgment with a gentle and compassionate attitude towards ourselves. By fostering an environment of kindness and acceptance within our minds, we create a nurturing space that encourages growth and self-acceptance. This shift in perspective allows us to approach life's unpredictable nature and inevitable ebbs and flows with greater resilience and stability, knowing that we are worthy of love and compassion, both from others and ourselves. Practicing grace and self-compassion involves extending the same empathy and understanding to ourselves that we readily offer others. For example, when you make a mistake, say, missing a deadline at work, rather than turning to harsh self-criticism, you might choose a more compassionate response, "*It's okay to make mistakes; I can learn from this and improve for next time.*" This mindset promotes kindness and acceptance, enabling you to grow from the experience rather than being consumed by negative self-talk. Pause for a moment and reflect deeply on how you can cultivate more grace and self-compassion for yourself before moving forward.

With the foundation for nurturing a healthy mind firmly established, through our exploration of overcoming mental blockages and limiting beliefs, understanding the key qualities of a thriving mindset, and practicing self-awareness, reframing, gratitude, grace and self-compassion, we are now poised to manifest abundance and fulfillment in our lives. By embracing these tools, we can begin to attract and sustain a flow of prosperity, both in the present moment and for the future. This intentional shift in mindset empowers us to make lasting, meaningful changes, opening the door to continuous growth, evolution and self-mastery.

Insights — The Art of Manifesting Abundance

Having explored powerful concepts in the pursuit of mastering your mind (and thoughts), we now stand at the threshold of a significant milestone. Throughout our experience together thus far, we have navigated the depths of consciousness, attained a deeper self-awareness regarding the nature of our thoughts, and confronted the intricate and robust relationship between our thoughts and spoken language (words). Additionally, we have identified the essential tools and practices needed to conquer mental blockages and cultivate a resilient, healthy mindset that endures over time. Your progress thus far is commendable, demonstrating the dedication, commitment and introspection required to fully engage with these deep and meaningful concepts. As we transition to the final segment of mastering your mind (and thoughts), we enter a pivotal phase: **The Art of Manifesting Abundance**.

Earlier in our journey, we examined various interpretations of abundance, encompassing both contemporary and spiritual perspectives. To recap, abundance goes beyond mere mindset; it represents a profound state of being and consciousness, an enduring blend of gratitude and a tangible sense of plentitude. At its core, it embodies the empowering idea of life's boundless potential, resonating with a Universe rich in endless possibilities. It surpasses conventional limits and societal norms, moving beyond religious doctrines and modern frameworks to reveal a unique path to true joy and fulfillment. Abundance is not only attainable but essential for genuine fulfillment. It simply takes a conscious decision, to ***decide, now***, to adopt this state of being as a lifestyle commitment and a powerful act of self-love.

The Decision: Embodying the State of Abundance

Decisions continuously confront us in every conceivable direction, demanding our focus and attention each day. Navigating this endless array of choices can be overwhelming, yet it is fundamental to our personal growth and fulfillment. From deciding what to wear or what to have for breakfast to making life-changing choices like defining a career path or choosing a life partner, we are constantly presented with opportunities to shape our destiny. Amidst these boundless possibilities, it becomes imperative to discern which choices resonate with our essence, deepest aspirations and highest quality of life. While some decisions may appear trivial, others carry the profound potential to steer our journey in significant ways. Therefore, it is crucial to develop practices that allow us to navigate these choices with clarity and intention. Before moving forward, think about this question: *What decisions can you make today that reflect your authentic self and steer you toward meaningful growth and fulfillment?* Pause now and reflect deeply on this question before moving forward.

One of the most effective methods for discerning the correctness of a decision is to envision your ideal future state and inquire: *Does this choice align with the life I envision?* Consider the decision's potential impact on your future self. *Will it enhance my well-being? Will it contribute to my overall joy and fulfillment?* A strong indication that you are making the right decision is when it strongly echoes your goals and aspirations, evoking a sense of alignment and certainty. Moreover, when a decision aligns with your life objectives, core values, belief systems and essence, it clearly indicates its appropriateness and relevancy. We will explore these concepts further in the next segment. Essentially, when a decision *feels right*, it seamlessly integrates with your authentic self, belief systems and values.

Our exploration of abundance is deeply intertwined with intentional decision-making and mindset, emphasizing how each shapes and reinforces the other. Each day presents an opportunity to embrace and embody abundance, yet doing so requires intentional action, disciplined focus and unwavering commitment. Even amidst challenges and uncertainty, maintaining a mindset of gratitude and abundance is essential. By steadfastly cultivating these attitudes, we navigate adversity with resilience and build a solid foundation for manifesting our goals and creating the life we desire. This journey calls for consistent effort and a devoted practice of fostering positivity and abundance in every dimension of our lives.

The Universe operates as a dynamic stage, constantly challenging us to navigate life's unpredictability with resilience and grace. Our response to life's challenges becomes a testament to our commitment to growth and self-mastery. By cultivating an unwavering sense of joy, abundance and gratitude, we not only demonstrate our readiness to overcome these tests but also position ourselves for profound personal evolution and fulfillment. Consider this journey akin to an epic video game quest, where each obstacle conquered represents a significant milestone in our character's development. With each triumph, we *level up*, gaining strength, wisdom and resilience. Much like the protagonist in a video game, we emerge from each challenge more empowered and equipped to navigate the next stage of our journey. In this way, embracing a persistent state of joy, abundance and gratitude becomes more than just a mindset; it becomes a transformative practice that propels us forward on our path towards self-realization and fulfillment. With each victory, we affirm our capacity to transcend obstacles and manifest our highest potential in the ever-unfolding adventure of life.

Just as navigating life's challenges with resilience and gratitude strengthens our inner growth, it also aligns us with the energetic principles we have discussed earlier, principles that govern our experiences. This connection naturally leads us back to the concept of the Law of Attraction, which highlights how our thoughts, emotions and actions shape the reality we attract. When we radiate abundance, embracing an energy and mindset of joy, gratitude and well-being, we naturally attract experiences that mirror this energy. For instance, approaching a challenging project with optimism and confidence can invite collaborative opportunities, supportive feedback and unexpected solutions, demonstrating how our intentions and beliefs actively shape the reality we create.

Now, let us put this theory into practice. Repeat after me, affirming with all the emotions and feelings you can summon: *Today and every day, I choose to reside in a state of abundance. Despite the challenges that may arise, I am committed to uncovering moments of joy and gratitude in my circumstances. I embrace a state of well-being, and regardless of the obstacles that may come my way, I will confront them with grace, composure and gratitude.* Repeat this affirmation as often as possible throughout the day to amplify its power and impact.

By consistently repeating this affirmation, or any variation that resonates with you, and fully embodying the feelings it evokes, you will deepen your ability to embrace the essence of abundance. Pay close attention to how you feel after each session of practicing this abundance affirmation. The aim is to cultivate a deeper sense of conviction with each repetition. Whether spoken aloud or reflected upon silently, let your affirmations flow with authentic sincerity and steadfast conviction. Through consistent practice, you will reinforce your dedication to embodying abundance and gratitude in your daily life. This practice trains your mind, body and spirit to fully embrace and embody abundance and joy, while simultaneously fortifying your resilience and optimism in the face of life's challenges.

As you engage in this practice, take the time to fully connect with the emotions elicited by these daily affirmations and core beliefs, recognizing your inherent ability to create a life filled with joy, fulfillment and well-being. *It is important to emphasize that words alone, without heartfelt emotion and genuine conviction, have limited transformative impact. To truly create change, these affirmations should be felt deeply and embraced from within.* In the upcoming section, we will explore how aligning your thoughts, spoken language (words) and intentional actions can lead to profound transformation. Additionally, we will explore powerful techniques designed to awaken deeper emotions, enabling you to tap into authentic feelings of abundance and gratitude and foster lasting breakthroughs in your life.

The Alignment: Thoughts (Beliefs), Spoken Language (Words), Action

All of existence is deeply interconnected. Every aspect of our lives has always been and will always be inextricably intertwined. Through our exploration of mind, body and soul alignment, we have come to recognize the intricate interconnection within our being. To truly thrive and experience abundance, it is essential to honor and prioritize the well-being of each aspect. Just as one cannot flourish without the integrated functioning of all parts, understanding the profound interplay between thoughts (beliefs), spoken language (words) and action is key to manifesting abundance. When these three facets work in concert, they create a foundation for conscious and intentional living, a concept we explore later, empowering us to mindfully shape and manifest the life we desire.

We have explored how our thoughts and beliefs exert a transformative influence over our emotions, language and actions. Our thoughts are not just fleeting mental events; they form the foundation of our entire experience. They shape our words, guide our actions and lay the groundwork for the habits we develop. These habits, in turn, sculpt our character and ultimately chart the course of our destiny. For example, consistently nurturing a positive belief in your abilities, such as affirming "*I am capable of achieving my goals,*" can empower you to take proactive steps like setting daily intentions, dedicating time to skill development and seeking opportunities that align with your aspirations. Over time, these habits reinforce confidence, drive consistent progress and create a life infused with fulfillment and purpose. With this profound understanding, we will be able to explore and reinforce powerful tools and practices designed to help you master your mind and sustain a perpetual state of abundance.

You can transform your mental landscape and manifest your deepest desires by aligning your thoughts and beliefs with your highest aspirations. This process begins with recognizing how our internal (and external) expressions, influenced by our thoughts, direct our actions. These actions gradually solidify into habits that define our everyday existence. Over time, these habits shape our character, guiding the trajectory of our lives. Thus, it becomes evident that the caliber of our thoughts (and beliefs) is the foundation of this intricate process. By grasping and leveraging the potential of this framework, we can accelerate our journey toward a state of abundance. Through deliberate management of our thoughts, beliefs and spoken language, and the conscious cultivation of positive actions, we lay the foundation for a life overflowing with abundance and profound fulfillment.

INTROSPECTION — THE ART OF MANIFESTING ABUNDANCE

Consider how your current thought patterns influence your daily decisions and overall sense of fulfillment. How do these thoughts shape your actions and habits? How can you consciously alter your thoughts to better align with your vision of abundance?

____

____

____

____

____

____

____

____

Think about a recent decision you made and how it aligns with your core values and long-term goals. Did this decision resonate with your essence and aspirations? How might you refine your decision-making process to ensure it supports your journey toward a life of abundance?

____

____

____

____

____

____

____

____

Imagine your life in a state of complete abundance and fulfillment. What does this ideal future look like, and how does it differ from your current reality? What steps can you take today to bridge the gap between where you are now and where you envision yourself?

____

____

____

____

____

____

____

____

Integration — The Art of Manifesting Abundance

Throughout our journey toward abundance, beginning with mastering our minds and thoughts, we have consistently returned to a powerful tool: **affirmations**. As a recap, these empowering declarations of truth hold immense transformative power, reaching beyond positive reinforcement. Affirmations serve as drivers for profound shifts in mindset, emotions and behavior. Consistently affirming our inherent worth, capabilities and potential instills a sense of confidence and self-empowerment within us. Affirmations can recalibrate our thought patterns and act as alchemists, transmuting negativity into positivity and nurturing a mindset steeped in abundance and possibility.

Earlier, we introduced a potent affirmation aimed at cultivating abundance in our lives: *Today and every day, I choose to reside in a state of abundance. Despite the challenges that may arise, I am committed to uncovering moments of joy and gratitude in my circumstances. I embrace a state of well-being, and regardless of the obstacles that may come my way, I will confront them with grace, composure and gratitude.*

Building upon this foundational affirmation, here are several additional affirmations to further strengthen your ability to manifest abundance:

I continuously manifest abundance.

I am worthy of abundance.

I live a life of abundance.

I am always prosperous.

I am open to limitless possibilities.

Abundance is all around me.

I am truly abundant.

These truth statements carry profound resonance and potential. When embraced with genuine sincerity and felt fully in the depths of our being, they serve as powerful tools to train our mind, body and soul to act as change agents. By aligning our thoughts, spoken words and actions with these affirmations, we awaken our natural capacity to attract and manifest the life of abundance we truly deserve. Affirmations are just one tool in our abundance toolkit. Equally potent are creative imagination, daydreaming and visualization, each providing distinct pathways to align with our desires and manifest them into reality.

Have you ever caught yourself mentally rehearsing a scenario before it materializes in reality? Think back to moments of anticipation, such as preparing for a first date. *Did you find yourself envisioning the interaction, exploring various scenarios in your mind?* If not a first date, perhaps you have experienced this phenomenon before a job interview. *Did you take on the roles of both interviewer and interviewee in your mental preparations?* If you have ever engaged in these imaginative rehearsals, you have already put **creative imagination** into practice. Engaging in such mental rehearsals allows us to mentally prepare for upcoming events and instills a sense of ease and calmness. By visualizing positive outcomes and vividly imagining scenarios overflowing with abundance and success, we prime ourselves to navigate real-life situations with confidence and grace.

As we have explored, the mind exerts remarkable power, shaping our emotions and even eliciting physical responses in the body. Take nightmares, for example: they can provoke intense feelings of fear, anxiety or terror, accompanied by physiological reactions like sweating, rapid heartbeat or shallow breathing. In some cases, the dream's intensity is so profound that it prompts vocalizations, such as shouting or speaking, upon waking. This example reveals the mind's extraordinary capacity to translate imagination into lived experience. However, mastering the ability to consciously influence this process requires practice and focused concentration. One effective approach involves identifying a situation that typically induces stress and using creative imagination and mental rehearsal to cultivate a non-stressful response. Through consistent practice, you can train yourself to leverage your mind's power, navigating challenging scenarios with greater calm and resilience. This intentional effort allows you to manifest more positive and higher-quality results across various areas of your life.

Let us engage in a simple creative imaginative exercise right now. Take a moment to imagine a future scenario that fills you with apprehension or anxiety. As you visualize this situation, focus on rehearsing it in your mind, but with a deliberate twist: imagine the best possible outcome unfolding before you, and immerse yourself in the emotions and sensations associated with this favorable result. Pause now and reflect deeply on the feelings that surface within you as you engage in this creative imagination practice. *What are the predominant emotions and feelings you are experiencing?*

If you find yourself enveloped in positive and empowering feelings such as success, confidence, peace and joy, embrace them wholeheartedly. Let these emotions sink in fully; feel them throughout your whole body and let yourself deeply connect with them in your consciousness (awareness). When you lean into these uplifting feelings and really let yourself feel them, you give yourself the energy and motivation to move forward with more purpose, clarity, strength and drive. When used with intention and focus, creative imagination can be an incredibly powerful tool. It empowers you to actively mold your reality by channeling the full capacity of your mind and imagination. By consciously nurturing positive emotional states, this practice supports the alignment of your thoughts and feelings with your deepest intentions, allowing your goals to come to life more effortlessly and helping you build a life rooted in abundance.

Building on the power of creative imagination, **daydreaming** and **visualization** also engage our internal thoughts and emotions, each serving a unique function in shaping our experiences. While creative imagination actively directs our thoughts toward specific goals or possibilities, daydreaming occurs when our attention drifts inward, allowing us to explore our own thoughts and feelings without a particular focus. Simply, creative imagination is goal-directed and focused, while daydreaming is more free-flowing and reflective. We lightly explored the practice of daydreaming in the *Insights* section of *Achieving Self-Awareness* when we discussed the Default Mode Network (DMN). To recap, the DMN is a network of brain regions that function like the brain's "idle" mode and is active during daydreaming, self-reflection and contemplation of personal experiences and memories. This state occurs when the mind is at rest, often engaging in introspection, mind-wandering and imagining scenarios that integrate memories, aspirations and future possibilities.

Daydreaming acts as a portal into our subconscious, uncovering the unspoken desires and unmet aspirations that lie beneath the surface of our conscious mind. For example, someone seeking a romantic partner might imagine walking hand-in-hand with their soulmate along a serene beach, experiencing deep connection and joy. Beyond idealized fantasies, daydreaming allows us to explore a spectrum of emotions and scenarios that reflect our inner world. In the context of manifesting abundance, we focus on using daydreaming to envision experiences aligned with our desired state. When practiced intentionally, it can evoke joy, excitement and fulfillment, laying a powerful foundation for advanced manifestation techniques like **visualization**.

Pause your reading for a moment and dive into active daydreaming now. Imagine your ideal future with unwavering focus, fully immersing yourself in the vivid details of your imagination. Allow your visions, emotions and sensations to fill your mind, body and soul with a rush of powerful energy. Surrender to these fantasies completely, allowing the profound feelings they stir to settle deep within you. Make it a habit to revisit these feelings often, allowing their potent energy to flow through your daily life. By consistently engaging in this practice, you tap into the ability to bring abundance and your deepest desires to life with crystal-clear focus and purpose.

In contrast to creative imagination and daydreaming, visualization is a bit more focused and targeted. It is a profound practice wherein you actively engage your mind in picturing the manifestations you desire, both within the realms of your personal life and beyond. It entails immersing yourself deeply in the imagery of accomplishing your goals, vividly envisioning the scenarios and sensations that accompany their fulfillment. Throughout this cognitive, emotional and spiritual experience, you direct your focus towards attaining these aspirations, exploring in detail what it would feel like to bring them to life. Through this intentional and immersive process, you visualize the end result and cultivate a profound sense of connection with your goals, empowering yourself to take inspired action towards their attainment.

While daydreaming allows you to conjure up an ideal scenario, such as sharing an intimate moment on the beach with your life partner, visualization takes it a step further by evoking deeper, more visceral feelings associated with that scenario. For instance, through a visualization practice, you can vividly imagine the sensation of your partner's hand in yours, the texture and warmth of their comforting grip. You might immerse yourself in the imagined surroundings, conjuring up the salty scent of the ocean breeze, the sound of gentle waves lapping against the shore and the radiant warmth of the sun on your skin. In this visualization, every detail comes to life with heightened clarity and intensity. You feel the love and connection between you and your partner, experiencing a profound sense of joy, contentment and peace. In this timeless moment, the physical, emotional and spiritual dimensions merge seamlessly, leaving you with a profound sense of fulfillment and assurance that this reality is within your grasp.

While both daydreaming and visualization involve creating mental imagery, they differ in intention, how deliberately the process is guided and the impact they have on our mindset and outcomes. Daydreaming entails allowing oneself to indulge in fantasies and desires, primarily for the sake of experiencing pleasure and enjoyment without necessarily aiming for tangible outcomes. It is typically a free-flowing, unstructured mental excursion into a realm of possibilities, often devoid of any deliberate intention to bring about specific results. In contrast, visualization is an intentional and purposeful practice wherein one imagines a desired outcome with the explicit intention of manifesting it into reality. Unlike daydreaming, visualization is characterized by a focused, directed effort to vividly envision a specific goal or objective. The key distinction lies in its *purposeful nature*, as visualization is a powerful tool for imprinting the desired outcome onto our subconscious mind, thereby priming it to manifest as tangible results in our external world...our lived reality.

Visualization operates on the principle that the subconscious mind cannot distinguish between vividly imagined scenarios and actual lived experiences. When we consistently visualize a desired goal with clarity, emotional intensity and full sensory engagement, we create neural patterns in the brain similar to those formed through real-life experiences. This repeated mental exercise effectively programs the subconscious mind to accept the envisioned outcome as possible, dare we say, even inevitable, aligning our thoughts, beliefs and behaviors in support of that goal. Over time, this alignment can influence our decision-making, confidence and the opportunities we attract into our lives. In this way, visualization becomes more than just a mental exercise; it becomes the driving force for real-world transformation. It can be considered a refined and intentional form of daydreaming, one that is distinguished by its purposefulness, focus and systematic approach to goal manifestation. Where daydreaming may be free-flowing and passive, visualization is deliberate and disciplined, rooted in the conscious intention to create change and manifest desired outcomes in the external world.

Let us pause and engage in a practice that blends both daydreaming and visualization. Take a moment to find a quiet spot to sit comfortably, allowing yourself to settle into a relaxed state. Close your eyes and begin by taking a series of deep, soothing breaths allowing each inhale to fill you with calmness and each exhale to release any tension. Now, turn your attention inward and focus on the desired outcome, object or situation you yearn to manifest in your life. Picture it vividly in your mind's eye, immersing yourself in every intricate detail with unwavering clarity. As you participate in this mental exercise, allow yourself to fully surrender to the emotions and sensations connected to your creative imagery. Begin by daydreaming, allowing your thoughts to wander freely through your chosen scenario without limitations. *What images spontaneously arise in your mind? What emotions bubble to the surface as you envision this desired reality?* Pause now and reflect deeply on these images and emotions as they cascade through your consciousness.

Now, let us deepen the practice by layering visualization onto your daydream scenario. Envision the scene with heightened clarity, focusing on the sensory details such as sights, sounds, smells and physical sensations. Imagine yourself fully enveloped in this scenario, experiencing it as if it were unfolding in the present moment. As you immerse yourself in this visualization, focus on the vividness and realism of the images and sensations. *How tangible do they seem to you? What emotions emerge across your physical, emotional and spiritual dimensions?* Fully engage with these sensations, embracing the limitless potential of the reality you envision. Commit to incorporating this practice into your daily routine, ideally engaging in it regularly to maximize its transformative impact in manifesting your desired outcomes and dream life. With consistent dedication, you will begin to access the profound power of creative imagination, daydreaming and visualization, turning your deepest desires and vision of abundance into lived reality.

To deepen your visualization practice, consider adding a vision board. Collect images, words and symbols that reflect your goals and dreams, creating a tangible representation of what you wish to manifest. The process of designing a board helps clarify your values, strengthen your focus and reinforce your intentions. At the same time, it is important to remember that a vision board is a tool, not the source of manifestation itself. Looking at images can inspire and organize your goals, but true manifestation comes from *embodying and dwelling in the state of already having what you desire.* Use your vision board to guide your focus and maintain clarity, while pairing it with visualization and feelings of already being or having. In this way, your board becomes a powerful companion in turning your vision into reality.

To begin this exercise, take a moment to reflect on your values, aspirations and what truly drives you, clarifying the goals you wish to pursue. Then gather images, words and symbols that represent these intentions and arrange them on your vision board in a way that feels meaningful and inspiring. Place your board somewhere visible so it can serve as a daily reminder of your focus and intentions. Remember, the vision board is a guide and source of inspiration, not the manifestation itself. Pair it with your visualization practice and the *feeling of already having what you desire.* Notice how your clarity, focus and sense of possibility grow as you engage with your board in this way.

Having explored the powerful practices of creative imagination, daydreaming and visualization, we now arrive at the final tool in the art of manifesting abundance: **embodiment**. You may be familiar with the saying, *"Dress for the job you want, not the job you have."* This popular adage captures the core of what embodiment means in the context of manifestation. It goes beyond simply visualizing or emotionally connecting with your desires; it calls for you to *become* the version of yourself who already lives that reality. It encourages you to **inhabit the consciousness** of your desires, feeling them as already real. In manifesting abundance, embodiment is about alignment, bringing your actions, language, presence and energy into congruence with the version of you already living the life you desire. It is the process of *living as if*, intentionally integrating the mindset, habits and vibration of your future self into your present-day experience.

For instance, imagine yourself embodying a sense of confidence, prosperity and vitality in every interaction, conversation and decision you make. This is not just a fleeting thought but the active practice of living in abundance. By deliberately channeling and radiating this energy, you raise your vibrational frequency and begin to align with the infinite potential of the Universe. As this inner shift takes root, your outer world naturally starts to mirror it, turning even ordinary moments into reflections of your highest self. In the next chapter, we will take this further by exploring the role of energy and vibration and how they shape your ability to manifest your goals and desires.

Embracing the practice of embodiment is a crucial step toward manifesting abundance. Let us initiate a simple embodiment exercise right now. Begin by envisioning the ideal version of yourself, the person you aspire to become. Visualize every detail: the way you look, the way you speak, the way you carry yourself and the energy you emanate. Dive deep into this mental imagery, letting it take hold in your mind and spirit. Now, breathe life into your vision. Actively integrate the behaviors, energy and presence of your ideal self into every aspect of your day-to-day life. Start by adopting habits and behaviors that align with the characteristics of your envisioned self. Whether cultivating confidence, expressing love and kindness or exuding positivity, consciously embody these qualities in your interactions, decisions and self-talk. Pause now and reflect deeply on how you can begin integrating a daily embodiment practice into your life starting now.

As Abraham Maslow profoundly stated, "*What a man can be, he must be.*" Embracing embodiment means showing up authentically as the person you aspire to be, not just in fleeting moments of inspiration, but consistently, day in and day out. It is about living in alignment with your highest vision of yourself, regardless of external circumstances or challenges. As you immerse yourself in the practice of embodiment, you initiate a profound journey of self-discovery and personal transformation. With each conscious action and decision aligned with your innermost desires, you begin to resonate more deeply with your higher self: the embodiment of your truest aspirations and potential. You do not achieve this alignment by luck; you make a deliberate choice to embrace the fullness of your being and step into the authenticity of who you are meant to be. Embrace this journey with joy, excitement and unwavering determination, recognizing that every choice, no matter how seemingly insignificant, will propel you closer to realizing your dreams.

Chapter Recap: The Abundance Pillars – Mastering Your Mind (Thoughts)

Chapter 2 explores key concepts for developing a healthy mindset that fosters abundance, personal growth and evolution.

Understanding Consciousness

Key Insights: Consciousness is our awareness and perception of reality; it shapes the way we understand and engage with the world around us.

Integration: Reflect on consciousness and how it shapes your worldview. Embrace practices like mindfulness to enhance consciousness.

Achieving Self-Awareness

Key Insights: Self-awareness means tuning into your thoughts, emotions and behaviors. It allows you to better understand what drives you and what truly matters to you.

Integration: Regularly engage in introspective practices such as journaling or mindfulness meditation to deepen your awareness of your inner state.

Where Are My Thoughts Coming From?

Key Insights: Thoughts arise from individual experiences and are shaped by the larger collective mind, which influences personal perceptions and beliefs.

Integration: Reflect on how external influences, such as relationships and environment, shape your thoughts, beliefs and perceptions.

Thoughts and Spoken Language (Words)

Key Insights: Thoughts and spoken language are interlinked. Words can shape perceptions and influence reality.

Integration: Be mindful of the language you use. Align your spoken words with your intentions and beliefs to foster positive outcomes.

Why Are Words So Powerful?

Key Insights: Words have the power to create and transform reality. They can reinforce beliefs, influence emotions and impact interactions.

Integration: Use affirmations and positive language to shift your mindset and cultivate desired changes in your life.

Mental Blockages and Limiting Beliefs

Key Insights: Mental blockages and limiting beliefs can hinder personal growth. They often stem from past experiences and self-doubt.

Integration: Identify and challenge limiting beliefs. Use introspective practices to overcome mental blockages and foster a positive mindset.

Cultivating A Healthy Mind

Key Insights: A healthy mind is characterized by clarity, resilience and emotional balance. It is resilient and adaptable. It supports overall well-being and personal growth.

Integration: Cultivate habits that support mental health, such as regular mindfulness, reframing, affirmations, self-reflection and balanced lifestyle choices.

The Art of Manifesting Abundance

Key Insights: Manifesting abundance involves aligning thoughts (beliefs), language (words) and actions with a state of abundance. It requires intentional decision-making and maintaining a positive mindset.

Integration: Practice affirmations, creative imagination, daydreaming, visualization and embodiment to support your goals. Ensure your daily choices and actions reflect your vision of abundance.

Introspection Exercises: Use the introspection exercises from each section to apply these principles to your life. Reflect on how consciousness, self-awareness and the influence of thoughts and language affect your daily experiences. Apply these insights to align your mindset, cultivate a healthy mental state and manifest abundance in your life.

Conclusion: Mastering your mind and thoughts, alongside the principles of consciousness, self-awareness and the art of manifesting abundance, is essential for personal growth and fulfillment. By understanding how your thoughts and language shape your experiences, you cultivate the power to create a more intentional, aligned and abundant life.

Chapter 3:

The Abundance Pillars – Mastering Your Essence (Self) and Energy

As we continue on our path toward abundance and fulfillment, we step into a powerful new phase of growth and transformation. With a strong foundation rooted in mental mastery, consciousness, self-awareness and a healthy mindset, we are now prepared to evolve from the inside out. Our commitment to living in a state of abundance becomes more than a mindset. It becomes an intentional way of being that guides how we care for ourselves, make decisions and relate to the world around us. This steady inner alignment serves as a governing force, continually leading us toward lasting fulfillment, purpose and peace.

In this chapter, our focus shifts from the landscape of the mind to the deeper terrain of **essence and energy**, the core of who you are and the frequency through which you experience life. Mastering your essence means reconnecting with your authentic self beyond conditioning, roles and external expectations. It invites you to nourish your body, honor your inner world and listen closely to the subtle intelligence within you. Mastering your energy, in turn, involves becoming aware of how your physical state, emotions, beliefs, experiences and spiritual connection shape your vibration and influence your lived reality.

Chapter 3 invites you into a holistic exploration of self. We begin with the body, recognizing physical well-being as the foundation of vitality and energetic balance. From there, we move inward toward your higher self and inner child, intuition, belief systems, values and lived experiences, each offering guidance, wisdom and insight into your evolving essence. As you deepen this relationship with yourself, you begin to access a more authentic sense of alignment, clarity and purpose.

This chapter also opens space for profound inner transformation through themes of spirituality, awakening, healing, releasing, enlightenment and transcendence. These are not abstract concepts, but lived processes, shifts in awareness that expand your capacity to experience peace, connection and meaning. Healing and releasing, in particular, play a vital role in this journey. By gently processing repressed emotions, past experiences and stored tension, you create space for greater wholeness and energetic flow. While this guidebook introduces these themes, you are encouraged to explore them further at your own pace, honoring the depth and sensitivity of this work.

Energy flows through every aspect of this chapter. Everything is energy, and we live in a frequency-based world. Every part of your body operates within its own energetic rhythm, constantly communicating and responding to both internal and external stimuli. Every word you speak, every thought you hold, the food you eat, the people you interact with, and the actions you take all carry energetic information that influences your state of being and lived experience.

As you become more aware of this energetic reality, you begin to recognize that abundance, well-being and fulfillment are deeply connected to the frequency you maintain. Thoughts, emotions, words and behaviors can either elevate or lower your vibration, shaping how you feel, what you attract and how you move through the world. Your role is not to seek perfection, but to cultivate awareness and intention, gently choosing, as often as possible, to maintain a higher, more coherent frequency that supports vitality, clarity, alignment and expansion. This awareness naturally strengthens self-empowerment, allowing you to channel your inner power and make choices aligned with your highest intentions and evolving truth.

Mindfulness, introspection and embodied practices serve as essential tools throughout this chapter. They help synchronize your inner world with the frequency of abundance, creating coherence between who you are, how you feel and how you live. As essence and energy come into alignment, manifestation becomes less about effort and more about **resonance**, allowing life to unfold with greater ease and authenticity. As you move through this chapter, approach it with openness, curiosity and compassion for yourself. This is an invitation to remember who you are beneath the layers, to honor your body and energy as sacred and to trust the intelligence guiding you forward. With each insight integrated and each practice embodied, you move closer to a life that feels aligned, expansive and deeply fulfilling. For additional grounding, you may wish to revisit *Your Essence (Self)* in *Chapter 1: The Core Principles of Abundance* as you continue this exploration.

As you move from here through the end of this chapter, you will explore a series of insights designed to deepen your connection with your essence and energetic nature. These include **Nourishing Your Body, Your Higher Self and Inner Child, Your Intuition, Belief Systems and Values, Self-Experience (Lived Experience), Spirituality and Spiritual Intelligence, Awakening, Healing and Releasing, Enlightenment, Transcendence, Self-Empowerment** and **Energy**. As before, you are encouraged to engage deeply with the introspection exercises and integration practices provided for each section, allowing these concepts to move beyond understanding and into lived, embodied experience.

Insights and Integration — Nourishing Your Body

As discussed in *Chapter 1: The Core Principles of Abundance*, an essential aspect of living abundantly is recognizing the deep connection and interdependence between the mind, body and soul, one of the core principles of abundance. These elements work synergistically to promote vitality and prosperity in our lives. Every aspect of our being (our essence) is interconnected, and to thrive abundantly, it is important to prioritize the well-being of each component of our holistic existence. While we have thoroughly explored the significance of a healthy mind in *Chapter 2: The Abundance Pillars – Mastering Your Mind (Thoughts)*, it is equally essential to ensure that our bodies are strong, healthy and vibrant. A resilient, well-nourished body creates the foundation for a thriving life, allowing your energy to flow freely and fuel the realization of your deepest desires.

For many, the ultimate goal is to live a long, vibrant and prosperous life, one that radiates vitality and balanced energy. Achieving such longevity requires more than a passive desire; it demands a devoted commitment to holistic health, wellness and **Nourishing Your Body** with conscious care, attention and respect. Reaching this state of sustained well-being calls for discipline and the consistent integration of intentional practices that strengthen both body and energy. Though the habits we are about to explore may seem simple and routine, they play a fundamental role in maintaining balance, vitality and the energetic foundation of a thriving life.

Prioritizing a balanced, nutrient rich diet is essential for sustaining optimal health, vitality and energy. A truly conscious approach to eating emphasizes *variety*, drawing from an array of whole foods: fresh fruits and vegetables, whole grains, lean proteins and healthy fats. Each food contains a unique mix of vitamins, minerals and bioactive compounds, naturally occurring substances that support the body's functions and promote overall well-being. **Diversity and balance are key**. Overly restrictive diets that eliminate entire food groups, unless medically necessary due to allergies or sensitivities, can be difficult to maintain and may limit the body's access to essential nutrients. Incorporating nutrient dense superfoods can further enhance your diet, offering concentrated sources of antioxidants, phytonutrients, plant-based compounds that support the body's functions and protect against disease, and other health promoting substances. Examples of superfoods include blueberries, kale, spinach, broccoli, quinoa, lentils, salmon, dark chocolate, turmeric and chia seeds. **The goal is a balanced, colorful plate rich in variety, supporting sustained energy and long-term health**.

Equally essential is being mindful of what to minimize or avoid. Highly processed foods laden with added sugars, artificial ingredients and preservatives can disrupt your body's natural balance and drain its energetic vitality. Similarly, seed oils like vegetable, soybean, canola, corn and sunflower oil are often highly refined and associated with inflammation when consumed in excess. Replacing them with more stable, nutrient-rich fats such as extra virgin olive oil, coconut oil or grass-fed butter helps restore balance and support optimal cellular function. By choosing whole, unprocessed foods and steering clear of harmful additives and inflammatory oils, you nurture a body and mind that are vibrant, resilient and aligned with long-term health. Planning and preparing nourishing meals in advance ensures that your energy remains steady, your body supported and your wellness goals consistently within reach.

In addition to eating consciously, maintaining proper hydration is equally essential for sustaining overall health and balanced energy. Water is the body's primary conduit of vitality. It supports digestion, circulation, energy production, temperature regulation and even the radiance of your skin. Most adults benefit from drinking approximately 2 to 3 liters (about 8 to 12 cups) of water per day, though individual needs vary based on activity level, environment and body composition. True hydration is about more than volume; it is about drinking water that replenishes, energizes and sustains your body at the cellular level.

Whenever possible, choose purified, mineral-rich or spring water over tap water to ensure your body receives not just hydration, but nourishment at the cellular level. Tap water can often contain contaminants such as chlorine, heavy metals and other impurities, which may interfere with the body's natural balance and overall vitality. Carrying a reusable water bottle can help you stay consistent with your intake, and adding a pinch of high-quality trace minerals or a squeeze of fresh lemon to your water can improve absorption, support electrolyte balance and enhance hydration, especially if you are active or sweat frequently.

Just as it is essential to focus on what fuels hydration and vitality, it is equally critical to recognize what can undermine it. Alcohol, though widely accepted in social settings, quietly erodes well-being: it dehydrates the body, disrupts restorative sleep, impairs digestion and dulls both mental clarity and emotional balance. By reducing or eliminating alcohol, you restore sharper focus, steadier energy and greater emotional resilience, qualities vital for living with purpose and creating a life of high-vibrational energy, intention and abundance. Because everyone's health and wellness needs are unique, consulting with a wellness coach, registered dietitian or qualified nutritionist can help you design a personalized nutrition and hydration plan that aligns with your lifestyle, activity levels and long-term goals.

Alongside proper nutrition and hydration, physical activity and mindful movement play a crucial role in supporting a strong, energized body and a balanced mind and spirit. Participating in exercises you enjoy, such as daily walking, jogging, running, lifting weights or practicing yoga, profoundly benefits your physical, emotional, mental and spiritual well-being. Engaging in regular exercise helps relieve stress, elevate your mood and build lasting strength and energy. A diverse and dynamic workout routine is recommended: cardiovascular exercises like jogging or running strengthen heart health and boost endurance, while strength training such as weightlifting is essential for preserving muscle mass, bone density and overall strength. To maintain a well-rounded fitness routine and support optimal health, incorporate both cardio and strength training into your weekly schedule and include daily stretches in the morning and evening to improve flexibility, release tension and enhance recovery. For more targeted and personalized plans, consider consulting with a fitness trainer who can tailor exercises to your goals, abilities and lifestyle.

While following a balanced fitness routine is important, it is equally vital to counteract the effects of long hours spent sitting, which have become typical in modern work environments. Make a conscious effort to move throughout your day, starting ***right now***. Pause for a moment, stand up and take a mindful walk, noticing your breath, your steps and the energy flowing through your body. These intentional moments of movement help keep you energized, flexible and resilient, while also clearing your mind and restoring focus.

Simple habits like taking the stairs instead of the elevator, stretching between meetings or walking during phone calls can create a profound difference in your health and energy. Even small moments of movement, stretching, standing or walking, compound into significant impact when practiced consistently. These intentional actions improve circulation, reduce stiffness and elevate your vitality. By making movement a regular part of your day, you not only strengthen your body, but also clear your mind, stabilize your mood and lay the foundation for long-term health, well-being and a life of abundance and fulfillment.

While fueling your body with nutritious food, staying hydrated and moving regularly are essential for physical vitality, true well-being also depends on your ability to rest and recharge. Adequate rest, sleep, relaxation and restorative pauses are critical for sustaining energy, supporting overall health and maintaining balance in mind, body and spirit. Rest can take many forms, whatever feels most nourishing to you. This might include an Epsom salt bath, a short nap, meditation or simply sitting quietly in nature. In a society that often glorifies hustle culture and hyper-productivity, we are intentionally shifting the narrative: *rest is not a luxury or a weakness, but a vital practice to harness your most abundant energy*. By prioritizing restorative moments, you create the conditions for greater clarity, creativity and resilience, enabling you to engage more fully with life and all its opportunities.

Building on the importance of intentional rest, another essential aspect of recharging your mind and body is ensuring you have quality sleep each night, which allows the mind and body to repair, restore and replenish energy. Creating a consistent bedtime and aiming for 7 to 9 hours of restorative sleep supports optimal recovery and vitality. Establishing a calming bedtime routine and optimizing your sleep environment, keeping it dark, quiet and cool, can significantly improve sleep quality. Equally important is exposure to natural light. Getting sunlight in the morning helps regulate your circadian rhythm, supports hormonal balance and promotes deeper, more restful sleep at night.

Additionally, incorporating relaxation, restoration and grounding techniques into your daily life such as breathwork, grounding in nature (including barefoot practices), mindfulness meditation and gentle movement, can profoundly lower stress, calm the nervous system and cultivate a deep sense of inner peace. As a reminder, breathwork helps regulate your body's energy, oxygenates your cells and brings immediate clarity to your mind. Grounding in nature, particularly walking barefoot on grass, sand or soil, reconnects you with the Earth's energy, reduces inflammation and fosters a tangible sense of presence. Mindfulness meditation trains your attention, allowing you to observe thoughts without judgment and deepen self-awareness. Gentle movement practices, including stretching or yoga, release physical tension and promote the balanced flow of energy throughout your body. These practices revitalize the mind, body and spirit, restoring balance and inner strength. The energy and health you embody outwardly is a direct reflection of the resilience and alignment within. Caring for your vessel allows you to experience life more fully, create with intention and connect deeply with your purpose.

A healthy body is the vessel through which you experience the fullness of life. With vitality and strength, you can engage wholeheartedly with the world, welcome new adventures and grasp every opportunity for growth and fulfillment. Nourishing and nurturing the vessel that holds your soul is a sacred act. *Your body is the channel through which you feel, express and engage with the world.* When it is treasured, respected and supported, you are better able to tap into the richness of this beautiful life and contribute effectively to your life's mission and purpose, topics we explore fully in *Chapter 4: The Abundance Pillars – Mastering Your Life and Collective Consciousness.*

As we discussed in *Chapter 1: The Core Principles of Abundance* in the *Insights — Mind, Body and Soul Alignment* segment, physical well-being is deeply intertwined with mental, emotional and spiritual health. It fosters psychological resilience, emotional steadiness and clarity on both mental and spiritual levels. Practices like balanced nutrition, hydration and regular movement not only uplift your mood and reduce stress, but also support restful sleep, sharpen cognitive function and elevate your overall energy and quality of life. A strong and healthy body cultivates inner strength, helping you recover from setbacks with greater ease. It also builds confidence and self-empowerment, allowing you to continue moving forward with purpose toward your goals and dreams, and ultimately, toward true abundance and fulfillment.

Nourishing your body and investing in your health transforms every aspect of life, empowering you to pursue passions and experience joy in everyday moments. A strong, vibrant body not only supports longevity and vitality but also fuels your ability to make lasting contributions to the world, a concept explored further in *Chapter 4: The Abundance Pillars – Mastering Your Life and Collective Consciousness.* Beyond being a physical foundation, a well-nourished body supports vibrant energy, emotional stability, mental clarity and deeper spiritual connection. When your body is aligned and in balance, energy flows freely throughout your entire system, clearing blockages, supporting spiritual growth and expanding your capacity for intuition and inner wisdom. This alignment between body and spirit sharpens your inner guidance, making it easier to access your higher self and trust your intuitive insights, concepts we will explore more deeply in the next sections. By caring for your physical health within a holistic self-care approach, you honor the sacred connection between mind, body and spirit, laying the groundwork for profound transformation, elevated consciousness and a life of true abundance.

Introspection — Nourishing Your Body

Reflect on the interconnectedness of your mind, body and soul in fostering a life of abundance and fulfillment. Consider how prioritizing your physical health contributes to your quality of life, overall well-being and vitality.

Consider how integrating balanced nutrition, proper hydration, consistent physical activity and restorative practices into your daily routine nurtures your body and supports your journey toward a vibrant, abundant and fulfilling life.

Reflect on how nurturing your physical health and sustaining your body's vitality creates a foundation for profound spiritual insights, heightened self-awareness and personal growth, allowing you to align more fully with your essence and the abundant flow of life.

Insights — Your Higher Self and Inner Child

Attaining a true state of abundance is a profound milestone, rooted in a deep understanding of, and alignment with, our essence, our most authentic self. This foundational concept is explored in *Insights — Your Essence (Self)* in *Chapter 1: The Core Principles of Abundance*. **You may wish to revisit that section before continuing.** As we have discussed, aligning with our essence is the gateway to uncovering our purpose and fulfilling the unique destiny we are here to live. Embracing our **Higher Self** is a pivotal part of this journey, a transformational shift that draws us closer to the abundant life we envision. *But what exactly is our higher self?* Simply, it is the wise, intuitive presence within us all, embodying our deepest essence and cutting through the noise of negative thoughts and low-vibrational energies that often obscure our lives. Unlike the ego or lower self, the higher self provides clarity and wisdom, helping us navigate away from anger, fear, worry and anxiety. Imagine your higher self as a protective shield, defending you against the detrimental forces of the human experience and directing you toward your highest potential, the grandest version of yourself.

Balanced within this higher awareness is another essential aspect of your being: your **Inner Child**. This part of you carries the essence of innocence, creativity and raw emotion. It holds the key to your truest desires, unmet needs and the pure, unfiltered joy and wonder you once experienced. Our inner child is not just a remnant of our past; it is a vital, living part of us that continues to influence our emotional responses and our capacity for playfulness, spontaneity and deep connection. While our higher self offers wisdom, guidance and insight, our inner child brings us closer to our vulnerability, reminding us of the importance of nurturing our emotional well-being and honoring our most authentic desires. Our higher self and inner child together create a dynamic balance within us. Our higher self guides us toward our highest potential with clarity and purpose, while our inner child keeps us grounded in our emotional truth, allowing us to access the purest forms of joy, love and creativity. Recognizing and integrating both aspects of self is crucial for a fulfilling journey toward abundance, as they each contribute unique insights and strengths that enrich our path to wholeness and self-realization.

Our higher self is a sacred channel of profound wisdom that supports us through the complexities of the human experience. As life presents us with emotional turbulence, anger, fear, worry or anxiety, the higher self invites us not to resist these feelings, but to observe and honor them as part of our human journey. Rather than becoming trapped in them, we are empowered to process and release them with clarity and grace. Guiding us from the inside out, the higher self liberates us from limiting patterns and reconnects us to our innate resilience and deeper knowing. From a broader spiritual lens, the higher self is not bound by the limitations of this single lifetime. It is often viewed as the eternal, intuitive presence that spans across lifetimes, carrying forward the distilled wisdom of countless experiences and lessons. In this sense, it is not only a guide, it is our essence in its most evolved and illuminated form.

When we are attuned to it, we begin to see beyond our immediate reactions and circumstances, and instead move through life with greater authenticity, confidence and peace. At the same time, deep healing, true integration and lasting transformation cannot happen through (higher self) wisdom alone. The inner child, the emotional core of our being, must also be acknowledged and nurtured. It is this part of us that first learned what love, fear, abandonment, joy and safety felt like. It lives within us not as a memory, but as an active influence on how we connect, protect and express ourselves. When triggered, it is often the inner child responding, not out of immaturity, but out of a deep, unmet need for safety, love or validation. This is where the higher self becomes a powerful reparenting force. It allows us to meet the inner child with compassion instead of criticism. Where the inner child may cry out or shut down, the higher self gently steps in to listen, hold space and bring truth to distorted beliefs formed long ago. This dynamic relationship creates a bridge between emotional honesty and spiritual maturity, a foundation for real, lasting healing.

When we cultivate this inner balance, we are able to access the fullness of our being. The creativity and joy of the inner child are no longer repressed, and the wisdom of the higher self is no longer drowned out by emotional noise. Together, they form a sacred inner alliance: one that empowers us to live from our essence, guided by intuition and grounded in emotional truth. By embracing practices like solitude, mindfulness meditation, introspection, self-reflection and journaling, key topics we will explore in the forthcoming *Integration* section, we deepen our connection to both the higher self and the inner child. We begin to recognize the voice of truth within us and trust its guidance. We learn to hold space for ourselves in all our forms: wounded and wise, playful and powerful. This sacred journey of self-realization guides us toward a profound sense of freedom, a fundamental principle of abundance, and empowers us to fully embody our authentic selves.

Introspection — Your Higher Self and Inner Child

Reflect on a moment when you felt disconnected, lost or unsure of your next step. How did your higher self guide you back to clarity or purpose? Describe the subtle guidance, inner clarity or deep sense of truth you felt and how this connection to your higher self shaped your thoughts, choices or the way you moved through the situation.

____

____

____

____

____

____

____

____

Reflect on a recent situation where you felt emotionally triggered or overwhelmed. What was the situation and how do you believe your inner child was influencing your response? Describe the emotions that surfaced, the unmet needs you may have uncovered and how acknowledging your inner child shifted your awareness or actions.

____

____

____

Reflect on a time when you chose to pause instead of reacting impulsively. What was happening in that moment and how did both your higher self and inner child show up? Describe how their interplay, wisdom and emotion, helped you navigate the situation with greater understanding, balance or authenticity.

Insights — Your Intuition

Now that we have acquainted ourselves with the concepts of the higher self and inner child and have learned how to discern their presence, the question arises: *How do we effectively tap into their wisdom and guidance?* One of the most accessible avenues is through tuning into that often-mentioned "gut feeling" (our **Intuition)**. *What exactly is intuition and how much weight should we assign to its guidance?* Have you ever experienced that subtle nudge from within as you navigate the twists and turns of life? It could very well be a soul-aligned pull, a sign that your higher self and inner child are actively reaching out to communicate with you. Intuition manifests in various forms, each carrying its own significance and message. Some perceive it as an innate sensation, a sudden wave of calm enveloping them. For others, it may materialize as physical sensations, such as a gnawing feeling in the stomach or a fluttering in the heart. Still, it presents itself as a magnetic force for many, drawing them towards a particular direction, decision or outcome. Regardless of its form, the message remains clear: *listen to it.*

Tapping into your intuition involves following the guidance and wisdom of your higher self and inner child, transcending the limitations of mere rational thought. *How can we recognize when our higher self, inner child and intuition are reaching out to us? What signals should we be alert to?* When your higher self and inner child are aligned and speaking through intuition, it often triggers a profound inner awakening, shifting your values, reshaping your beliefs and transforming how you experience life itself. For example, you may begin to challenge long-held societal ideals centered around job titles, material success and outward status. Rather than chasing validation through external achievements, you feel an undeniable pull inward, toward meaning, integrity and emotional fulfillment. Your intuition begins to guide you away from the need for approval and toward a life rooted in authenticity. As you deepen your connection with your essence and higher self, you begin to shape a new framework of values and beliefs, one that reflects your soul's truth, not the world's expectations.

Imagine you have spent years chasing the benchmarks of success defined by the world: prestigious titles, financial gain and public recognition. On paper, you have arrived. But internally, something feels hollow and incomplete. As your connection with your higher self and inner child deepens, a quiet but undeniable truth begins to surface: these external markers no longer define you. You start to question the cost of living out someone else's version of success. A subtle, soul-level shift begins to unfold, one that draws you inward, toward a life of authenticity, meaning and alignment. Rather than striving for status, you find yourself gravitating toward *purpose*. You may feel called to pursue work that lights you up from within, even if it lacks the prestige or salary once sought. You begin to measure success not by applause, but by alignment with your values, your passions and your truth.

Relationships become more intentional, your time more sacred. Perhaps you leave the corporate spotlight to launch a mission-driven nonprofit, mentor young creatives or build something heart-centered that nourishes you and serves others. This is not a loss; *it is a homecoming*, a return to your essence, who you have always been to your core. In choosing fulfillment over validation and impact over image, you access a level of joy that is real and lasting, one no title or paycheck could ever offer. It is here, in this sacred alignment, that you meet your true self and realize **this is the abundance you were always meant to embody**.

Other powerful signals that your higher self, inner child and intuition are reaching for your attention often appear as an irresistible pull toward creativity and nature. You may feel magnetically drawn to paint, write, compose music or express yourself through poetry, not for achievement, but as a soul-level release, a way for your essence to speak without filters. These are not hobbies; **they are portals**. When you surrender fully to the creative flow, you enter a sacred space: one that reveals truths about who you are and what you are here to become. This call to create is not random; it is your higher self and inner child whispering through inspiration, inviting you to *return home to yourself.*

In a similar way, moments spent in nature can act as portals as well. If you ever find yourself breathless before a quiet forest, moved by the rhythmic pull of the ocean or stilled by the vast silence of a mountain trail, recognize that nature is not merely a backdrop; **it is both a mirror and messenger**. Its vibrations echo the frequency of your soul, reflecting the truth of who you are beneath the noise of the world. In these sacred spaces, distractions dissolve. You hear more clearly. You feel more deeply. You remember more honestly. Nature does not just ground you; *it expands you.* It opens a channel, silent but powerful, through which the voice of your essence can rise. So, when something stirs in you amidst the wind, the water or the trees...*listen.* That pull is not random. It may be your higher self or inner child speaking the language of your soul, calling you inward toward wisdom, creativity and profound inner peace.

Beyond the call toward self-expression and the natural world, you may also experience a powerful pull to make a meaningful impact on those around you. If you feel a compelling desire to serve, uplift or leave the world better than you found it, whether quietly or boldly, this too is a sign. It is a nudge from your higher self and intuition, guiding you into alignment not only with your own truth but with the greater rhythm of humanity's collective heartbeat. While deep inner work often begins in solitude, its impact is never isolated. *The more we connect with our essence, the more naturally we feel moved to create ripples of healing and evolution beyond ourselves.* Perhaps this calling shows up as a passion project, a shift in career or simply the need to extend kindness where it is most needed. This guidebook, itself, is a living embodiment of that principle, shaped not only by personal insight, but by the merging of collective wisdom, soul-aligned vision and timeless spiritual truth. It exists as a sacred offering, meant to guide others along their path of transformation and metamorphosis.

As you deepen your connection with your higher self, inner child and intuition, you may find your awareness expanding beyond personal boundaries. If global concerns like hunger, inequality, environmental destruction or collective consciousness stir something deep in your chest, *honor that.* That stirring is sacred. It is your higher self, inner child and intuition (your essence) reminding you that your life holds purpose not just for you, but for the collective good. Take a moment now. Reflect on the creative pursuits that awaken your passion. Then ask yourself: *How might these gifts, your voice, your hands, your heart, be used to serve something greater than you?* **That answer may be the very key to your next chapter**.

Introspection — Your Intuition

Reflect on any recent shifts in your values, beliefs or perspectives. What prompted these changes and how have they impacted your approach to life and decision-making? Describe how your intuition may have played a role in guiding you toward these new understandings.

____

____

____

____

____

____

____

____

Think of a recent decision you made based on a gut feeling or intuitive sense. Describe the decision-making process and how your intuition influenced it. What were the outcomes and how did following your intuition affect your sense of fulfillment or alignment with your higher self?

____

____

Consider any recent creative pursuits or activities that have deeply resonated with you such as art, writing or connecting with nature. How did these activities make you feel and what insights or inspirations emerged during these moments? Think about how these creative expressions connect with your intuition, higher self and inner child, and consider how they guide you toward a deeper understanding of your essence and purpose.

Integration — Your Higher Self, Inner Child and Intuition

To truly connect with our higher self, inner child and intuition, and follow their guidance, it is crucial to spend intentional time in **Solitude**. Time in this sacred space helps us reduce distractions and lets us tune into the wisdom within. *But what exactly is solitude?* It is important to distinguish solitude from loneliness, as many people tend to conflate the two. Solitude is a peaceful, deliberate practice where you enjoy your own company, reflect on yourself and your life, and recharge. It is about valuing personal space, in your own energy, and nurturing your own needs. In solitude, you can make deep connections with your inner self and gain insights into your deepest desires and motivations. It is here where you can do the healthiest processing as moments of solitude often provide the necessary space for profound healing, a topic we will explore more deeply in an upcoming section.

In contrast, loneliness brings a profound sense of sadness and emptiness, arising from a lack of meaningful connection with others. Unlike solitude, which is a chosen and enriching state, loneliness is typically unwelcome, creating a heavy sense of isolation that burdens both heart and mind. It arises from a perceived disconnection, not just physically, but emotionally and spiritually. Over time, persistent loneliness can contribute to feelings of unworthiness, depression and anxiety. It lacks the intentionality, empowerment and self-reflective quality that solitude offers. While solitude invites us inward for growth and renewal, loneliness often leaves us longing outward for connection and validation, sometimes making it difficult to sit with ourselves in a peaceful or purposeful way.

Solitude, as a practice, provides invaluable time to explore your inner world free from external influences. It helps you better understand what truly drives you and gives you the opportunity to reevaluate whether your current lifestyle and daily habits align with your authentic self and your future vision. Beyond fostering self-reflection, solitude serves as an important source of replenishment, particularly for introverts whose energy levels can be significantly impacted by external stimuli. Solitude can contribute to improved mental and emotional health by facilitating self-compassion and self-love and fostering the establishment of personal rituals that promote overall well-being. *Intentionality is essential when embracing solitude.* It is important to use this time for introspection, inner work and cultivating healthy rituals, habits and practices that contribute to a joyful and fulfilling life. In solitude, it is vital to commit to uncovering who you truly are and to become deeply acquainted with yourself; that is the true gift it offers.

To create space for intuition in your solitude, it is important to consciously quiet the constant noise of daily life and let your inner voice be heard. When constantly engaged in activities, our minds can become cluttered, making it challenging to connect with our intuition. Therefore, it is essential to carve out dedicated time each day, whether a few minutes or an hour, to cultivate this connection. One approach is to incorporate **mindfulness meditation** into your daily routine. Let us take a moment to revisit the practical steps for establishing a mindfulness meditation practice, as discussed in the *Integration* section of *Achieving Self-Awareness.*

Start by finding a quiet, comfortable space where you will not be disturbed. Sit upright, relaxed, with your hands resting in your lap. Take a moment to settle in, let your body soften and your mind begin to slow. Turn your attention inward. Focus on your breath as it moves in and out through your nose. Feel the rise and fall of your chest and belly. Stay with this rhythm, attuning to the flow of now. As thoughts or sensations arise, notice them without judgment. Do not chase or resist; just observe and let them pass. If your mind drifts, gently return to your breath. Give yourself space to simply sit and be. In this stillness, clarity can surface. *Intuition speaks in quiet moments*; create the space to hear it.

Introspection and **self-reflection** are essential practices to incorporate into your daily rhythm whether in solitude, during mindfulness meditation or in quiet moments throughout the day. As discussed, introspection is the practice of looking inward to gain a more profound understanding of yourself. It invites you to self-reflect and examine your deepest motivations and desires. Through this inward journey, you begin to uncover your true essence: who you are at your core. Set aside intentional time each day, whether ten minutes or an hour, to sit in stillness, without an agenda, simply being fully present with yourself. By consistently creating space for introspection and self-reflection, you open the door for intuition to emerge. Over time, this practice helps you tap into your inner knowing, bringing greater clarity and insight into your everyday life. *Introspection* exercises are included throughout each section of this guidebook to help you strengthen your connection to your intuition and deepen your journey of self-discovery.

During moments of introspection, consider practices like **journaling**, expressing **gratitude**, and reciting **affirmations** to deepen your connection with your higher self. One powerful journaling exercise is to ask yourself: "*What would my higher self say or do in this situation?*" Take a few quiet minutes to write freely, allowing your thoughts, feelings and intuitive guidance to surface without judgment. Reflect on any insights or patterns that emerge and note one small action inspired by this guidance that you can apply in your daily life. Gratitude further strengthens this connection by shifting your awareness toward abundance and presence, while affirmations help realign your thoughts with your core truth. Revisit the *Integration* sections throughout this guidebook to reinforce these practices and fully activate your intuitive awareness.

Although this list is not exhaustive, these tools provide a valuable glimpse into the various ways you can connect with the intuitive guidance of your higher self. Each practice is an essential aid on your journey toward aligning with your essence and sacred calling. Integrating these practices into your daily routine awakens your ability to tune into the quiet whispers and transformative wisdom of your intuition. This consistent engagement helps deepen your connection with your inner knowing, core values and spiritual guidance, ultimately supporting you in living an abundant life that reflects your authentic self and aspirations.

Insights and Integration — Belief Systems and Values

As we move through *Mastering Your Essence (Self) and Energy*, our attention shifts to uncovering and understanding our core **Belief Systems and Values**. We begin to reveal the underlying frameworks that embody our inner truths and inherent wisdom by deepening our understanding of our true selves. Our belief systems and values form an elaborate network of interconnected convictions that structure how we perceive and engage with the world around us. These beliefs, deeply ingrained within our consciousness, serve as guiding principles that dictate our attitudes, behaviors and decision-making process, a concept we examined in *Insights — The Art of Manifesting Abundance*. To revisit this idea, intentional decision-making is most powerful when it is rooted in alignment with our core belief systems and values. When a decision reflects these foundational elements of our being, it resonates deeply with our essence, our most authentic self.

In the segment *Insights — Where Are My Thoughts Coming From?* we explored how thoughts can evolve into belief systems and deeply held convictions over time. When you reinforce thoughts through repetition, personal experiences or social and cultural influences, they take root in your consciousness. These persistent thought patterns gradually become ingrained, solidifying into core beliefs that shape our perception of the world and guide our actions, choices and interactions with others. As these beliefs become more entrenched, they can influence our worldview, directing our behavior and decision-making processes. This transformation highlights our thoughts' profound role in constructing the foundation of our reality and influencing how we navigate our lives.

It is important to recognize that belief systems are not rigid or fixed; they are living, evolving and continually reshaping themselves. Understanding the dynamic nature of belief systems is essential, as they continually adapt and evolve throughout our journey of self-discovery and growth.

Our beliefs are constantly tested and refined, shaped by new experiences, deepened through insights, and transformed by the process of personal growth and maturation. These ongoing processes shape and mold our beliefs, influencing how we perceive the world and our place within it. The fluidity of belief systems highlights their responsiveness to inner growth as well as external influences, including societal norms, cultural paradigms and interpersonal relationships. These external factors serve as agents of change to our existing beliefs, continually prompting us to reevaluate our perspectives on life, meaning and purpose.

A real-life example of how belief systems evolve can be seen in someone raised in a conservative religious household, where strict beliefs about morality and life purpose were instilled from a young age. As they grow older and move to a diverse urban area, they encounter a wide range of worldviews, cultural practices and spiritual beliefs that differ from what they were taught. Forming close relationships with people from different backgrounds challenges their original beliefs. Through meaningful conversations, personal experiences and deep introspection, they question the rigid definitions of right and wrong they once held. They start exploring various spiritual practices, reading literature from different philosophies and engaging in open-minded discussions. Gradually, their belief systems shift, integrating new ideas and values that align more closely with their evolving understanding. This example of realignment reflects how belief systems are not fixed but are constantly reshaped by internal growth and external influences, leading to a more nuanced perspective on existence.

Many of us carry belief systems that were never truly ours, adopted from society, our families or media without ever examining whether they resonate with our authentic selves. Over time, these inherited beliefs may feel restrictive or misaligned with our core values and sense of purpose. An example of this can be seen in someone who grew up in a family that emphasized conventional career success as the ultimate measure of worth. As they enter adulthood and experience different environments, perhaps through travel, higher education or diverse work settings, they begin to notice that these beliefs no longer reflect their personal aspirations or values. Through reflection, conversations with mentors and peers, and exposure to alternative ways of living, they consciously evaluate which beliefs serve them and which do not. Slowly, they develop a belief system that honors their essence, shaping a worldview that feels authentic, empowering and aligned with who they truly are rather than the expectations imposed upon them.

While our beliefs can evolve from personal insight and experience, much of what we hold comes from the world around us. In contemporary society, belief systems arise from a multitude of sources, including religion, culture, politics, philosophy and spirituality. Religion, one of the most pervasive frameworks, provides guiding principles that help individuals navigate their lives, with countless structures around the world offering unique approaches to understanding existence, morality and the human experience. Spirituality, often distinct from organized religion, allows for a personal connection to transcendental experiences and inner wisdom. Beyond religion and spirituality, societal norms and cultural values shape beliefs by defining acceptable behavior and social expectations. Political ideologies offer additional lenses for interpreting the world, influencing perspectives on governance, justice and social order. Philosophy adds another dimension, equipping us with guiding structures to examine the fundamental questions of life, ethics and human nature.

It is important to note that although society and culture offer guidance and structure, *the beliefs that truly define us emerge from our lived experiences, our deepest values and our ongoing process of introspection.* Even this guidebook, in its essence, could be seen as a belief system, presenting key insights, principles, concepts and frameworks for consideration. What matters most is cultivating a belief system that reflects your authentic self, rather than one shaped by external pressures or societal expectations. When you take ownership of your personal convictions and values, you create an opportunity to build a belief system that aligns with your true self and supports your personal growth and fulfillment.

Exploring and identifying your beliefs and values can be a deeply profound and enlightening journey that shapes your internal governance. Identifying your current belief systems, for instance, involves a combination of **self-reflection** and **observation**. Begin by reflecting on your core values and guiding principles. Ask yourself: *What do I truly believe about life, success and joy?* **Journaling** can help uncover patterns in your thoughts and reactions, revealing underlying subconscious beliefs operating beneath the surface. For example, you might journal about a recent situation that triggered a strong emotional response. As you reflect, you might uncover recurring patterns, for example, feeling undeserving of praise or recognition. Such patterns often point to deeper, subconscious beliefs like "*I must constantly prove my worth.*" By *observing* this reaction and exploring it through journaling and self-reflection, you begin to uncover and better understand the belief driving it.

Additionally, **seeking feedback** from trusted friends, mentors or coaches can offer fresh perspectives and reveal blind spots in your thinking. Often, the people closest to you can identify patterns or limiting beliefs you may not immediately notice yourself. **Mindfulness practices**, such as meditation or breathwork, help you tune into the present moment, allowing subconscious beliefs to surface through increased awareness of your thoughts and emotional responses. It is also helpful to reflect on how cultural norms, societal expectations and family dynamics have shaped your worldview over time. Consider journaling about pivotal life events, both positive and challenging, and the beliefs that may have formed as a result. By integrating self-reflection, observation, journaling, feedback and mindfulness, you gain a more complete picture of your belief systems and how they influence your daily choices, relationships and overall well-being.

Here is a real-world example that brings all of these practices together. Imagine an individual who highly values independence. Through introspection, they notice a recurring pattern: a preference for solitary tasks and a tendency to avoid collaborative projects at work. By journaling their reactions to teamwork and reflecting on their satisfaction with independent achievements, they uncover the central role personal autonomy plays in their life. Further observation of their choices, such as opting for freelance work over a traditional job, combined with feedback from colleagues and mindful reflection, highlights how this belief in independence shapes both their career path and personal decisions. Pause for a moment and consider how this example might mirror your own experiences, using it as a guide to uncover the underlying beliefs influencing your choices.

Once you have identified your core beliefs, you may feel called to explore or refine them further to develop your belief systems. One powerful way to do this is by opening yourself up to new ideas, perspectives and ways of thinking. Traveling, for example, allows you to encounter various experiences and interact with a variety of individuals from different demographics and backgrounds, helping you discern and align with thoughts and experiences that resonate with your inner truth. Additionally, seeking out role models who exemplify values and lifestyles you admire can inspire and motivate you to cultivate empowering belief systems. Embracing life fully, engaging with diverse communities and welcoming nuanced experiences all contribute to the evolution of your belief systems over time. It is essential to allow this process to unfold naturally and with intention as it is a dynamic and ever-evolving journey.

Now what about our values? They undergo a similar transformative process and evolution. As a reminder, values represent the qualities and principles we hold in the highest regard, the aspects of life that are most sacred to us, both internally and externally. Our value system, which encompasses all our values, profoundly shapes our perceptions and interactions with the world. At its core, our value system directs us toward what we truly consider essential in our lives. Living by our values creates a powerful magnetic force, drawing people and circumstances that resonate with our authentic self, fostering genuine joy and fulfillment. Simultaneously, it pushes us away from anything that contradicts our core values and true identity. Values are paramount because they act as the compass by which we navigate our thoughts, emotions, decisions and actions. Aligning our lives with our values profoundly influences our connection to our essence and our choices. *Our value system is a vital filter, connecting us with individuals and circumstances that align with our deepest beliefs.*

Just like with your belief systems, identifying your values requires a process of honest ownership and thoughtful exploration. A powerful introspective question to consider when seeking to identify your core governing values is: *What matters most to me?* This question (and answer) is a gateway to understanding your core priorities and guiding principles. A simple approach for understanding your values and value system is to **categorize your life** into key areas or themes and evaluate the significance of each in relation to your overall well-being and fulfillment. Consider categories such as health, relationships, career and personal growth. Reflecting on these areas helps identify which aspects of your life are most important to you and how they impact your decision-making process.

For example, when examining the realm of health, pause to reflect on what mental, emotional, physical and spiritual well-being genuinely mean to you. Consider how you define a healthy lifestyle, what practices support your vitality and how your mental, emotional, physical and spiritual state influences your overall quality of life. Consider factors such as nutrition, hydration, exercise, sleep and overall wellness. Rate the importance of maintaining optimal health, recognizing its impact on your ability to pursue other goals and enjoy life's experiences. Similarly, in the context of relationships, examine the value you place on various connections, whether with family, friends, romantic partners or your broader social circle. Consider the importance of love, trust, communication, mutual support, emotional safety and belonging in your life. Pause now and reflect deeply on how prioritizing your well-being and nurturing meaningful relationships contributes to your sense of joy, connection and personal growth, key principles of abundance. Through this process, you begin to uncover the values that shape your decisions, fuel your motivations and define what matters most to you. These reflections lay the foundation for identifying your core value system, one that aligns with your authentic self and guides you toward a more intentional, fulfilling and abundant life.

By drawing inspiration from the core principles of abundance, which we explored in *Chapter 1: The Core Principles of Abundance*, you can deeply enrich and fortify your belief and value systems. These foundational principles, rooted in your essence (self), mind, body and soul alignment, joy and peace, love and connection, growth and evolution, freedom and gratitude, offer a powerful blueprint for creating a life rich in abundance, fulfillment and meaning. As you align your beliefs and values with these essential energies, you gain access to profound clarity around your core priorities, desires and aspirations. This alignment creates a strong inner framework that empowers you to navigate life with authenticity, intention and a deep sense of purpose.

Introspection — Belief Systems and Values

Consider a time when you encountered a challenging situation that prompted you to reassess and refine your belief systems. How did this experience influence your perceptions, attitudes and behaviors? What insights did you gain about yourself and your values through this process of self-discovery and evolution?

____

____

____

____

____

____

____

____

Explore the various sources from which belief systems stem in contemporary society, such as religion, spirituality, politics and philosophy. Reflect on how these diverse influences have shaped your own belief systems and worldview. How do you navigate the interplay between external influences and your inner truths when forming your belief systems?

____

____

Evaluate the importance of different categories in your life, such as health and wellness, relationships, career and personal growth as it pertains to your value system. Rate each category based on its significance to your overall well-being and fulfillment. How do these categories contribute to your sense of joy, purpose and fulfillment in life?

Insights — Self-Experience (Lived Experience)

As your beliefs and values evolve, the wisdom cultivated through **Self-Experience (Lived Experience)** empowers you to face life's uncertainties and complexities with greater confidence and discernment. This wisdom, deeply personal and inherently subjective, is shaped by your unique background, emotions, perspectives and observations. It encompasses the invaluable lessons learned through lived experiences, including moments of trial and error, triumphs and setbacks and the awareness of right and wrong paths. Self-experience is not just a passive collection of memories; it actively molds our understanding of the world and ourselves. Every interaction, every win and loss, contributes to a growing bank of insight that shapes our beliefs, values and perspectives, and, by extension, our thoughts, emotions and actions. This guidebook's core concepts are deeply rooted in the collective self-experience of individuals worldwide, highlighting that the most meaningful and transformative insights often arise from personal experience and the compounded wisdom passed down from others.

As we begin to explore more abstract ideas such as spirituality and spiritual intelligence, soon to be discussed, self-experience plays an even more vital role in bringing meaning and clarity to these concepts. Unlike empirical evidence, which we can observe and measure, we often validate spirituality and spiritual intelligence through profound personal experiences that go beyond the physical realm. These experiences might include deep meditation, a profound connection with nature, intuitive nudges, spiritual awakenings or acts of love and compassion that resonate with spiritual truths. Although spirituality and spiritual intelligence cannot be empirically measured, countless individuals attest to profound personal experiences that affirm their depth, presence and transformative influence.

Imagine someone navigating a period of intense struggle, weighed down by uncertainty and self-doubt, who takes a quiet walk in nature and suddenly experiences a moment of profound clarity. In that instant, they may feel guided by a higher power, by the wisdom of their own inner self or by an unexplainable sense of knowing, inspiring a decision that aligns with their deepest purpose and sacred calling. This single moment of insight can shift their perspective, opening new possibilities and redirecting the trajectory of their life in meaningful ways. While such experiences cannot be quantified or measured by scientific methods, their impact is unmistakable: they serve as powerful reminders of the presence and relevance of spirituality and spiritual intelligence, reinforcing the belief that *personal growth and understanding often emerge through lived experience, reflection and attunement to the deeper currents of life.*

In spirituality and spiritual intelligence, self-experience is a powerful source of understanding and validation. It allows individuals to explore and affirm truths that resonate with their deepest selves, offering guidance and wisdom that science and empirical evidence alone cannot provide. As we explore our essence, it is important to recognize how self-experience shapes our beliefs, guides our actions and reveals our path forward. While science provides important insights into our physical world, our lived experiences and perceptions play an equally important role in shaping how we understand ourselves, our beliefs and our place in the Universe. Ultimately, self-discovery and spiritual growth are deeply intertwined with self-experience. Through our own experiences, we discern what is true, meaningful and aligned with our innermost beliefs and values. By embracing and integrating these experiences, we gain a deeper understanding of ourselves and the world around us, walking a path that is uniquely our own, rich with insight, purpose and fulfillment.

Introspection — Self-Experience (Lived Experience)

Reflect on a recent experience in which you gained a meaningful personal insight or deeper understanding. What circumstances or choices brought you to this realization, and how did it influence your perspective, decisions or actions? In what ways does this moment of clarity connect to your broader journey, your personal growth and the patterns of your lived experience?

Describe a notable personal experience that profoundly affected you, such as a moment of deep reflection, a significant life event or an encounter that shifted your perspective. How did this experience shape your self-understanding or influence your life path?

____

____

____

____

____

____

Think about a challenging experience you have faced. How has navigating this challenge contributed to your self-awareness or personal development? What insights have you gained from this experience, and how has it shaped your understanding of yourself?

____

____

____

____

____

____

____

____

Insights — Spirituality and Spiritual Intelligence

We have begun exploring the expansive territory of **Spirituality** and briefly touched on the concept of **Spiritual Intelligence** in connection to self-experience. We will now take a closer look at the foundation of spirituality and spiritual intelligence to understand how they shape and support the discovery and nurturing of our authentic self. When integrated, spirituality and spiritual intelligence reveal the path to a more authentic, meaningful and enriched life. Spirituality is a multifaceted journey that spans a broad spectrum of beliefs, practices and experiences, all dedicated to cultivating inner peace, meaning and fulfillment. It reflects a person's continuous pursuit to uncover deeper truths and build an intimate connection with their true self and a higher presence or purpose beyond themselves. People may experience this in different ways, whether through faith, quiet meditation or a deep sense of oneness with nature. These different paths help you explore your spirituality in your own way, often leading to profound insight and a stronger sense of connection to life's deeper meaning. Spiritual practices and experiences contribute to personal growth and serve as important elements in understanding your essence, a core principle of abundance.

Spirituality is a deeply personal and expansive experience. For some, it is found through the structure and tradition of religion. For others, it is discovered through more introspective or embodied practices like mindfulness meditation, breathwork, journaling or simply being present in nature. Regardless of how one connects with it, spirituality often serves as a powerful anchor, a source of meaning, clarity and inner peace. While this guidebook does not focus extensively on the topic of spirituality, acknowledging its energy and presence in your life can offer profound insight on your path to self-discovery. It can help guide your exploration of your authentic self and support your pursuit of fulfillment, alignment and true abundance. Embracing even a subtle sense of spiritual connection, whether through stillness or self-inquiry, can enrich your journey of personal transformation in meaningful ways.

For a tangible example of spirituality in everyday life, begin with stillness and mindfulness meditation. Consider the experience of Maria, who feels a deep sense of stress and disconnection in her daily life due to her high-pressure job and busy schedule. Seeking a way to find inner peace and reconnect with herself, Maria begins practicing mindfulness meditation. Each morning, she sets aside time for stillness, focusing on her breath and observing her thoughts without judgment. As she continues this practice, she starts to notice subtle shifts in her perspective. She becomes more present in her daily activities, appreciating small moments of joy and finding a sense of calm amidst chaos. Through mindfulness meditation, Maria experiences a profound sense of inner tranquility and connection to something greater than herself. This practice helps her navigate life's challenges more easily, fostering a sense of alignment and fulfillment. Her journey shows how spirituality, through practices like stillness and mindfulness meditation, can help you better understand yourself and find a deeper sense of inner peace.

Building on the foundation of spirituality, spiritual intelligence, often referred to as spiritual quotient (SQ) or SI, is a specific capacity that transcends the material world, enabling you to perceive and understand deeper layers of consciousness, meaning and wisdom. Simply put, spiritual intelligence is your ability to connect with your inner self, uncover life's greater purpose and live in alignment with your values, purpose and higher awareness. Consciousness and self-awareness, central themes in this guidebook, play an essential role in understanding spiritual intelligence. *As we grow and strengthen our connection to ourselves, spiritual intelligence begins to unfold.* It lays the groundwork for accessing our inner wisdom and approaching life with greater clarity, purpose and coherence. As the world shifts into a new era of awakening and expanded collective consciousness, the depth and importance of these truths come into sharper focus. *Individuals who exhibit consciousness and self-awareness demonstrate a profound capacity for spiritual intelligence, reflecting a deep understanding of their inner truths, beliefs, values and life purpose.*

As we deepen our understanding of spirituality and spiritual intelligence, we naturally arrive at the transformative experiences that awaken and shape the soul. The journey ahead will explore the interconnected phases of awakening, healing and releasing, enlightenment and ultimately, transcendence. These stages are not always linear, but together, they form the energetic blueprint for mastering your essence. Awakening often begins with a powerful realization, an inner shift that reveals the limitations of past beliefs and opens the door to higher consciousness. At times, however, deep healing may come first, as unprocessed pain must be acknowledged before awakening can fully take root. In most cases, healing and releasing follow the awakening, clearing emotional and energetic blockages that stand in the way of expansion. From this foundation, enlightenment arises as a deeper recognition of the self's connection to the greater whole. Finally, in transcendence, we rise above mental divisions and separateness, deeply connecting with universal intelligence and fully embodying the unified awareness toward which spiritual intelligence guides us.

These powerful experiences are at the heart of spirituality and spiritual intelligence, representing an unwavering pursuit of deep insights, meaningful connections and a richer understanding of ourselves and the world. They reinforce the dynamic journey of self-discovery, personal growth and the acquisition of wisdom that defines these realms. By incorporating these transformative moments into our journey of mastering our essence and energy, we align ourselves to a path of genuine fulfillment and liberation, marking a pivotal evolution in our quest to deeper meaning and authentic self-realization.

Introspection — Spirituality and Spiritual Intelligence

How have specific spiritual practices or experiences, such as mindfulness meditation, religious faith or connection with nature, influenced your inner peace and alignment with your authentic self? Describe a moment when one of these practices profoundly impacted your understanding of yourself.

____

____

____

____

____

____

____

____

How do you recognize and engage with deeper layers of consciousness, meaning and wisdom? Think back to a recent moment when you felt led by spiritual intelligence, an elevated awareness or deeper inner truth. How did this experience shape your perspective and actions?

____

____

Examine the concepts of spirituality and spiritual intelligence and its impact on your personal growth. How do self-awareness and consciousness influence your ability to perceive deeper layers of meaning and wisdom? Reflect on how these elements have guided you toward greater self-discovery and alignment with your true self.

Insights — Awakening

Building on our exploration of spirituality and spiritual intelligence in mastering your essence and energy, we now turn our attention to the concept of **Awakening**. In beginning our study of awakening, we see its profound link to enlightenment, a concept we will examine more fully later. Both awakening and enlightenment are marked by a profound awareness of the interconnectedness and unity of all existence, transcending the limitations imposed by egoic attachments and self-identifications. In both spiritual and philosophical traditions, awakening can be viewed as a *spiritual initiation*, a sudden moment of deep realization or a gradual unfolding of insight. Either way, it reflects a shift in awareness, one that reveals your true essence and your connection to everything around you. It is about seeing beyond the surface of everyday life and tapping into deeper truths that often go unnoticed. This shift opens the door to a more expansive understanding of yourself and the Universe, helping you move past old limitations and into a clearer, more meaningful way of being.

While awakening is often portrayed as a single, transcendent moment, lived experience tells a different story. For most, awakening unfolds gradually through repeated moments of awareness, collapse, insight and integration. It is not linear, nor is it constant. There are periods of clarity followed by contraction, joy followed by grief, expansion followed by deep rest. This ebb and flow is not a sign of failure, but evidence of a nervous system, psyche and soul recalibrating to a higher truth. Awakening asks us not to escape our humanity, but to inhabit it more fully, with presence, compassion and patience.

During an awakening, individuals often experience a profound expansion of consciousness, heightened awareness and deep spiritual insights, frequently accompanied by a lasting sense of inner peace that can be difficult to convey through ordinary language or logic. As we discussed earlier, linguistic relativity suggests that language shapes how we perceive and communicate reality. In the context of awakenings, the limits and nuances of language influence how we interpret and express these transformative experiences. The words available to us both reflect our inner state and constrain how we articulate it, reinforcing the idea that language shapes our understanding of the world.

Since the words we use influence how we understand transformative experiences, it helps to examine the tangible signs of a personal awakening. *How, then, will you know if you are in the midst of one?* One of the clearest signs of awakening is a growing pull toward solitude and time in nature, reflecting a deep inner need for introspection and reconnection with the natural world. These shifts often point to profound inner transformation. Solitude becomes a sacred sanctuary for peace and reflection, offering space for deeper self-discovery and alignment. It allows for an intimate connection with your inner essence, revealing insights into your true desires, motivations and authentic self. Similarly, nature, with its unique vibrations and energies, provides a powerful backdrop for mindfulness and creative exploration, further enhancing your understanding of your inner self. Whether you are hiking through majestic landscapes or strolling along serene shores, pay attention to the sensations and emotions these environments evoke within you. Take a moment to pause and reflect deeply: *Have you ever felt a profound yearning for solitude or a natural pull toward the peace of nature, hallmarks of an awakening?*

Let us examine a real-life case of awakening through Sarah's experience. Despite her impressive career accomplishments and material comforts, Sarah, a successful corporate executive, felt a deep and pervasive dissatisfaction. After a particularly stressful period at work, she chose to take a sabbatical and escape to a remote mountain retreat. There, immersed in nature, Sarah spent her days hiking through vibrant forests and meditating beside gentle streams. This period of solitude and connection with the natural world triggered a profound shift in her perspective. Sarah began to experience a heightened awareness and clarity about her life and core values. Her surroundings' stillness and natural beauty allowed her to reflect deeply on her true desires and motivations. Through introspection, she realized that her corporate career, while outwardly successful, was misaligned with her deeper passions and values; she was no longer experiencing joy. This epiphany led her to make a significant life change: she left her corporate job to pursue a career in environmental conservation and community development. Sarah experienced a transformative shift in consciousness during her awakening, as her time in solitude and nature revealed more profound truths about herself. This newfound clarity guided her towards a more authentic and fulfilling path, reflecting the profound impact of her awakening and leading to a greater sense of inner peace and purpose.

Beyond solitude and a pull toward nature, other powerful signs of awakening often include a persistent inner restlessness, an intense yearning for meaningful change in your life, sudden shift in values, a deep questioning of long-held beliefs, heightened emotional sensitivity, a profound connection with your intuition and higher self, and a desire for genuine connection and authenticity. You may also notice an increase in synchronicities, meaningful coincidences, a growing awareness of energy, and a sense of disconnection from relationships or patterns that no longer serve you. Crucially, awakening often stirs the need for healing and releasing, bringing unresolved wounds to the surface so they can be acknowledged, processed and ultimately transformed. This essential inner work will be the focus of our next segment.

Acknowledging that the path to awakening carries its own challenges is an important part of the journey. This profound shift in consciousness can, at times, result in disorientation, confusion and the emergence of repressed emotions and unresolved traumas, necessitating the process of healing and releasing. As the ego dissolves, individuals may face identity crises and existential questions such as "*Who am I?*" "*Why am I here?*"

and "*What is the purpose of it all?*" These questions can evoke a sense of uncertainty and confusion as one navigates through their inner world in search of meaning. Awakening may also result in social alienation, difficulty connecting with others not on a similar spiritual path and existential anxiety related to the meaning of life and death. Physical symptoms like fatigue, headaches and changes in appetite can also manifest during this process. Though challenging, these experiences are essential to the transformative process of awakening. Embracing these difficulties with patience, grace, self-compassion, resilience and openness can lead to profound growth and personal evolution, key principles of abundance. Getting support from spiritual mentors or community groups can be valuable as you work through this process, offering guidance and mutual support as you move toward a more authentic and evolved version of yourself.

Awakening represents a profound shift in consciousness that reveals your true essence, deepens your connection to life and invites greater clarity, purpose and authenticity. It manifests through both subtle and tangible signs: yearnings for solitude, immersion in nature, heightened intuition, meaningful synchronicities and an inner call for transformation. While this process can bring disorientation, emotional intensity and existential questioning, these challenges are essential drivers for growth, self-realization and the cultivation of inner peace. By embracing awakening with awareness, reflection and support, you move toward a more authentic, aligned and expansive way of being, laying the foundation for the healing and releasing work that follows.

Introspection — Awakening

Think about times when you struggled to articulate your transformative experiences. How do you believe the limitations of language have impacted your ability to express or understand your spiritual insights fully? What strategies might help you better convey or grasp these profound experiences?

____

____

____

____

____

____

____

____

Identify and reflect on any recent inclinations towards solitude or nature. How do these inclinations reflect a more profound awakening or a need for introspection? What might they reveal about your current state of awareness and personal transformation?

____

____

____

Consider the challenges you have faced during your journey of awakening, such as confusion, disorientation or existential questions. How have these challenges contributed to your personal evolution? What lessons have you learned from navigating these difficulties and how have they shaped your growth?

Insights and Integration — Healing and Releasing

Awakening often sets in motion a profound process of **Healing and Releasing**, as buried emotions and unresolved traumas begin to surface to be seen, felt and transformed. This energy and shift in consciousness can bring feelings of confusion or emotional upheaval, signs that deeper layers of the self are ready to be acknowledged and let go. Engaging in healing and releasing is essential to mastering your essence and aligning your energy with greater clarity and purpose. When you heal and release what no longer serves you (limiting beliefs, pain, fear, resentment, self-doubt), you realign with your true nature and higher consciousness. This alignment fosters coherence between your thoughts, emotions and actions, allowing your energy to flow with clarity and purpose instead of being weighed down by inner conflict. Throughout this process, many individuals feel called to **solitude** and **reflection**, often arising in response to emotional, psychological or physical pain or imbalance. Whether rooted in close relationships or past trauma, true healing and release are key to living with freedom, joy and emotional clarity.

Healing and releasing encompasses the psychological, emotional, cognitive and spiritual dimensions of well-being. Psychologically, it involves addressing and resolving emotional wounds and traumas. Emotionally, it requires acknowledging repressed feelings, cultivating resilience and developing self-compassion to restore inner safety and stability. Cognitively, healing and releasing restores balance by reshaping negative thought patterns, managing stress and enhancing clarity and emotional regulation. Spiritually, it involves connecting with a deeper sense of purpose and inner peace, uncovering one's true self and experiencing moments of transcendence, rising above ordinary limitations to perceive life from a broader, unified awareness, a concept we will explore in greater depth. Integrating the psychological, emotional, cognitive and spiritual dimensions fosters a holistic approach to healing and releasing, guiding you toward a more balanced, empowered and fulfilling life.

As we continue to explore the psychological, emotional, mental and spiritual dimensions of healing and releasing, we build a powerful foundation for deeper insight, clarity and lasting inner peace. Each of these realms offers unique tools and practices that guide us toward wholeness and self-mastery. Psychological healing and releasing often begins with addressing past traumas and unresolved emotional experiences through practices such as **therapy**, **introspection** and **journaling**. It involves developing greater self-awareness, identifying and challenging limiting beliefs and reshaping the narratives that shape our thoughts, behaviors and perceptions of the world. By confronting and integrating these experiences, we free ourselves from patterns that may have unconsciously governed our decisions, laying the groundwork for more conscious, intentional living, a concept we will explore in more depth later.

Emotional healing and releasing requires acknowledging and processing deeply held feelings, such as grief, anger, fear or sadness that may have been buried or overlooked. It invites us to sit with these emotions fully, without judgment, and to understand the messages they carry about our unmet needs, past experiences and internal conflicts. Through practices like **mindful reflection**, **journaling** and **self-compassion**, we learn to move through these emotions with patience, gentleness and self-love rather than resistance or avoidance. This process gradually restores emotional balance, strengthens resilience and cultivates a sense of inner safety. As we integrate and release these emotions, we become more grounded in ourselves, better able to respond to life with clarity, presence and authenticity.

Cognitive healing and releasing centers on identifying and shifting negative or limiting thought patterns that may unconsciously shape our perceptions and behaviors. It involves the development of a clear and balanced mindset, enhancing focus and developing the ability to respond thoughtfully rather than react impulsively to stress or external pressures. Through practices such as **mindfulness meditation**, **introspection** and **journaling,** we learn to observe our thoughts without judgment, redirect unhelpful patterns and strengthen our capacity for discernment and conscious decision-making. This process not only reduces mental clutter and stress but also fosters a more resilient and empowered mindset, enabling us to navigate life's challenges with greater awareness and intentionality.

Finally, spiritual healing and releasing invites us to reconnect with a deeper sense of meaning, purpose and inner peace. It encourages us to explore our true essence and to cultivate a relationship with the stillness and wisdom that reside within. This process often involves opening ourselves to something greater than the individual self, whether experienced as divine guidance, universal intelligence or the interconnectedness of all life. Spiritual healing and releasing nurtures a sense of awe, gratitude and reverence for life, helping us transcend limiting beliefs, ego-driven patterns and fears that block our growth and evolution. Through practices such as **solitude**, **mindfulness meditation**, **introspection**, **journaling** and **gratitude**, we learn to attune to our inner guidance, recognize the sacredness in everyday moments and align our actions with our deepest values and highest purpose.

These powerful practices facilitate inner transformation, release negative energy, dismantle maladaptive cognitive patterns and beliefs and cultivate self-awareness. Engaging in these approaches fosters a deeper connection with your inner wisdom, intuition, higher self and spiritual essence. Many of these tools and practices have been explored extensively in our journey together. It is beneficial to revisit these tools in the *Integration* segments of this guidebook to support and enhance your healing journey. Together, the psychological, emotional, cognitive and spiritual dimensions of healing and releasing form a holistic foundation for profound transformation. By engaging with each of these layers, we cultivate wholeness, alignment and authenticity, strengthening the inner framework that supports well-being, insight and lasting peace. As we continue to explore and integrate these realms, we open the door to greater clarity, self-mastery and a life lived in resonance with our true essence.

To see how these layers of healing unfold in everyday life, consider Alex, a professional in his early 30s navigating a major personal loss. In the aftermath, he shows several signs that point to a need for deep holistic healing. Psychologically, Alex experiences lingering sadness, feelings of hopelessness and difficulty finding motivation for activities he once enjoyed. Emotionally, he may feel overwhelmed by grief, anger and fear, and struggle to process these intense feelings with patience and self-compassion. Cognitively, he finds himself ruminating over past events, experiencing heightened anxiety and struggling to concentrate and make decisions at work. On a spiritual level, Alex may feel disconnected from a sense of meaning, purpose and inner peace, questioning his values and feeling out of alignment with his authentic self.

These signs reflect the intertwined nature of psychological, emotional, cognitive and spiritual imbalances, highlighting the importance of addressing them through therapy, reflective practices, self-care routines and supportive communities. Engaging with each of these dimensions of healing allows Alex to restore balance, gain clarity and reconnect with his essence, opening the door to recovery, growth and holistic well-being. Take a moment now to reflect: *Is there a personal experience in your own life that could benefit from healing and releasing?*

Holistic healing and releasing invite you to let go of what no longer serves you such as past traumas, grievances, attachments or resentments that weigh on your heart, mind and spirit. This process emphasizes **forgiveness**, **acceptance**, **surrender** and the conscious choice to *release* burdens that inhibit your growth, inner joy and authentic expression. By integrating the mind, body and spirit, you create a space where healing and releasing work together, fostering a sense of wholeness, alignment and connection to your higher self and the Universe. *Letting go* is not about erasing the past, but about transforming its hold over you, empowering you to live with clarity, freedom and vitality across all dimensions of being.

One of the most accessible and transformative practices for facilitating both healing and release is **mindfulness meditation**. This practice, which has been a consistent part of our journey together, supports the gentle release of stored emotions, habitual thought patterns and inner tension. By cultivating present-moment awareness without judgment, mindfulness meditation nurtures psychological clarity through self-awareness, fosters emotional healing by allowing buried feelings to surface and dissipate, and cultivates mental calm by easing stress and mental fragmentation. Through regular practice, it strengthens your capacity to release attachments to fear, resentment or limiting beliefs, restoring balance across the inner self and allowing renewal to flow through mind, body and spirit.

As awareness deepens, mindfulness naturally extends beyond the mind and into the body. The body often carries what the mind cannot fully process, expressing unresolved emotional or spiritual experiences through tension, discomfort or fatigue. When we bring presence to these sensations, through breath, stillness or intuitive movement, we create an opening for release that is both gentle and profound. Practices such as **mindful movement**, **yoga** and **somatic dance** allow emotions stored in the nervous system to move, unwind and integrate, supporting healing at a physical level while reinforcing emotional and psychological balance.

Movement-based and breath-centered practices complement meditation by restoring vitality, regulating the nervous system and strengthening the body's innate capacity to heal. Expressive outlets such as **dance** or **singing**, along with time spent outdoors, **walking**, **absorbing sunlight** and **connecting with nature**, further support this process by lifting mood, increasing energy and grounding awareness in the present moment. Together, mindfulness and embodied practices form a holistic pathway for release and integration, deepening your attunement to your inner wisdom and spiritual essence. Pause now, take a deep breath, and gently *come home to yourself*, embracing the transformative power of awareness, embodiment and letting go.

Building on the mind-body connection cultivated through mindfulness and movement, we can also support healing through intentional physical practices. Modalities such as **red light therapy**, **sauna** and **cold plunges** support cellular repair, improve circulation, reduce inflammation and regulate the nervous system, all of which contribute to greater overall healing. In addition, feeding your body with intention, as we covered earlier, plays a crucial role in physical healing and releasing. Revisit the *Insights and Integration* section on *Nourishing Your Body* to apply these principles and support your healing journey. These practices serve as reminders that the *body holds wisdom* and deserves the same attention and care we give to our inner world. When we engage in physical healing, we naturally support mental clarity, emotional release and spiritual connection since healing one part of ourselves inevitably uplifts the whole.

As we honor the body's wisdom, it becomes clear that true healing and alignment also depend on the regulation of the nervous system: the vital link between mind, body and energy. Your nervous system is the energetic bridge between your inner world and the outer reality you create. Its state determines the frequencies you emit, shaping not only how you perceive life, but also what you attract and allow yourself to receive. *The more regulated your nervous system becomes, the greater your capacity to hold higher frequencies: love, joy, creativity and abundance.* You do not manifest what you desire; you manifest what your body feels safe to receive. When your body feels calm and grounded, it sends a signal of safety to the Universe, opening the flow of expansion and opportunity. Regulation is not merely relaxation; it is energetic mastery in motion. Through grounding, slow breath and mindful presence, you teach your body that *expansion is safe*, that *peace is power* and that *stability is strength.* When your nervous system rests in balance, your vibration resonates with abundance itself. From that state of embodied safety, life begins to respond differently: more fluidly, more generously, more aligned with your highest frequency of being.

When approached with mindfulness and intention, holistic healing, releasing and regulation can lead to profound transformation and eventual enlightenment, a concept we will explore more deeply soon. *True restoration of balance in mind, body and spirit does not come through bypassing pain, but by bravely moving through it.* Healing, releasing and evolution all require us to meet ourselves fully, not just in moments of peace, but especially in discomfort, where the richest insight and growth reside. Avoidance may numb our awareness temporarily, but it allows old wounds to remain active beneath the surface. Only by confronting what hurts can we begin to *release* and *let go*, freeing ourselves from the weight of past experiences. This act of **conscious courage** is what empowers us to transcend limitation, reclaim our energy and evolve into our fullest, most liberated and healed selves.

Introspection — Healing and Releasing

Reflect on a specific experience that has left a lingering emotional impact. How does this experience continue to influence your thoughts, emotions or behaviors today? Write about the emotions it evokes, and any unresolved feelings or thoughts associated with it.

Reflect on a persistent negative thought or belief rooted in a past painful experience. In what ways has this pattern shaped how you see yourself, influenced your choices or impacted your relationships? Envision what healing from this wound might look like and how you could begin transforming this limiting belief into one that empowers and uplifts you.

____

____

____

____

____

____

Write a brief letter or message to yourself from the perspective of your future healed self. In this letter, provide guidance and comfort about how to move forward from the pain you have experienced. Using the tools discussed, offer yourself grace, self-compassion and practical steps for healing and releasing.

____

____

____

____

____

____

____

____

Insights — Enlightenment

Our exploration of essence (self) and energy has taken us through transformative teachings, each one purposefully designed to reveal deeper layers of self-awareness and mastery. As we continue on this path, we come to the powerful concept of **Enlightenment**, a state of expanded awareness, inner clarity and profound understanding of the true nature of reality and existence. Enlightenment moves beyond the bounds of everyday awareness, bringing with it a deeper sense of clarity, wisdom and inner peace. While often associated with spiritual growth, the concept also spans philosophical and intellectual realms, with roots that stretch across a wide range of spiritual and cultural traditions worldwide. People often link it with spiritual awakening, self-realization and the quest for spiritual liberation or nirvana, a profound state of freedom from suffering and desire.

Within the realm of spiritual intelligence, enlightenment signifies the highest state of spiritual realization, the awakening of deep awareness, boundless wisdom and unity with the greater whole of the Universe. It signifies a transformative shift in consciousness, marked by liberation from the illusions of the ego and material world. While awakening can be seen as the *initiation*, a stirring or realization that opens the door to higher consciousness, enlightenment reflects a more *sustained, embodied state* of that realization. *Now, how can you discern if you have already experienced enlightenment?* A significant shift in consciousness often characterizes this profound state, reflecting a deep sense of interconnectedness with all of existence. Indicators of enlightenment include enduring inner peace and tranquility amidst external challenges, an expanded awareness that acknowledges the unity of all things, and a transcendence of egoic limitations. Additionally, enlightenment is often marked by an intensified focus on the present moment, free from distractions of past regrets or future anxieties. It may also manifest as a profound sense of love, compassion and empathy for all beings, accompanied by a genuine desire to alleviate suffering. Pause and reflect deeply: *Have you ever felt similar transformations within that reshaped how you see yourself and the world?*

Imagine a partnership in which one or both individuals have carried years of tension, frustration or resentment. Perhaps disagreements or unmet needs and expectations have built up over time, affecting the connection and the joy each person experiences with one another. Through practices like open communication, mindfulness and introspection, both partners begin to recognize that much of the tension stems not from the other person's actions, but from their own insecurities, unmet needs and past experiences such as trauma. This realization allows them to release blame and resentment, replacing it with empathy, grace, compassion and understanding, not only toward each other but also toward themselves. This shift in perspective represents a form of enlightenment, as it involves a transformative awareness that reshapes how they relate to one another and themselves. The partnership begins to experience a renewed sense of alignment, emotional freedom and mutual respect, having transcended previous limitations and embraced a deeper, more conscious way of being together.

If you have not yet encountered enlightenment but are eager to pursue it, you might wonder where to begin. The path to enlightenment typically starts with dedicated practices that foster inner growth and expand consciousness. Powerful practices we have explored, such as solitude, self-awareness, mindfulness meditation, journaling and gratitude, are fundamental instruments in pursuing enlightenment. Return to the *Integration* sections of this guidebook whenever you need as they offer powerful tools to reinforce your growth and anchor these practices in your ongoing journey.

As a recap, solitude offers a space for profound reflection and connection with your inner self, free from the distractions of the outside world. Developing self-awareness sharpens your understanding of your thoughts, emotions and behaviors, driving personal growth and clarity. Mindfulness meditation helps you develop present-focused awareness, enabling you to transcend habitual thought patterns and connect with a more profound sense of being. Journaling facilitates introspection, tracks personal evolution and reveals insights that foster self-discovery. Practicing gratitude shifts your focus from scarcity to abundance, nurturing a positive mindset and a deeper appreciation for life. Revisiting these core practices, as outlined throughout this guidebook, can provide invaluable support as you continue your journey toward enlightenment and mastering your essence and energy.

Introspection — Enlightenment

Reflect on what enlightenment means to you. Have you experienced moments of profound insight or inner peace that shifted your perspective on life? Describe these experiences and how they have influenced your understanding of reality and yourself.

____

____

____

____

____

____

____

____

Consider times when you felt a deep sense of interconnectedness with the world or liberation from ego and material concerns. How did these experiences manifest in your life and what lasting changes did they bring about in your sense of self and your interactions with others?

____

____

____

Evaluate how solitude, self-awareness, mindfulness meditation, journaling and gratitude have supported your journey toward enlightenment. Which practices have been most impactful and how can you deepen or expand these practices to further enhance your personal growth and awareness?

Insights — Transcendence

As we continue to explore transformative concepts such as awakening, healing and releasing and enlightenment, we arrive at a powerful culmination: **Transcendence**. This stage represents the pinnacle of mastering your essence and energy, marking the highest point of personal evolution beyond the limitations imposed by mind and ego. Transcendence is more than a heightened state of awareness; it represents a fundamental shift beyond dualistic thinking, where reality is seen through opposing extremes like good and bad. At this advanced stage, perception becomes unified and awareness expands into a more integrated understanding of our deep interconnectedness with the Universe. Simply, you move beyond black-and-white thinking and access a clearer, more connected sense of reality. This shift synthesizes the key lessons from earlier stages: *awakening*, marked by the initial realization of higher consciousness, *healing and releasing*, which involves processing and freeing oneself from past wounds; and *enlightenment*, which brings profound insight into the nature of existence.

To illustrate transcendence, consider the journey of an individual who, after extensive personal growth and self-exploration, arrives at a profound realization. Having engaged deeply in practices like mindfulness meditation, introspection and emotional healing, this person reaches a transformative state where they no longer perceive themselves as an isolated, separate entity. Instead, they experience a profound connection with a larger, universal whole. At this stage, this individual senses a deep, abiding peace and clarity, understanding that their personal identity is not a distinct and isolated self but a mere expression of a greater cosmic unity. The boundaries that once defined their egoic self, the divisions between themselves and others, the separations they once felt, begin to dissolve. They immerse themselves in a state of pure awareness, where an overwhelming sense of oneness and interconnectedness with the entire Universe replaces the usual distinctions between self and others. This realization represents a significant shift from individualistic perspectives to a holistic, unified experience of existence. Reflect deeply: *Have you felt these shifts within yourself?*

Achieving transcendence requires intentional practices that elevate your state of consciousness. Mindfulness meditation, for example, enables you to observe your thoughts and emotions with calm awareness and impartiality, helping you move beyond entrenched ego-driven behaviors. Engaging in self-reflection through solitude, using practices like introspection and journaling, cultivates a deeper awareness of your inner world and its intrinsic connection to the greater whole. Engaging in acts of service and compassion further advances transcendence by shifting your focus from the individual self to the collective, nurturing a sense of unity and interconnectedness. Transcendence is a pivotal aspect of spiritual intelligence, signifying your ability to surpass egoic constraints and access profound truths about yourself and the nature of reality. In this elevated state, you experience deep peace, clarity and a sense of oneness, where your identity yields to a broader, universal consciousness. By incorporating practices that promote transcendence, you can enhance your spiritual intelligence, leading to increased fulfillment, meaning and a profound connection with the more extensive network of existence.

Introspection — Transcendence

Consider a situation where your ego-driven reactions may have limited your understanding or connection with others. How could approaching this situation from a place of pure awareness and compassion have changed the outcome or deepened your sense of unity?

____

____

____

____

____

____

____

____

In what ways have you begun to move beyond dualistic thinking, where you no longer see the world in terms of rigid opposites (e.g., right/wrong, good/bad)? How has this shift influenced your understanding of your place in the Universe and your connection to the broader existence?

____

____

____

Reflect on when you experienced a significant shift in consciousness, where you felt a deeper understanding of your true self and your connection to the Universe. What insights or lessons emerged from this experience and how have they influenced your spiritual journey?

Insights and Integration — Self-Empowerment

Having explored the fundamental principles of mastering your essence and energy, including nourishing your body, understanding your higher self and inner child, connecting with your intuition, examining belief systems and values, engaging with self-experience and immersing ourselves in spirituality and spiritual intelligence through awakening, healing and releasing, enlightenment and transcendence, the next step is to focus on self-empowering yourself to achieve your deepest desires and live a life aligned with your authentic self. In this segment, we will explore how to leverage this **Self-Empowerment** to navigate your life as your *evolved self*. We are now prepared to channel our personal growth and hard-won insights to navigate life with greater mastery, and, ultimately, to resonate with and elevate collective consciousness. Our approach to self-empowerment will center on two key aspects: **Harnessing Your Core Power** and **Awakening Your Inner Voice**.

When we explore the concept of self-empowerment, our focus naturally gravitates toward the core element within: *power. Now, what is power?* In its purest form, power is the capacity to shape our own actions, influence others and impact the unfolding of events. It manifests in countless forms, through physical strength, authority, influence and wisdom. Throughout history, power has been a double-edged sword, reflecting the duality of human nature. On one end, it has catalyzed profound positive change. Consider leaders like Mahatma Gandhi, whose peaceful resistance empowered a nation toward independence or Martin Luther King Jr., whose voice and vision fueled the civil rights movement. Power, in these instances, inspired hope, unity and societal transformation. Yet, on the other end, power has also been wielded as a tool of manipulation, domination and oppression, seen in the regimes of Adolf Hitler or Joseph Stalin, where power in the form of fear and control devastated millions.

Power, with its dynamic and multifaceted nature, is the force that shapes the very structure of relationships, societies and individual destinies.

Whether it uplifts or destroys depends on the consciousness with which it is held and the integrity of those who channel it. *But what, then, is self-empowerment in relation to power?* Often, when we think of power, our minds turn to figures of authority, leaders who inspire, icons who embody strength and role models who lead by example. These individuals do not just possess power; they channel it in ways that *empower* others, demonstrating that true power lies in the ability to elevate oneself and others. Similarly, self-empowerment is about tapping into your intrinsic strength, the source of inner energy that allows you to take control of your life and guide it toward your highest aspirations. It embodies agency and self-mastery, urging you to design your own destiny and shape the life you are meant to live with intention and purpose.

Self-empowerment entails placing unwavering trust in yourself and your intuition, recognizing the inherent power and profound truth within your internal voice. It involves relying on your inner knowing rather than seeking external validation. When embodying self-empowerment, you make choices that ignite inspiration and motivation and decisions that resonate with your core beliefs and values, propelling you toward greater achievements, fulfillment and your ideal quality of life. To harness your core power in connection to self-empowerment, which we will discuss next, it is important to recognize and channel your innate skills, talents and strengths to create positive change in your life and in the lives of others. This process begins with **self-awareness** and **self-acceptance**, acknowledging your unique qualities and embracing your potential for growth and transformation.

Central to this endeavor is **developing a mindset of resilience and optimism**, empowering you to face life's challenges with grace and determination. By **reframing** setbacks as opportunities for learning and growth, you can turn obstacles into stepping stones for personal development. Participating in practices like **affirmations**, **visualization** and **goal-setting** aids in clarifying your aspirations, empowering you to take deliberate steps towards their realization. Additionally, **fostering**

supportive relationships and **seeking guidance** from mentors can provide invaluable encouragement and perspective along your journey of self-empowerment. Through continuous self-reflection and personal development, you can access the full extent of your core power and inner voice and embrace a life of abundance, fulfillment and purpose.

Harnessing Your Core Power

So, where do we start in accessing your inner strength and ***harnessing your core power?*** **Self-awareness**, a tool we have consistently emphasized throughout this guidebook, serves as a vital foundation. Having a deeper and more accurate understanding of yourself enables you to optimize your strengths while addressing areas for development. By uncovering your strengths, you can leverage them to maximize your potential and achieve your desired goals. Conversely, by identifying your areas for growth, you can actively work to improve yourself and evolve, leading to a more well-rounded and empowered self. You can begin to initiate this self-discovery process by recognizing your top five strengths and top five developmental areas. Start by identifying and writing down your top five strengths, competencies and talents. Then, map out how you can leverage these strengths to awaken your core power effectively.

A sample list of strengths might include:

1. **Resilience**: Ability to seamlessly bounce back from challenges, setbacks and adversity
2. **Adaptability**: Flexibility and openness to change
3. **Emotional Intelligence**: Understanding and managing emotions and those of others
4. **Empathy**: The ability to genuinely connect with others and their emotions
5. **Leadership**: Encouraging and motivating people to achieve shared goals

This individual can begin to leverage these strengths and attributes to channel their core power in the following ways:

1. **Resilience**: By embracing resilience, one can bounce back from challenges, setbacks and adversities, maintaining the strength to persevere and uphold internal fortitude over time.
2. **Adaptability**: Welcoming change and remaining flexible empowers this individual to navigate new situations and obstacles easily, ensuring they stay empowered and in control of their life's journey.
3. **Emotional Intelligence**: Skillful management of emotions empowers this individual to navigate interpersonal dynamics and conflicts with grace, patience, compassion, resilience and empathy, thereby preserving internal strength during challenging moments.
4. **Empathy**: Cultivating compassion and understanding towards others enhances their ability to form meaningful connections, fostering trust, collaboration and mutual respect, all essential aspects of personal and interpersonal empowerment.
5. **Leadership**: Encouraging and motivating people to achieve shared goals, this individual can effectively activate their internal power by providing guidance, encouragement and direction to achieve collective objectives.

Take a moment now to identify and record your top five areas for development. Then, outline specific steps to address and improve these areas, focusing on actionable steps for growth.

A sample list of developmental areas could include:

1. **Self-doubt**: Lack of confidence in abilities, skills and talents
2. **Fear of failure**: Avoidance of risks and challenges due to a fear of not succeeding
3. **Lack of resilience**: Difficulty coping with setbacks and adversity
4. **Lack of emotional intelligence**: Difficulty understanding and managing emotions
5. **Lack of empathy**: Insensitivity towards the feelings and experiences of others

To help this individual improve in these developmental areas and access their internal power, they can take the following steps:

1. **Self-doubt**:

- Practice **affirmations** to build confidence in talents and abilities
    - Replace negative self-talk with **positive affirmations**
- **Set achievable goals** and **celebrate small victories** to boost self-esteem

2. **Fear of failure:**

- Utilize **reframing** and **develop a growth mindset** to embrace failure as a learning opportunity rather than a setback
- **Take thoughtful risks** and **step out of comfort zone** to face fears little by little

3. **Lack of resilience:**

- **Build a solid support network** of friends, family or mentors who can offer guidance and encouragement when times get tough
- **Practice mindfulness** and **stress-reduction techniques** such as **mindfulness meditation** or breathing exercises such as **breath-work** to build emotional resilience
- **Reflect on past experiences** of overcoming adversity to reconnect with inner strength and fortitude
- **Focus on solutions** rather than dwelling on problems and **maintain a positive outlook** even in the face of setbacks

4. **Lack of emotional intelligence**:

- **Increase self-awareness** by paying attention to your thoughts, feelings and behaviors in various situations
- **Practice active listening** and **empathy** by tuning into others' emotions and perspectives
- **Develop effective communication skills** to express emotions constructively and assertively
- **Seek opportunities for emotional growth** through therapy, coaching or self-help resources

5. **Lack of empathy**:

- **Practice perspective-taking** by imagining yourself in another person's shoes and considering their feelings and experiences
- **Practice kindness and compassion** towards others to develop empathy and understanding

- **Explore different perspectives and experiences** to broaden your knowledge of various cultures, backgrounds and viewpoints
- **Practice active listening** and **validate others' emotions** to demonstrate empathy and support

---

Through this process of self-awareness and the intentional harnessing of your inherent strengths, talents and capacities, combined with a thoughtful commitment to growth in areas needing development, you can cultivate and strengthen your internal resilience and core power. As you identify and refine these aspects of yourself, it becomes important to set realistic, manageable and meaningful goals that align with your values and aspirations. To avoid feeling overwhelmed by the scale of a significant goal, such as writing a book, break it down into smaller, actionable tasks. Rather than being daunted by the idea of thousands of words or hundreds of pages, start by clarifying the core message you wish to convey or brainstorming potential titles and outlines. Then, divide the project into smaller sections or chapters, treating each as a mini-goal or milestone. By setting achievable targets, like completing one section per day or week, you can maintain momentum and motivation throughout the process. *Embrace the journey and find fulfillment in the progress you make, rather than solely focusing on the final outcome or destination. It is not about the tangible achievement itself but rather the transformation you undergo throughout your evolutionary journey.* ***It is about who you become in the process that holds the most value.***

Harnessing your core power represents a pivotal milestone on your journey to self-empowerment and mastering your essence and energy. As you cultivate self-awareness, you begin to recognize both your strengths and areas for growth, while simultaneously nurturing lasting confidence, resilience and inner assurance. Self-acceptance, together with self-compassion, serves as a foundational cornerstone of this journey. Rather than relying on external validation, you develop an unshakable trust in your own abilities, empowering you to pursue your aspirations with both determination and kindness. Building on this foundation, we now turn to the process of awakening your inner voice, a vital step in aligning with your true self and navigating life with clarity, purpose and inner gentleness.

Awakening Your Inner Voice

With a strong foundation of self-empowerment and a deep connection to your essence, it is time to focus on a crucial aspect of inner evolution: **Awakening Your Inner Voice**. Having aligned with our higher self, rooted in wisdom and intuition, and explored ways to harness our internal power, the next step is to awaken your inner voice. This process will deepen our intentional connections with ourselves and others, guiding us to live more purposeful and authentic lives. *So, what exactly is our inner voice?* Just like the concept of our higher self, your inner voice, often called intuition or inner wisdom, is the voice of your deepest self. This inner voice manifests as thoughts, feelings or instincts, offering insight, clarity and direction in diverse situations. This inner guidance system serves as a conduit for communicating your genuine desires, beliefs and values. In essence, your inner voice channels the guidance and direction of your higher self and intuition. It is unique to you and reflects your authentic self, offering support and wisdom on important life decisions and paths. Tuning into your inner voice can help you make choices that align with your essence and lead you to a more fulfilling and authentic life.

How can we attune ourselves to our inner voice and harness its power for self-empowerment? Throughout this guidebook, we have explored various methods to tap into our inner wisdom. One effective approach is to seek **solitude** and embrace **stillness**. By distancing ourselves from external distractions and immersing in quiet contemplation, we create space to listen to the whispers of our intuition and discern the desires of our inner voice. Practicing **mindfulness meditation** enhances this process by fostering present-moment awareness, enabling us to connect deeply with our internal landscape and observe our thoughts, feelings and emotions as they unfold. Additionally, **self-reflection** and **introspection**, whether through **journaling** or meaningful **self-dialogue**, provides valuable opportunities to communicate with our inner voice and intuition, gaining insights and clarity along the way.

As you awaken your inner voice on the path to self-empowerment, **self-validation** becomes an essential foundation. Trust your inner voice to provide validation and affirmation, shifting away from the need for external approval. Let your intuition and inner wisdom guide your choices, empowering you to act with confidence and clarity. Authentic **self-expression** is vital, express your truth honestly and sincerely, assert your opinions boldly and establish firm boundaries. This strengthens your inner voice as a reflection of your true self, embodying both authenticity and integrity. Additionally, **self-advocacy** is crucial. Listen to your inner voice and honor its guidance, standing up for your beliefs, asserting your rights and championing your well-being with unwavering conviction. Embrace **creative expression** by tapping into your inner voice as a source of inspiration and innovation. Allow your intuition and imagination to shape your creative endeavors, trusting the unique insights and ideas that arise deep within you. This holistic approach to self-empowerment, rooted in your inner voice, fosters a life of purpose, integrity and authenticity.

To integrate these insights, use the following tools and exercises:

1. **Journaling**: Regularly journal about your inner voice and self-validation experiences. Document moments of clarity and how you acted upon them.

2. **Affirmations**: Create affirmations that reinforce your trust in your inner voice, such as "*I trust my inner voice to guide me with confidence and clarity.*"

3. **Visualization**: Visualize scenarios where you can apply these insights. Imagine the steps you need to take and how you will act with authenticity.

4. **Boundaries Exercise**: Practice setting and maintaining firm boundaries in different areas of your life. Reflect on how this strengthens your sense of self and integrity.

Take a moment to pause and explore one or all these exercises to effectively integrate the insights you have gathered in this segment.

With a profound understanding of your inner voice and its role in personal empowerment, you are now ready to apply this insight to broader, collective goals. By channeling your awakened inner voice into collaborative goal setting, you can work with others to define objectives that align with shared values. Through open and transparent dialogue, you can identify common goals and create a unified vision for collective action. By leveraging your combined strengths, you can maximize your potential by encouraging individuals to contribute their unique abilities toward achieving these goals. To ensure progress, foster shared accountability by holding each other responsible for both individual and collective actions, with clearly defined roles and timelines. Cultivate leadership within the group to enhance integrity, resilience and authenticity, driving collective empowerment through exemplary actions. The upcoming sections of this guidebook will explore these principles further, showing how they relate to living a life of meaning, purpose and collective consciousness, an elevated state of awareness in which individuals recognize their interconnectedness with others and act in ways that support the well-being of the greater whole.

Introspection — Self-Empowerment

Reflect on your journey of exploring the fundamental principles of mastering your essence. How has this exploration shaped your understanding of self-empowerment?

____

____

____

____

____

____

____

____

Identify two key aspects of self-empowerment mentioned: harnessing your core power and awakening your inner voice. How do you plan to focus on these aspects in your personal transformational journey?

____

____

____

____

Explore strategies for harnessing your core power and awakening your inner voice. How do you plan to incorporate practices such as identifying your strengths and developmental areas, solitude, stillness, mindfulness and self-reflection into your daily routine?

Insights — Energy

We have reached the final segment of the *Mastering Your Essence (Self) and Energy* chapter, a crucial milestone in your journey toward self-empowerment and evolution. Before we proceed, **I invite you to truly acknowledge and congratulate yourself for reaching this point**. The concepts and principles we have explored together are not just surface-level ideas; they are deep, transformative insights that require intentional inner work, reflection and introspection. Engaging with them is no easy feat and your commitment to this process is commendable. It is important to recognize that not every concept mentioned in this guidebook may resonate fully with your current beliefs or life experiences. Maintaining an *open mindset* and *curiosity* is key. Authentic growth begins with the willingness to receive new insights and let them guide your evolution and the **Energy** you share with the world. By staying receptive to new perspectives, you allow yourself the opportunity to reveal new layers of understanding and self-realization.

As we further explore the mastery of our essence, we begin to truly understand the energy and vibrations we project through our thoughts, emotions, words and actions. Energy is not just a vague concept; it is a fundamental force that flows through everything in existence. Recognizing the impact of energy on our journey toward abundance and fulfillment is essential. Consider the powerful idea that *energy is never lost*; it is constantly being transformed and redirected. This means that every thought you think, every emotion you feel, every word you speak and every action you take contributes to the energy you put out into the world. This energy, in turn, influences the circumstances and experiences you attract. Pause now and reflect deeply on how this understanding of energy's transformative nature can empower you to consciously shape your life, guiding you toward greater abundance and fulfillment.

Now, what exactly is energy? Beyond the definitions we learned in school, energy is the fundamental force behind all transformation and change. In physics, it manifests in several key forms. *Kinetic energy* drives motion, from flowing rivers to orbiting planets. *Potential energy* is stored power, like a stretched rubber band or a boulder on a hill, waiting to be released. *Thermal energy*, felt as heat, transfers between objects of different temperatures, such as a spoon warming in hot tea. *Chemical energy*, held in molecular bonds, fuels everything from human metabolism to car engines. *Electrical energy*, produced by moving electrons, powers modern life, from smartphones to city grids. By understanding the diverse ways in which energy operates, we can better appreciate its role not only in influencing the physical world around us but also in guiding the energetic flow within our minds, bodies and spirits. Recognizing this interconnectedness allows us to become more intentional with how we direct, conserve and cultivate our own energy, laying the groundwork for transformation and personal evolution.

When we explore our human experience, energy is far more than just a scientific concept; it is what keeps everything in motion, from the beat of your heart to the turning of the earth. It is behind every shift, spark and change we experience, both around us and within us. Energy is multifaceted, encompassing the physical, mental, emotional and spiritual dimensions of our lives. On a physical level, energy powers our bodies, sustaining vital functions and enabling movement. It is what keeps our heart pumping, our lungs breathing and our muscles moving, enabling us to interact with the world. Yet, energy is not confined to the physical realm. Energy guides our thoughts, emotions and actions, while these same thoughts, emotions and actions continually shape the energy we radiate outward. It is the driving force behind our mental clarity, focus, creativity and the way we navigate our cognitive and emotional landscapes.

From a spiritual perspective, energy transcends the tangible and enters the realm of the subtle and the unseen. It is the invisible thread that runs through all of life, quietly linking every being and object across the Universe into one great, connected whole. This spiritual energy is often referred to as "*vibes*," a term that captures the essence of the frequencies or vibrations that each person and experience emits. These vibrations influence our mood, outlook and the energy we attract and repel in our lives. Within this holistic framework, energy is recognized as a powerful influence on our overall well-being, physically, mentally, emotionally and spiritually. Practices we have discussed such as mindfulness meditation, yoga, breathwork and other forms of energy work are designed to integrate and elevate this energy, helping us to achieve more excellent balance, higher states of consciousness and profound spiritual growth. By consciously cultivating and directing our energy, we can enhance our vitality, sharpen our mental acuity, deepen our emotional resilience and foster spiritual growth, ultimately leading to a more fulfilled and balanced life.

As human beings, we are intricate systems of energy, composed of particles constantly vibrating at varying frequencies, deeply influenced by our psychological state, emotional disposition and overall well-being. Much like ripples on water, these frequencies radiate outward, subtly influencing the energy around us and helping to shape the quality of our experiences and interactions. The empowering part of this truth is that our thoughts and emotions deeply affect the tone and strength of our energetic frequencies, giving us meaningful influence over how we feel and what we attract into our lives. As we explore energy and vibrations further in the upcoming segment, we will uncover how our conscious awareness and intentional cultivation of positive states of being can empower us to emit frequencies that attract abundance, love, joy, peace and fulfillment into our lives.

Energy exerts a profound influence on universal laws, particularly two fundamental principles: the Law of Attraction and the Law of Vibration. The Law of Attraction, as discussed, suggests that like energies attract each other, meaning that the positive or negative energy we emit draws similar energy back to us. This principle highlights how our thoughts and emotions emit vibrational frequencies that resonate with corresponding energies in the Universe, shaping our experiences and interactions. The Law of Vibration, closely related, asserts that everything in the Universe vibrates at its own frequency, constantly emitting energy. This principle reveals that everything in existence is connected through energy, and the vibrations we emit can directly influence the reality we create. *Now, how can we leverage this energetic power to manifest the life we desire?* Pause and reflect deeply on how you can begin to channel your energy to attract the life of your dreams.

High and Low Vibrations

Consider the powerful link between your thoughts, emotions, vibrations and the reality you manifest. The energy you project through your thoughts and emotions actively shapes the experiences you draw into your life. This insight reveals the essential need to recognize and mindfully manage the vibrations you send into the world, as they mold your reality and influence the collective energy of those around you. In this section, we will explore the dynamics of **High and Low Vibrations,** uncover their significance and learn how to channel your energy intentionally. By mastering this process, you can synchronize your vibrations with your goals, ensuring that your energy drives your intentions forward rather than hindering them.

High and low vibrations refer to the frequency or quality of energetic states. High vibrations align with positive emotions and states of being, while low vibrations correspond to negative emotions and states of being. High vibrations typically reflect feelings and emotions such as joy, peace, love and gratitude, foundational elements and cornerstones of abundance. These states are associated with positivity, growth and well-being. When individuals experience high vibrations, they often feel uplifted, inspired and connected to a greater sense of purpose and meaning. By embracing and radiating positive energy, we attract people, circumstances and opportunities that align with that vibration, setting in motion a virtuous cycle of continual growth, joy and deeper fulfillment.

The real power of transformation lies in the interplay between the energy we radiate and the thoughts and beliefs we nurture, especially when they come together in alignment. To recap, the thoughts we consistently entertain can solidify into deep-seated belief systems over time, profoundly shaping our reality. This intersection of positive energy and empowering beliefs magnifies our ability to attract and manifest the abundance we seek, aligning our external experiences with our internal state of being. Pause and reflect deeply on a time when your positive energy and vibrations drew in favorable situations. *How did that experience make you feel?*

Low vibrations, conversely, are marked by emotions such as fear, anger, sadness, anxiety or despair. These states often lead to negativity, stagnation and disharmony. When you find yourself in a low-vibrational state, it is common to feel drained, stressed or disconnected from yourself and others. It is important to be mindful of these low vibrations since they profoundly influence your internal state and attract corresponding energy that diverges from your desired goals and abundance. When in a low-vibrational state, the energy you emit can perpetuate experiences of lack, conflict and resistance, keeping you out of alignment with the life you truly desire to create. When you become aware of these vibrations and intentionally raise them, you shift the energy you project, bringing in positive experiences and opportunities that match your higher purpose. Doing so significantly enhances your overall well-being and creates a more fulfilling life.

In an upcoming segment, we will explore various tools and practices designed to help you channel your energy in alignment with your goals and aspirations. The key lies in recognizing your ability to shape your thoughts, emotions, behaviors and, by extension, the energy you radiate. This awareness is a transformative force, a spiritual "*shortcut*" that allows you to master your internal landscape. It gives you the power to intentionally direct your thoughts, emotions and actions, aligning them with your deepest aspirations. In doing so, you create coherence between your inner energy and outward life, paving the way for purpose, abundance and lasting fulfillment.

Mastering your essence and energy is a fundamental step in achieving abundance and fulfillment in your life. By embracing your authentic self, you naturally radiate at a high vibration and frequency, which attracts corresponding experiences and opportunities. By truly understanding who you are, your core beliefs, values and true essence, you can leverage the power of your inner vibrations. With this understanding, you can shape your reality to reflect your deepest desires and true purpose. With this mastery, you can move through life with intention, attracting positive experiences and opportunities that resonate with your higher self. By consciously directing your energy and maintaining high vibrations, you create a more fulfilling life for yourself and contribute to the collective well-being of those around you. Mastering your essence and energy is the key to accessing the abundance and fulfillment that are inherently yours. Ultimately, this mastery allows you to align fully with your life's path and participate consciously in the unfolding of collective consciousness, the subject of our final chapter.

Introspection — Energy

Reflect on your journey through the *Mastering Your Essence (Self) and Energy* chapter. What concepts or principles resonated with you the most and why?

____

____

____

____

____

____

____

____

Consider the role of high and low vibrations in your daily experiences. Can you recall times when you were in a high vibrational state? How did it affect your mood and interactions with others? Do the same introspective exercise for a time when you were in a low vibrational state.

____

____

____

Reflect on your understanding of energy and vibrations now compared to before engaging with this chapter. How has your perspective shifted, if at all?

Integration — Energy

How can we draw upon the insights and tools from *Chapter 2: The Abundance Pillars – Mastering Your Mind (Thoughts)* to consistently channel and sustain high-vibrational energy through our thoughts, emotions, words and actions? Our mental landscape, including our thoughts and underlying beliefs, forms the foundation of our emotional state, verbal expressions and behaviors. This truth highlights the importance of *focusing on our mindset as the primary driver of positive energy*. Our thoughts and beliefs about ourselves deeply influence the energy we emit. This dynamic between our energy and self-beliefs is pivotal in shaping our personal experiences and interactions with others. By aligning our thoughts, beliefs, emotions and actions with positive energy, we can leverage this transformative power to foster personal growth and achieve our goals. This section integrates earlier insights and tools to support continued growth. To begin, we will look at an example, navigating the emotional aftermath of a breakup, as a gateway to our first energy alignment tool: **reframing**.

After a profound breakup, many find themselves engulfed by grief, loss and feelings of inadequacy, emotional currents that resonate at lower vibrational frequencies and weigh heavily on the spirit. Yet within you lies the ability to consciously shift your perspective, allowing it to become a doorway to healing and transformation. Rather than allowing these emotions to define your experience, you can choose to view the breakup as a turning point for transformative change. Recognize that life's challenges and obstacles often conceal valuable lessons and opportunities for personal and spiritual advancement. By adopting a high vibrational perspective, you open yourself to the potential for growth and self-discovery, turning what may initially appear as a setback into a powerful opportunity for personal evolution.

Now that we have explored reframing through the lens of a breakup, take a moment to apply this practice more intentionally to your own life.

Reframing allows you to reinterpret challenges in ways that cultivate resilience, gratitude and emotional clarity. Rather than being overwhelmed by adversity, you begin to see it as a meaningful initiator for growth. In doing so, you create space for greater peace, optimism and a higher vibrational state. Pause and reflect: *What is one recent challenge you have faced? How could you shift your perspective to generate positive vibrations, enhance emotional resilience and create greater inner alignment?*

Gratitude and **affirmations**, foundational tools we have explored together, are immensely powerful for amplifying positive energy. As a reminder, practicing gratitude is an incredibly effective method for boosting our vibrational state. By taking a moment each day to recognize and appreciate our blessings, no matter how small, we turn our attention to the beautiful and positive aspects of our lives. This simple act elevates our vibrational energy, transforming our thought patterns toward abundance and joy. Keeping a gratitude journal can further amplify this practice, providing a dedicated space to record and verbalize what we are thankful for. *It is important to reinforce that gratitude reaches its fullest potential from fully living and breathing it in every moment.* Pause now and reflect deeply on your life journey so far. Consider the challenges you have faced, the doubts you have overcome and the victories and setbacks you have experienced. Reflect on the growth you have achieved and the love you have encountered along the way. Fully immerse yourself in the profound sense of gratitude that arises as you reflect on the richness of your life journey. Looking back, it becomes clear how remarkable your life has been.

Affirmations are another powerful tool for channeling your energy to master your essence to achieve abundance and fulfillment. As a recap, they act as a profound pathway for inner growth, allowing you to shift from negative, limiting thoughts to self-empowering, affirmative statements aligning with your core beliefs, values and aspirations. When you constantly repeat affirmations, you direct your energy toward reinforcing positive thinking patterns. This practice elevates your mindset and your emotional state while driving behavior that supports your goals. For instance, if you often find yourself plagued by self-doubt, affirming "*I am capable and worthy of success*" channels your energy away from self-limiting beliefs and towards confidence and self-assurance. In the same way, if you wrestle with feelings of not being enough, affirmations like "*I embrace my strengths and celebrate my achievements*" shift your focus to a more positive self-view and energize you to embrace your true potential.

Adding affirmations to your daily routine allows you to take control of your inner thoughts and direct your energy toward abundance and new opportunities. By aligning your thoughts with affirmations that resonate with your deepest desires, you create a vibrational frequency that attracts positive experiences and opportunities into your life. To further enhance your practice, revisit the *Integration* sections of both *Thoughts and Spoken Language (Words)* and *The Art of Manifesting Abundance* in our guidebook. These sections offer detailed examples for crafting effective affirmations and integrating them into your life. Pause now and reflect deeply on how you can use affirmations to direct your energy more effectively and foster a mindset that aligns with your vision of abundance and fulfillment.

Acts of kindness complete our toolkit for raising vibrational energy and attracting a life of abundance and fulfillment. Engaging in spontaneous and intentional acts of kindness profoundly influences our vibrational frequency and our surroundings. When we extend generosity and compassion to others, we uplift their spirits and enhance our own vibrational resonance. These selfless actions create a ripple effect, fostering a deep sense of interconnectedness and positivity within ourselves and our communities. Acts of kindness brighten others' lives and show us that our actions possess the power to shape the world's energy. By making these practices a vital part of our daily routines and lifestyle, we help create a more positive and uplifting environment for everyone. View all these practices as dynamic tools in your journey to elevate your vibrational frequency and master your essence and energy. Apply them with intention and mindfulness as you work towards mastering your life and collective consciousness, which will be the focus of our next chapter.

Chapter Recap: The Abundance Pillars – Mastering Your Essence (Self) and Energy

Chapter 3 invites you to align with your true essence and energetic frequency, guiding you toward a life of abundance and fulfillment.

Nourishing Your Body

Key Insights: Physical health is the foundation of vitality and well-being, crucial for experiencing abundance. A healthy and balanced diet, regular exercise and sufficient rest support a vibrant, energetic life and help you achieve a life of fulfillment.

Integration: Prioritize activities that support physical health, understanding their influence on your sense of abundance. Make lifestyle choices that promote physical well-being to enhance your overall fulfillment.

Your Higher Self and Inner Child

Key Insights: When you tune into both your higher self and inner child, you awaken inner wisdom that leads you toward authentic fulfillment and purpose.

Integration: Practice mindfulness and introspection to reconnect with your higher self and inner child. In quiet moments of solitude, their wisdom becomes clearer, gently guiding you toward decisions that honor your deepest truth.

Your Intuition

Key Insights: Intuition is a subtle form of guidance from your higher self, influencing your decisions and actions. It manifests as inner feelings or pulls towards authenticity.

Integration: Tune into intuitive nudges by reflecting on shifts in beliefs, values and desires. Embrace solitude and mindfulness to minimize distractions and enhance intuitive insights. Engage in creative pursuits and connect with nature to strengthen your intuitive connection.

Belief Systems and Values

Key Insights: Belief systems shape how we perceive the world and guide our interactions based on our values. These frameworks influence our sense of purpose and fulfillment.

Integration: Reflect on your core beliefs and values to understand their impact on your decisions. Challenge and expand your beliefs through diverse perspectives and introspection. Align your actions with your core values to enhance fulfillment.

Self-Experience (Lived Experience)

Key Insights: Self-experience involves learning from personal trials and reflections, shaping our beliefs and perspectives. It provides valuable insights into our essence and decisions.

Integration: Reflect on recent personal experiences that offered significant insights. Recognize how these moments of clarity have influenced your decisions and perspectives. Use this wisdom to align your actions with your evolving essence.

Spirituality and Spiritual Intelligence

Key Insights: Spirituality and spiritual intelligence guide us toward a deeper understanding of consciousness and meaning, fostering inner peace and fulfillment.

Integration: Engage in spiritual practices and explore spiritual intelligence to enhance your self-awareness and connection with the Universe.

Allow these practices to deepen your understanding of your essence and inspire personal growth.

Awakening

Key Insights: Awakening involves a profound shift in consciousness, revealing deeper truths and interconnectedness. It represents a transformative phase of self-awareness.

Integration: Reflect on transformative experiences that have shifted your awareness. Use mindfulness and other practices to deepen this awareness and integrate new insights into your life.

Healing and Releasing

Key Insights: Healing and releasing involve processing and letting go of repressed emotions and traumas. This process is crucial for achieving emotional and spiritual well-being.

Integration: Give yourself the space to process unresolved emotions from past experiences. With the support of solitude, quiet reflection and mindful presence, you can begin to release old pain and strengthen your sense of wholeness.

Enlightenment

Key Insights: Enlightenment is the awakening to a profound spiritual truth and a deep sense of unity with the Universe, a state marked by insight, clarity and interconnectedness.

Integration: Reflect on moments of profound insight and interconnectedness. Engage in practices that support and expand your spiritual understanding to integrate these realizations into your life.

Transcendence

Key Insights: Transcendence is the expansion beyond personal limits, revealing deeper purpose and universal truth through a shift in awareness and perspective.

Integration: Reflect on instances where you experienced a breakthrough or shift in perspective. Use these insights to seek ongoing growth and expand your view of purpose and universal truth.

Self-Empowerment

Key Insights: Self-empowerment involves channeling your core power and awakening your inner voice to make choices aligned with your essence and goals. It represents taking decisive actions that support your personal growth and self-realization.

Integration: Take a moment to reflect on recent decisions where you tapped into your inner power and followed your inner voice. Let these moments serve as a guide for future choices, reinforcing your dedication to living in alignment with your authentic self. Continue cultivating practices that strengthen your inner resolve and support actions rooted in your highest intentions.

Energy

Key Insights: Energy is the fundamental force driving transformation, influencing your thoughts, emotions, words and actions. It shapes your experiences and interactions with the world. Understanding and managing high and low vibrations can significantly impact your well-being and fulfillment.

Integration: Consider how your thoughts and emotions influence your energetic state, either raising or lowering your vibration. By becoming more intentional with your energy, you can align with uplifting, high-frequency experiences that support your well-being. Gently acknowledge and release sources of low vibration to create a more balanced, vibrant and harmonious life.

Introspection Exercises: Use the introspection exercises from each section to apply these principles to your life. Reflect on how nurturing your physical health, connecting with your higher self and tuning into your intuition influence your sense of abundance. Consider how belief systems, values, personal experiences and spirituality shape your understanding and decisions. Examine how awakening, healing and releasing and enlightenment have transformed you and how transcendence and self-empowerment align you with your essence. Assess the impact of your energy on your life experiences.

Conclusion: Integrating insights from nourishing your body, connecting with your higher self, intuitive guidance, core belief systems and values, and attuning your energy creates a foundation for a life rooted in purpose and fulfillment. By aligning with your essence and embracing the transformative processes of awakening and healing, you open the path to a more abundant, meaningful existence. As you cultivate self-empowerment and direct your energy with intention, you elevate your well-being and begin to embody your highest potential.

CHAPTER 4:

The Abundance Pillars – Mastering Your Life and Collective Consciousness

Throughout our journey together, we have sharpened our mental faculties, mastered our mind and thoughts with precision and explored the depths of our essence. We have unraveled the complexities of the energy we emit and learned to channel it with deliberate power. Along the way, we have mastered the art of manifesting abundance, understanding that *abundance is not a distant aspiration but a conscious decision to embody it* ***now****, through the energy you hold, the beliefs you affirm and the way you show up in the world.* We have explored big questions about who we are, how we think and how we interact with life, initiating a transformative journey of self-discovery and growth. And yet, this is only the beginning. Ahead lies the invitation to expand beyond old limits, to access deeper truths and greater wisdom that will guide you toward a life rich with abundance, purpose and profound fulfillment.

With a strong foundation now established through mastery of your mind, alignment with your essence, and intentional direction of your energy, you are fully prepared to enter the next phase of this journey: **Mastering Your Life and Collective Consciousness**. In this chapter, we explore abundance not merely as personal fulfillment, but as a holistic, integrated way of living. We will redefine wealth and abundance through a more expansive lens, one that honors presence, fulfillment in everyday moments and the sacred routines and practices that nourish the soul. You will learn to live consciously and intentionally, aligning daily habits and actions with your core beliefs, values, talents, passions and Ikigai: your unique reason for being.

We will also examine the value of simple living and mindful choices, understanding how reducing clutter and focusing on what truly matters enhances clarity, peace and freedom. Daily practices, rituals and routines will be explored as tools for embedding purpose and intentionality into every moment of life. Through introspection and self-reflection, you will refine your vision of your ideal life, bridge the gap between your current reality and aspirations and embody a purpose-driven life in alignment with your deepest values.

A central focus of this chapter is the cultivation of meaningful relationships, community and collective consciousness. We will explore how transcending the ego allows you to move from self-centered desires to contribution, empathy and connection. Aligning your personal mission with collective needs amplifies both fulfillment and impact, allowing you to co-create with others in ways that enhance community well-being. Love, connection and self-love will be highlighted as essential foundations for meaningful human interaction, while intentional consideration of life partners and collaborative contributions will demonstrate the power of alignment with shared purpose.

Finally, this chapter integrates insights on contribution, co-creation and sustaining abundance. You will learn to combine personal empowerment with a conscious awareness of the collective, recognizing that your growth and fulfillment are intricately linked with the well-being of the larger world. Through this alignment, you amplify your ability to live a life that is not only personally rich but also positively impacts the broader field of human experience.

What follows is an invitation to engage deeply with practical tools, introspection exercises and guiding principles to help you **live with lasting purpose and meaning**. You will move from vision to action, applying the insights you have gained into everyday life, and cultivating habits, decisions and contributions that strengthen both your personal fulfillment and the collective consciousness. By integrating these teachings, you step fully into the role of a conscious creator, shaping a life that is abundant, purposeful and profoundly connected to the world around you.

As you move through this chapter, I encourage you to engage with the insights and teachings on **Redefining the Concept of Wealth and Abundance, Conscious and Intentional Living, The Value of Being Present, Finding Fulfillment Each Day, Sacred Routines and Practices, Simple Living, What Does Your Ideal Life Look Like?, Ikigai, Identifying Your Talents and Passions, Embodying Your Purpose-Driven Life, Cultivating Your Community, Transcending the Ego, Collective Consciousness, Contribution, Love and Connection (Recap), Your Life Partner,** and **Sustaining Abundance: Co-Creation.**

As before, I encourage you to deeply engage with the introspection exercises and integration practices provided for each section. While the depth and scope of these practices may feel expansive, approaching them with intention and presence allows you to gradually integrate their power into your daily life, creating profound, lasting transformation for yourself and those around you.

Insights — Redefining the Concept of Wealth and Abundance

Let us now **Redefine the Concept of Wealth and Abundance**. True wealth and abundance are not abstract concepts; they are living realities that emerge from inner fulfillment, intentional living and alignment with purpose. **They are conscious states of being**. They extend beyond fleeting feelings to become sustained expressions of gratitude, joy and inner fullness. At their core, wealth and abundance are rooted in the belief that life offers limitless possibilities and reflects a deep resonance with a Universe that continuously provides when we release the grip of scarcity and surrender control. By embracing these states, we access a profound sense of peace and personal empowerment, allowing us to move through life's unfolding with trust, clarity, presence and grace.

In contemporary society, many equate financial wealth and material possessions with true abundance and fulfillment, however this perspective deserves closer examination. True abundance extends far beyond bank accounts and material possessions. It is not defined by what we own, but by how *deeply we feel*, how *connected and fulfilled we are*, and how *aligned we are with something greater than ourselves*. It is deeply rooted in joy, gratitude and self-awareness, core principles extensively discussed throughout our journey, and it manifests through robust health and wellness, vibrant and supportive relationships and self-love and love from others. It thrives in personal growth and embracing a state of inner prosperity. True abundance is also reflected in our ability to support and uplift others, contributing to the collective well-being. Above all else, authentic wealth begins with mental, physical and spiritual well-being, which serves as the foundation for a profoundly fulfilling and abundant life. A deeper understanding of abundance shows that *true richness comes from within* and reflects the quality of our inner and outer experiences, not just the accumulation of material goods. It is through nurturing our growth and the well-being of those around us that we genuinely embody and expand our sense of abundance.

It is important to clarify that our discussion does not imply that individuals with substantial financial resources or material possessions cannot experience true abundance and fulfillment. Instead, we seek to challenge the often simplistic and dichotomous assumptions surrounding wealth and success. Contemporary perspectives frequently lead people to equate abundance solely with financial, material or career achievements, overlooking the deeper, more meaningful paths that cultivate genuine fulfillment and a rich, purpose-driven life.

Reflect on the powerful question from *Insights — Joy and Peace* in *Chapter 1: The Core Principles of Abundance*: *How valuable are material possessions or professional achievements if, despite having them, we feel empty, unfulfilled and hollow inside?* You have probably encountered people who seem to have it all, financial stability, professional success or social recognition, yet they may still experience a subtle sense of something missing, such as self-love, meaningful connections or a clear sense of purpose. Often, this gap is reflected in the energy they project, hinting at attachments to external validation or ego-driven patterns. Later, we will explore the nature of the ego and how it shapes our experiences and sense of fulfillment.

When we move beyond equating material wealth with true abundance, our focus naturally shifts toward *inner fulfillment*. Genuine wealth transcends external markers and is cultivated through consistent practices of joy, love, gratitude and inner peace. Nurturing meaningful relationships with family, friends and community fosters a depth of fulfillment that money alone cannot provide. Likewise, dedicating ourselves to contributing to the collective good amplifies our sense of purpose and enriches our overall quality of life. By prioritizing inner growth, through ongoing learning, self-reflection, creative expression and self-improvement, we elevate our experience and often uncover our true mission and calling. This devotion to inner evolution deepens our lived experience and sets the stage for a purposeful, aligned existence, a topic we will explore in greater detail in a later segment.

Decide, now, to fully embrace a state of abundance that permeates every aspect of your being and life. Identify opportunities for joy and growth in every moment, from the ordinary to the extraordinary, and infuse even the mundane with purpose and fulfillment. In redefining abundance, move your focus away from material wealth and toward the deeper states of joy, gratitude and love, where true freedom resides. Freedom, a foundational principle of abundance, arises not from external possessions but from the small, treasured moments embedded within the rhythm of daily life. Reflecting back on *Insights — Freedom* from *Chapter 1: The Core Principles of Abundance*, recognize that abundance, fulfillment and liberation often emerge through the intentional choices we make and our mindful engagement with everyday responsibilities. Whether it is finding joy in dancing to music while folding laundry, sharing a light-hearted moment with a colleague or engaging in playful interactions with your children, these simple pleasures reveal the essence of a prosperous life. Take a moment to reflect on a time in your life when you felt genuinely rich, not in money, but in meaning. *What was happening around you? What made that moment feel so full and abundant?* Let yourself reconnect with the emotions and insights that made it unforgettable.

This redefined concept of abundance, rooted in profound joy, love, connection and gratitude, has the power to elevate the mundane into a source of deep fulfillment. It invites you to look beyond material possessions and recognize that true richness lies in the depth of your emotional and spiritual experiences. *Through building resilient trust in the innate abundance within you, you come to realize that everything essential for a rich and fulfilling life is already within your reach.* Embracing this expanded understanding of wealth, one that transcends mere material accumulation, opens the door for a transformative journey. This journey culminates in a deep and enduring experience of abundance, where every facet of your life flourishes with purpose, joy and a lasting, profound sense of fulfillment.

Introspection — Redefining the Concept of Wealth and Abundance

Reflect on a moment in your life when you felt deeply fulfilled, not through material means but through joy or connection. Describe the experience, your emotions and why it was so impactful. Consider how this moment helps redefine your understanding of true wealth.

For one week, identify and record three moments each day where you experience joy, love, gratitude and/or connection. At the end of each day, note how these moments contribute to your sense of abundance, fulfillment and richness.

Identify five experiences or moments from today for which you feel genuine gratitude, focusing on the feelings they evoked rather than material items. Reflect on how each one deepens your sense of abundance and shapes your broader understanding of wealth.

Insights — Conscious and Intentional Living

Each day invites a choice: to live with intention and purpose, or to quietly drift through life without conscious direction. Without a clear understanding of our beliefs, values and essence, striving for a mindful, purpose-driven life can feel daunting and out of reach. When you commit to **Conscious and Intentional Living**, you fortify your inner foundation and grow stronger with every practice that supports your self-discovery and transformation. With clarity on your inner landscape, goals and vision, conscious living becomes not only possible but necessary as you pursue an abundant and fulfilling existence. It is important to extend grace and patience to yourself, especially if you are still building the inner foundation and energy infrastructure, the internal energetic system that supports your mindset, beliefs, emotional well-being and spiritual alignment, needed for intentional living.

Ultimately, living consciously and intentionally comes down to alignment: aligning your thoughts, emotions and actions with your beliefs, values and aspirations. For example, our daily habits and choices should actively reflect, and reinforce, our greater vision and mission, a concept we will explore further in *Insights — Sacred Routines and Practices*. Ultimately, it is about authenticity, remaining true to ourselves and actively choosing to thrive in balance with our beliefs and sense of self. It is a lifestyle characterized by awareness, mindfulness and purposeful action. It involves being fully present in each moment, making deliberate choices and taking responsibility for the consequences of those choices.

At the heart of conscious and intentional living is self-awareness, clarity of intention and a commitment to personal growth and fulfillment. It involves continually examining your beliefs, values, habits and behaviors and actively seeking to align them with a deeper sense of purpose and meaning. It often includes mindfulness meditation, self-reflection, gratitude and simplifying your life to focus on what truly matters, a concept we will discuss soon. Overall, conscious and intentional living empowers you to live authentically, in alignment with yourself, others and the world around you. Refer back to *Chapter 2: The Abundance Pillars: Mastering Your Mind (Thoughts)* and *Chapter 3: The Abundance Pillars – Mastering Your Essence (Self) and Energy*, especially the segments on *Achieving Self-Awareness* and *Belief Systems and Values*, to effectively integrate these concepts into your life. Pause now and reflect deeply on how you can begin to align your daily life with your inner beliefs, values and intentions.

We will dive deeper into conscious and intentional living, focusing on how to cultivate presence and find true fulfillment in our daily experiences, rather than fixating solely on outcomes and destinations. Each day is a meaningful gift, a fresh opportunity to honor yourself, nurture your well-being and contribute positively to the world around you. In our discussion, we will also examine the significance of establishing sacred daily routines, practices and habits that promote overall wellness and align with your vision for your ideal life. These intentional actions lay the foundation for a deeply full, joyful and satisfying existence. Additionally, we will explore the principles of simplicity and minimalism, showing how clearing out physical and mental clutter can make you feel lighter and more agile, helping you get more done with less. Prepare for more richness as we achieve profound alignment, intentionality and mindfulness to attract our desired life, the life we have always deserved to live.

Introspection — Conscious and Intentional Living

Take a moment to consider how your daily habits and routines reflect your core beliefs and values and where there might be discrepancies that prevent you from living in alignment with your true self.

Reflect on how you can better align your long-term aspirations and goals with your everyday actions and decisions to ensure that each step is intentional and contributes meaningfully to your vision for an ideal life.

What internal barriers or limiting beliefs might be hindering your ability to live consciously and intentionally, and what actionable steps can you take to address and overcome these obstacles to create a more authentic and purposeful existence?

Insights — The Value of Being Present

The present moment holds a profound truth: depression tethers us to the burdens of the past, while anxiety pulls us toward the uncertainties of the future. *True and lasting peace, however, can only be found in the here and now.* When we allow ourselves to fully be in the moment, we let go of the heaviness of the past and the worry about what is ahead. This insight reveals the profound significance of the **Value of Being Present**, showing how it serves as a foundation for deep inner peace and authentic fulfillment. Tolle, in his influential work *The Power of Now*, explores this concept in depth, revealing how anchoring ourselves in the present moment can awaken profound inner shifts. His teachings reveal the transformative power of presence and its ability to reshape the way we experience life. For those seeking to deepen their understanding of this empowering practice, Tolle's work serves as a valuable guide for channeling the power of the present moment.

In *The Power of Now*, Tolle emphasizes that *only the present moment truly exists*, with the past and future being mere reflections or projections of the present. He explores the importance of fully embracing the present rather than dwelling on past events or seeking fulfillment in future outcomes. By practicing non-attachment and releasing the expectation that joy and fulfillment depend on external factors or future achievements, you can cultivate a deep appreciation for life in the present moment, regardless of your circumstances (Tolle, 1999). Following this excerpt, we will unpack the concept of non-attachment in our *Integration* segment to further explore and reinforce this idea. Pause now and embrace the present moment with full force, understanding that it is all that truly exists.

Fully embracing the present moment unveils the extraordinary potential within your current reality. The here and now offers a priceless opportunity to honor the gift of life and to step into the highest expression of yourself. When we fail to be fully present, lingering on past regrets or anxiously anticipating the future, we limit our ability to manifest our aspirations and slow the unfolding of our greatest potential. Take physical fitness as an example. To build a toned, healthy physique efficiently and sustainably, it is important to embrace full presence during each workout. Channel your energy into every lift and exercise, paying close attention to your form, technique and breath. By fully inhabiting each moment, mindfully moving, breathing and feeling your body, you maximize the benefits of your effort, achieving better results and enhancing overall well-being. **Presence amplifies both the practice and its outcomes.**

Similarly, if your ambition is to publish a book, it is important to immerse yourself fully in the present moment throughout your creative process. By focusing your energy on each word, sentence, paragraph, and your overall message as you craft and refine your manuscript, you leverage the maximum potential of your current efforts. Being present in each stage of writing ensures that your work is infused with love, clarity and authenticity, laying a solid foundation for your future success. This dedicated engagement to presence not only enhances the quality of your manuscript but also propels you closer to your goal, demonstrating how essential it is to *fully invest in the present to shape the future you desire effectively*. **This level of dedication and intentionality is vitally important and must not be overlooked**. Your present actions and choices, whether they involve fitness, writing or investing in other personal goals, directly shape both your current progress and the trajectory of your future achievements. *The quality of the energy you invest now will reflect in the overall quality of your results.* In a subsequent segment, we will explore sacred routines and practices designed to embody and amplify this idea, providing you with transformative strategies for intentional living, and the powerful actualization of your goals.

Now, consider how this principle applies in high-pressure situations. Imagine facing a major event, such as delivering a presentation to a demanding client, with anxiety. To maintain calmness and poise, it is essential to rise above the worry and nervous tension that can easily overwhelm you. By integrating creative imagination, visualizing positive outcomes and vividly imagining scenarios filled with success, as discussed in the *Integration* segment of *The Art of Manifesting Abundance* in *Chapter 2: The Abundance Pillars – Mastering Your Mind (Thoughts)*, you can free yourself from worry or negativity. This shift enables you to tap into self-trust and confidence, crucial for delivering a successful presentation. Grounding yourself in the present moment and embracing creative imagination allows you to focus your energy where it truly matters, on the here and now. This focus not only enhances your effectiveness but also emphasizes the importance of the present moment as the foundation for success. In the upcoming *Integration* segment, we will explore techniques to help you stay rooted in the present while approaching future challenges with greater clarity and confidence.

Fully embracing the present moment brings countless rewards, enriching life, and deepening engagement, which leads to more meaningful and fulfilling experiences. In today's social media-dominated culture, many prioritize documenting events over fully immersing themselves in the experience. Research highlights how much of our lives are spent on social media, raising important questions about the impact on the quality and depth of our experiences. Firsthand immersion in our life's experiences often surpasses the act of capturing footage for later viewing, footage that, more often than not, is never revisited. Next time you feel the urge to reach for your camera or phone, pause instead. Savor the moment fully and take the time to immerse yourself in the thoughts, feelings and emotions that arise in your present experience. Pause now and reflect deeply on a recent experience you recorded on your phone, one where you now wish you had been fully present instead.

As previously mentioned, excessive worry about the future or dwelling on the past is strongly associated with anxiety and depression. Embracing the present moment has proven to be a simple and powerful antidote, reducing the stress and anxiety that often accompany life's challenges, and fostering a sense of sustained calm. In his book, *The Power of Now*, Tolle reinforces this idea by suggesting that there are no actual problems, only situations that either require present attention or can be accepted until they naturally resolve or are ready to be addressed. In essence, he suggests that worrying is an unnecessary burden that inflicts needless pain, tarnishing the beauty and sanctity of the present moment (Tolle, 1999). By firmly grounding yourself in the *now*, you build a protective barrier against these negative thoughts and emotions, shielding your cognitive, psychological, emotional and spiritual well-being from unnecessary harm.

Another powerful benefit of embracing the present moment is its transformative impact on relationships and the deep connections we form with others. Fully engaging in conversations without distractions is a profound act of love and respect, especially in today's fast-paced world. Although challenging at times, offering your undivided attention significantly enhances relationships and fosters a deeper connection and nourishment that people often overlook. Moreover, being present sharpens self-awareness, enabling you to observe your thoughts, emotions and actions with greater clarity. This heightened awareness initiates personal growth and self-discovery, propelling you toward a more intentional and fulfilling life. Embracing the power of presence opens the door to experiencing life in its truest essence, infusing each moment with mindfulness, clarity and purposeful intent. From this moment forward, make a deliberate effort to notice when you drift away from the present, and actively engage in practices that bring you back to the here and now. Consider this a preview of the tools and strategies we will explore in the *Integration* segment, where we will take a closer look at techniques for nurturing and activating the power of presence in your daily life.

Introspection — The Value of Being Present

Reflect on a recent experience where you focused on the past or future. Write down how this affected your experience. Then, rewrite the scenario, imagining how being fully present would have changed your emotional state or outcome.

____

____

____

____

____

____

____

____

Choose a simple daily activity, like eating or walking, and immerse yourself fully in the experience. Pay close attention to the sights, sounds, smells and sensations of the experience, and gently observe any distractions that arise. Afterward, reflect in writing on how being fully present shifted your experience.

____

____

____

Imagine a future event that triggers your anxiety. Visualize managing it with complete presence, infusing the scenario with positive outcomes, and concentrating on the here and now. Reflect on how this mindset could impact your real-life situation and identify practical steps to maintain your focus on the present moment.

Integration — The Value of Being Present

To sustain a lasting state of presence, it is important to understand what it truly means to be grounded in the moment. This involves recognizing the value of fully engaging with the *here, now*, and appreciating how presence enriches our well-being and shapes our lived experience. Developing **self-awareness** around presence is foundational for maintaining it consistently in your daily life. Let us begin by engaging in a simple introspection exercise. Identify moments when you find yourself drifting away from the present. Observe what is happening during these times. *Where does your mind tend to wander? What emotions arise as you lose touch with the moment?* By identifying the patterns that pull you out of the present moment, you uncover the barriers to your presence and can begin dismantling them. This level of self-awareness becomes the foundation for showing up more fully and consistently in the *sacred now*. Pause now and reflect deeply on these two questions before moving forward.

Throughout your day, make a conscious effort to bring your attention to the present moment. Notice and embrace the sights, sounds, smells and sensations around you. Absorb these moments and express **gratitude** for your life and daily experiences as often as possible. Gratitude, as a reminder, is a powerful tool that shifts your focus from what you lack to appreciating what you already have. Consistently practicing gratitude rewires your cognitive patterns, enriching your overall quality of life. This practice not only redirects your attention from worries and distractions but also brings you back to a state of joy and calm, rooted in the present. Over time, the cumulative impact of cultivating gratitude fosters a profound transformation, enhancing your ability to navigate life with increased peace and resilience.

Examine your history of presence: when you were wholly immersed in the moment, and when your attention fractured or faded. This practice invites you to explore your lived experiences with honesty identifying the recurring patterns and triggers that pull you out of presence. By revealing what disrupts your focus, you gain the clarity needed to reclaim your attention. This heightened self-awareness becomes a powerful tool for strengthening your ability to remain grounded in the moment. This insight allows you to use **mindfulness** practices to reliably re-center yourself whenever you drift from the moment. Incorporating techniques such as **mindful breathing** and **grounding exercises** can help you return to a state of presence. Consistently applying these techniques is essential for strengthening your ability to remain grounded in the present.

Regular mindfulness practices are a powerful way to train your mind to focus on the present moment and pay attention to your thoughts, emotions and physical sensations as they arise. Examples include **mindfulness meditation** or **breathwork**. These exercises are practical yet powerful tools in promoting mental clarity, calm and peace. For a refresher on these practices, revisit the *Integration* segment of *Achieving Self-Awareness*. Similar to mindfulness practices, grounding exercises encourage sensory engagement by prompting you to notice your environment's sights, sounds, smells, textures and tastes, thereby redirecting your focus to the present moment. A simple grounding exercise that helps stabilize your awareness in the present moment involves the 5-4-3-2-1 technique:

- Identify and name **five things** you can **see** around you
- Acknowledge and mentally note **four things** you can **touch** or **feel**
- Recognize and verbally state **three things** you can **hear**
- Observe and describe **two things** you can **smell**
- Focus on and savor **one thing** you can **taste**

Dedicating even one intentional hour a day to mindfulness or grounding practices can elevate your emotional well-being and nourish a profound sense of calm. Grounding reconnects you to the present moment, engaging the brain's advanced capacities, such as clarity, discernment and conscious decision-making, so you can respond to life with greater presence and peace. These sophisticated brain functions empower you to consciously manage your energy, attention, behavior and emotions. Grounding disrupts the automatic fight-or-flight response, the body's instinctual reaction to perceived threats, which can trigger stress and disconnection. By connecting deeply with the present moment, you quiet these survival-driven impulses and move into conscious awareness, fostering greater mental clarity, emotional balance and a deeper sense of presence.

Building on the benefits of grounding, incorporating **mindful movement** practices such as walking, stretching or yoga offers another powerful way to connect deeply with your body and breath, fostering a richer engagement with the present moment. **Mindful walking**, for instance, is a simple yet profound practice that involves focusing your attention on each step you take. By doing so, you bring awareness to the physical sensations of walking, such as the lifting and lowering of your feet, the shifting of your weight, and the contact between your feet and the ground. This awareness encourages a gentle attunement to your body, helping you notice subtle shifts in tension, balance and posture, while also calming the mind and cultivating a sense of inner presence.

To begin this practice, find a quiet and safe place to walk, free from interruptions. Stand still for a moment, close your eyes if comfortable, and take a few deep, intentional breaths to center yourself and tune into your body. As you start walking, bring your full attention to each step, noticing the sensation of your feet connecting with the ground and the subtle shifts in your body as you move. Allow thoughts, worries or distractions to arise without judgment, gently returning your focus to the rhythm of your walk. If you wish, you can coordinate your breathing with your steps, inhale for a set number of steps and exhale for the same count, creating a natural, meditative flow. Pay attention to your posture: keep your shoulders relaxed, your spine aligned, and your movements fluid. Notice the sights, sounds and smells around you without clinging to them, allowing yourself to be fully immersed in the present moment. Walk at a pace that feels natural, neither rushing nor dragging, and allow this mindful practice to cultivate awareness, calmness and a deeper connection to your body and breath.

Continue walking mindfully for a few minutes or longer, and when you are ready to finish, take a moment to express and embody **gratitude** for the experience, solidifying the practice by acknowledging how it shifted your awareness and carrying that sense of presence into the rest of your day. Mindful walking is a simple and powerful way to bring mindfulness and presence into your everyday routine, promoting a sense of calm and groundedness. Engaging in these practices invites you to attune fully to the subtle, flowing sensations of your body, moving with gentle awareness and graceful presence. It is important to approach these practices with a mindset of patience and non-reactivity, allowing any unexpected thoughts or sensations to surface and pass without judgment. Embracing a sense of **non-attachment**, you can fully immerse yourself in the flow of movement, experiencing each breath and posture with profound awareness and presence.

Let us explore the concept of non-attachment. Rooted in various spiritual and philosophical traditions, such as Buddhism, Taoism, Hinduism and Stoicism, non-attachment involves releasing our hold on desires, outcomes and material possessions. It emphasizes living in alignment with the natural flow of life. Being present involves non-attachment, which means releasing your grip on thoughts, emotions and external outcomes that can pull you away from fully experiencing the moment. This practice helps you let go of past regrets and future worries, so you can fully enjoy the present without being weighed down by what has already happened or what may (or may not) happen. This perspective aligns closely with Tolle's teachings, which suggest that such preoccupations stem from the mind's illusions rather than reality. By fostering non-attachment, we learn to observe our thoughts and feelings without becoming consumed by them, leading to inner peace and freedom from unnecessary mental and emotional distress. Embracing non-attachment enhances our experience of presence, enabling us to appreciate each moment with greater calm, clarity, openness and mindfulness.

One effective path to non-attachment is practicing **acceptance**, allowing reality to be as it is without resistance or judgment. Acceptance does not mean resignation; rather, it involves being *fully present with what is* and *letting go of the need to control it.* It entails releasing expectations and attachments to specific outcomes while embracing uncertainty with ease. **Rather than ruminating on how things ought to be, concentrate on responding to situations with optimism, openness and adaptability, acknowledging that every life occurrence carries purpose, meaning and value, with your perception shaping the significance of these events.** By fully embracing your life in the here and now, you can cultivate joy and gratitude for the present moment and the countless blessings that surround you every day.

The value of being present is at the very heart of conscious and intentional living and mastering your life and collective consciousness. By focusing deeply on the present moment, we move beyond past regrets and future worries, enabling us to truly experience and appreciate the richness and beauty of each moment. This state of presence empowers us to live with greater discernment, authenticity, purpose and fulfillment by allowing us to observe our thoughts, emotions and impulses without distraction or judgment. *By fully engaging with each moment, we can make conscious choices that reflect our essence and core principles.* Embracing the present fosters a deeper connection to ourselves and the world around us, enhancing clarity, mindfulness and intentionality in every action. *As we make presence a central practice in our daily lives, we reveal the transformative potential to navigate each moment with grace and purpose, ultimately enriching our lived experience and deepening our engagement with the essence of our being.*

Insights — Finding Fulfillment Each Day

The allure of our dreams, milestones and goals often commands our attention, propelling us forward with intensity. Yet in the pursuit of these aspirations, we can easily overlook *the journey itself*, the unfolding process that shapes growth and meaning. Consider ambitious fitness goals as an example. Rather than fully savoring each moment of your workouts, it is easy to become consumed by urgency and restlessness. Our focus often narrows to hitting specific targets, lifting heavier or running faster, leaving little room to appreciate the experience and the growth unfolding in the process itself. Similarly, when writing a book, fixating on the final publication can eclipse the satisfaction and fulfillment found in each word, sentence, paragraph, page and chapter completed along the journey. Even in romantic relationships, the focus might be on the grand event of walking down the aisle, rather than nurturing the daily companionship, communication, trust and connection that sustain a lasting bond. *True fulfillment emerges from the daily efforts and intentional habits nurtured throughout the journey.* **Finding Fulfillment Each Day** means recognizing that *joy does not wait at the end* but is found in *embracing each moment of the process, where real growth and transformation occur.*

As highlighted in *Integration — The Value of Being Present*, embracing non-attachment is essential for experiencing daily fulfillment. It involves developing a mindset free from excessive fixation on outcomes or desires, allowing satisfaction and joy to emerge from within rather than from external sources. By practicing non-attachment, you learn to appreciate what you have without clinging, fostering a profound sense of liberation, inner peace and heightened presence. This approach enables you to experience abundance and fulfillment regardless of external circumstances, supporting conscious, intentional living and holistic well-being.

To deepen your daily sense of fulfillment, adopt a deliberate and intentional approach, expanding on the examples explored earlier. In your fitness journey, redirect your focus from striving for a "perfect" body to fully engaging in each workout with mindfulness, consistency and presence. Rather than rushing through your routine, slow down and concentrate on mastering each movement with precision and presence. *It is not about perfection; it is about progress.* **Every improved rep, every bit of refined form, every added weight is a win worth celebrating**. These small, consistent victories build momentum and meaning. *True fulfillment emerges not from the outcome, but from the daily commitment to growth and finding joy in the process itself.*

If you are pursuing a creative endeavor, such as writing a book or engaging in art, prioritize the essence of your message or theme. Let your inner muse guide you, finding inspiration in the act of creation rather than being solely driven by the desire for a finished product. Embrace the daily discoveries and insights that unfold during your creative process, cherishing the journey of exploration and self-expression as a source of joy and fulfillment. In relationships, prioritize building a solid foundation rooted in genuine friendship rather than idealizing marriage or lifelong commitment. A deep connection fosters trust, improves communication and provides the emotional support and security essential for a lasting partnership. A solid friendship ensures both partners are aligned in their values and committed to mutual growth. *By focusing on the process and journey, you cultivate a deeper sense of presence, meaning and fulfillment that extends beyond any specific outcome.*

Equally important, embracing mindfulness and presence is essential for experiencing true daily fulfillment. By grounding your attention in the present moment, you open yourself to fully experiencing and appreciating each aspect of your life, transforming even routine activities into sources of joy and satisfaction. Practices such as mindfulness meditation, breathwork, mindful movement and savoring small daily moments can profoundly enhance your well-being. For example, taking a few intentional breaths while noticing the flavors and textures of your meals can turn eating into a deeply mindful experience. Similarly, practicing active listening in conversations fosters deeper connection and presence with others. By integrating mindfulness into your daily life, through meditation, mindful walking or simply engaging fully in your activities, you nurture grounded awareness, foster lasting fulfillment, and enrich the quality of your everyday experiences.

By shifting your focus from outcomes to the journey itself, embracing presence, mindfulness and non-attachment, you transform everyday actions into meaningful experiences. Whether in fitness, creativity, relationships or simple daily routines, true fulfillment is discovered in the intentional engagement with each moment. This approach nurtures growth, deepens connection and cultivates lasting joy, allowing you to live fully and intentionally, finding abundance not at the finish line, but throughout the unfolding process of life itself.

Introspection — Finding Fulfillment Each Day

Reflect on today's experiences. Which moments made you feel most fulfilled and why? How did these moments align with your values and goals? What changes can you make to enhance your sense of fulfillment in your daily routine?

____

____

____

____

____

____

____

____

Which daily task, eating, walking or brushing your teeth, can you turn into a mindful practice today by fully engaging your senses? As you focus on textures, flavors or sensations, how does it shift your awareness and connection to the present moment?

____

____

____

Each day, briefly reflect on your goals and feelings. Practice letting go of excessive attachment to outcomes and find contentment in the present moment and current efforts. Write about your experience incorporating this reflection into your daily life.

Insights — Sacred Routines and Practices

Our future is shaped not by a single defining decision, but by the habits we uphold day after day: the **Sacred Routines and Practices** that quietly transform our lives. These personal practices form the foundation of a life filled with intentionality, abundance and fulfillment, shaping our steps with conscious direction. Without a clear vision or purpose, a concept we will explore in a later segment, living with intention becomes challenging. We may struggle to remain grounded in our mission or to sustain meaningful daily practices. However, once your vision and purpose come into focus, and your goals are clearly defined, your daily actions can align with what you truly value, propelling you toward the life you are meant to live. This alignment between our habits and goals empowers us to shape our future with deliberateness, ensuring that each moment contributes to the realization of our larger dreams. By consciously nurturing habits that support our vision, we create a purposeful trajectory toward living the life we desire.

Now, what are sacred routines and practices? These intentional, meaningful actions, many inspired by timeless spiritual practices, extend far beyond automatic habits like reflexively checking your phone or brewing coffee on autopilot. Sacred routines and practices are carried out with *full presence* and *mindful awareness*. Practices we have explored, such as meditation, breathwork and mindful movement, have been passed down through early civilizations as tools to connect with universal wisdom, expand consciousness and align with the natural world. Whether it is a daily breathwork session drawn from yogic pranayama, silent meditation rooted in Vipassana or Zazen or a reflective journaling ritual, these sacred acts offer moments of stillness, to slow down, turn inward and remember who we truly are. They serve as portals to self-awareness, emotional clarity and spiritual alignment, grounding us in the present while connecting us to something greater. Over time, they build a resilient internal foundation that helps us navigate life with intention, clarity and grace.

Sacred routines and practices often serve as lifelines, grounding us and preventing descent into unproductive or harmful patterns. By consistently engaging in these daily practices, we cultivate a supportive rhythm that directs our time, energy and attention toward what truly matters, enabling us to move through life with clarity, focus and purpose. In contrast, drifting through life unconsciously diminishes our capacity to foster meaningful growth and personal evolution, both of which are essential pillars of abundance. The power of integrating sacred practices into your daily life cannot be overstated; it is the foundation upon which lasting fulfillment and intentional living are built.

The true power of sacred practices lies not in perfection or rigid daily adherence, but in the intentional integration of these practices into your life through a consistent framework. It is the system, the structure and the alignment you create around your practice that sustains growth, awareness and transformation over time. For example: Imagine someone who sets aside time each morning for meditation. Some days they meditate for twenty minutes, other days only five and occasionally they skip a day entirely. The focus is not on perfect consistency; it is on having a framework, a dedicated time, a space and a habit of returning to the practice, that ensures meditation remains a meaningful and accessible part of their life. Over weeks and months, the benefits compound, even without perfection. While the importance of sacred practices is evident, it is equally important to recognize that strict adherence is not required. If you happen to miss a day of yoga, exercise or meditation, grant yourself **grace** and **self-compassion**. What truly matters is maintaining consistency over time, developing a system you can return to, rather than striving for perfection in every single instance. Pause now and reflect deeply on sacred routines and practices you would like to enhance or introduce into your daily life today.

Sacred rituals do not need to be confined to isolated moments or perfect conditions; they can be integrated into the rhythm of your daily life. You can amplify your growth, healing and holistic wellness by combining sacred practices into a single, intentional moment. This is how we reclaim time and intention. Imagine meditating in the warmth of the sun, practicing breathwork and allowing nature and your breath to align your energy. Or take a mindful walk, soaking in sunlight while reciting affirmations and mantras that uplift and transform your inner dialogue. Even in the midst of a busy lifestyle, whether you are driving, commuting on the metro or moving between responsibilities, you can still engage in breathwork or repeat affirmations to ground and refocus. This layered approach to wellness, inner work and transformation allows you to optimize your day without sacrificing either your responsibilities or your well-being. It is not about perfection; it is about presence, devotion and honoring yourself in the moments you already have.

Mainstream culture often tells us that wellness must look a certain way: polished, scheduled and practiced in designated spaces like yoga studios, meditation centers or curated retreats. We are led to believe that in order to truly care for ourselves, we need memberships, mats, apps and rituals that fit a specific aesthetic. However, the deeper truth is that sacred practices do not require fancy spaces or structured routines. They can happen anywhere, at any time, in the quiet of your car before work, during a walk, while washing dishes or in the stillness of your bedroom before bed. What matters most is not the setting, but the presence and intention you bring to the moment. When you pause to breathe deeply, listen inwardly or move your body with care, you are already engaging in meaningful practice. True wellness begins when we reclaim everyday moments as opportunities for connection, reflection and nourishment, wherever we are.

Start now by establishing a sacred ritual or routine that brings you joy, fulfillment and a deep sense of well-being, whether physical, cognitive, emotional, spiritual or all-encompassing. As a reminder, this practice does not have to exist in isolation. In fact, you can amplify its impact by intentionally integrating multiple practices at once. Meditate while basking in the sun, combine breathwork with movement or repeat affirmations as you walk through nature. Even amidst a busy lifestyle, you can incorporate practices like breathwork or reciting mantras into your day, whether during your commute or while moving through everyday tasks. Begin by incorporating one or more of these practices into your weekly routine and then gradually invite them into your daily lifestyle. Over time, these rituals will feel less like tasks and more like sources of grounding, something you eagerly return to that nourishes your well-being. As you build this relationship with your sacred practices, remember to extend grace and patience toward yourself. True growth is not about perfection; it is about showing up with intention, even on the hard days. Embrace the unfolding process with self-compassion, knowing that each small step forward contributes to lasting transformation.

Introspection — Sacred Routines and Practices

Reflect on your current daily habits. Are there any routines already bringing you a sense of fulfillment and purpose? Identify one existing habit that you can elevate into a sacred practice by infusing it with deeper intention. How can you align this practice more closely with your values and long-term goals?

____

____

____

____

____

____

____

____

Choose a new sacred routine that resonates with your vision of an abundant and fulfilling life. This routine could be anything from a daily meditation, creative expression or a gratitude practice. Commit to integrating it into your life, starting small and gradually increasing its presence in your daily routine. How do you envision this new practice supporting your personal growth and well-being?

____

____

Consider your approach to maintaining sacred routines. Reflect on a time when you missed a day or struggled to keep up with a practice. How did you respond to yourself at that moment? Explore how you can balance consistency with self-compassion, ensuring that your routines remain a source of joy and fulfillment rather than pressure.

Insights — Simple Living

Building on the foundation of sacred routines and practices, we now turn our attention to the transformative power of **Simple Living**, examining its core principles, how it manifests in daily life, and the profound, lasting impact it can have on your well-being and sense of fulfillment. Within this discussion, we will unpack the concept of minimalism and challenge the pervasive belief that material possessions are essential for true joy and fulfillment. It is important to understand that these concepts are not rigid rules but offer valuable alternative perspectives. As a gentle reminder, throughout this guidebook, the aim is to *stay curious* and *open-minded* rather than feeling pressured to adopt and integrate every idea discussed. These principles provide guidance for anyone at an impasse, seeking fresh direction or longing to live a more meaningful and purposeful life.

Now, what does simple living really entail? The answer to this question may vary for each individual. For some, simple living might mean intentionally focusing on what truly matters and brings value to your life. This can take the form of decluttering, not just physical possessions, releasing items that no longer serve you, but also clearing mental clutter, including unproductive thoughts and lingering emotional baggage. For others, it may mean slowing down a fast-paced lifestyle by setting boundaries around work, creating technology-free moments during the day or savoring daily rituals like preparing a home-cooked meal or taking a quiet walk in nature.

Simple living encourages prioritizing experiences over possessions, cultivating meaningful relationships instead of chasing status, and making choices that honor sustainability and conscious consumption. This shift in lifestyle and state of being emphasizes quality over quantity, promotes mindful decision-making and supports the removal of distractions that dilute our energy and joy. By embracing a more minimalist or intentional mindset, we are capable of accessing a deep sense of freedom, a cornerstone of abundance. A clutter-free space and clear mind eases stress and fosters peace and agility as you move through life. *With fewer obligations and material concerns, we reclaim time and energy for what genuinely brings us joy and fulfillment.*

Now, how do these ideas apply to your immediate environment and personal space? Many believe that our physical space is a reflection of our inner world. When your mind feels scattered or overwhelmed, your surroundings might echo that state: cluttered, disorganized or unsettled. While this is not always the case, and everyone's situation is different, there is often a strong connection between how we feel internally and how we care for the spaces we inhabit. Pause now to consider how you have organized your personal space. *Does your space support your sacred routines and daily practices? Does it feel restrictive or does it offer a sense of peace and calm, a place where you can truly exhale?*

The way your living space is arranged plays a powerful role in shaping your lifestyle and daily flow. When your environment is clean, organized and intentional, it naturally supports your routines, making it easier to move through your day with focus and ease. *Beyond function, your space also carries energy.* The mood, feeling and vibration of a room or space can either uplift you or weigh you down. A calm, uncluttered space invites peace and clarity, while a chaotic one can stir up anxiety and distraction. When your surroundings reflect what inspires and grounds you, they do not just look good; they feed your creativity, fuel your motivation and support your emotional and spiritual well-being.

Part of living simply, mindfully and intentionally is evaluating the utility and value of the items you possess. Prioritizing belongings that serve a purpose aligns with a minimalist approach to living, ensuring that each item genuinely contributes positively to your life. The prevailing culture of over-consumption has propagated the notion that more possessions equate to greater joy and fulfillment. In response, minimalism advocates for intentional living and mindful consumption. Instead of chasing material wealth and tangible possessions, minimalists prioritize experiences, relationships and personal growth, recognizing their intrinsic value. *By carefully curating what enters your life, you can foster a deeper appreciation and gratitude for everything you possess, in all aspects of your life.* Pause to reflect on the things you own. *Do they genuinely bring you joy, a sense of peace or serve a meaningful purpose in your life?*

One transformative practice to integrate consistently is conducting a mindful inventory of your surroundings. Examine each item in your space and ask yourself whether it genuinely contributes value, through practicality, purpose or authentic emotional significance. If something no longer serves you or enhances your well-being, *release it*. This applies not only to physical items but also to lingering thoughts, past emotional baggage or anything else that weighs you down. Consider donating possessions that could bring value or joy to someone else. This act clears your space while extending generosity. Intentionally surround yourself with objects that support your daily life or hold meaningful memories. Everything else may simply occupy space. *Letting it go* creates room for greater clarity, peace and intentional living. *The more you release what no longer supports your growth, the more space you open for what truly resonates with your values, purpose and highest self. Letting go clears the path for the energy needed to welcome what genuinely belongs in your life, physically and spiritually.*

Simplistic living involves not just managing physical belongings and releasing the weight of the past but also addressing the impact of content consumption on your mental well-being. In today's digital age, social media, news outlets and entertainment platforms constantly bombard us with information, not all of which is nourishing to our growth and peace of mind. This overwhelming influx can lead to mental clutter, contributing to stress, anxiety and distraction. Simplistic living encourages a mindful approach to content consumption by evaluating the quality and relevance of the information you engage with. This means being selective about the media you consume, prioritizing content that aligns with your values and supports your mental health. Reducing exposure to harmful or sensationalized information, and focusing on uplifting, educational or inspiring content can help you maintain and sustain a clearer, more positive mindset. By being intentional and curating your digital environment, you can prevent it from becoming a source of mental overload and instead use it as a tool to enhance your well-being and personal growth.

It is essential to recognize that while living a simplistic lifestyle, as defined in this segment, offers numerous benefits, it is ultimately up to each individual to define what genuinely brings them joy, peace and fulfillment. As we further explore the pillar of mastering your life and collective consciousness, it is important to ask yourself a simple question: *What drives your life?* Ideally, this powerful introspective question will reveal an answer which will help guide you towards greater intentionality in your daily habits, behaviors and the routines you adopt, and ensure they resonate with your overarching vision and life goals.

Introspection — Simple Living

Examine your living space and how it makes you feel. Take 15–30 minutes to observe whether your environment supports your daily routines and uplifts your mood. Identify what feels peaceful and what feels distracting or heavy. Note small changes that could make the space more calming and functional. This reflection helps you create a more supportive and intentional atmosphere that nurtures your well-being.

Review your physical possessions and digital content. Clear out things you do not need and think about the kinds of content you are engaging with online. Assess how these elements affect your mental state and make adjustments to reduce clutter and focus on what truly matters. This process fosters a more intentional and balanced lifestyle.

Reflect on how your current lifestyle aligns with the principles of simple living. Evaluate whether your daily routines, physical space and digital content contribute to a sense of clarity and fulfillment. Identify areas where you can simplify or declutter to better align with a simplistic lifestyle approach, promoting a more purposeful and balanced life.

Insights — What Does Your Ideal Life Look Like?

Before moving forward, pause. Breathe. Ask yourself with honesty: ***What does your ideal life look like when you are fully, unapologetically yourself?*** Picture it. Feel it. Let that vision lead the way. Your answer is not meant to be fixed. **As you grow, reflect and evolve, your definition of an ideal life will evolve with you**. New experiences shift your values, reshape your beliefs and expand your sense of what is possible, and that is exactly how it should be. For this moment, center yourself in the here and now of your journey. Visualize the life that feels true to who you are today. See it in vivid detail: the sights, the sounds, the textures and scents. Notice who is with you. *What fills your days? Where do you live, and what kind of energy surrounds you?* Most importantly, *feel it. What emotions arise in this life that feels fully aligned with your essence?* Give yourself full permission to imagine without boundaries. Let this vision become as expansive and extraordinary as you allow it to be.

Visualization is a powerful pathway for creating the life you desire. As a reminder, it is more than simply imagining a goal; it is the intentional practice of stepping into the experience of *already having it*. When you fully immerse yourself in the emotions, the environment and the reality of your success, you train your mind and body to recognize that vision as possible. By repeatedly focusing your attention on this future you, you strengthen the mental pathways that guide your choices, actions and habits into alignment with that outcome. Visualization turns dreams from distant ideas into a direction your life naturally begins to move toward. For additional guidance and reinforcement of this practice, refer to the *Integration* segment of *The Art of Manifesting Abundance* in *Chapter 2: The Abundance Pillars – Mastering Your Mind (Thoughts)*.

Now that you have reflected on your ideal life and begun embodying it through visualization, you are ready to take the next step in expanding your vision. Next, we will explore the concept of *Ikigai*: your reason for being. Together, we will uncover what you are gifted at, what you love and what gives your life meaning and direction. From this foundation, you will begin to shape your personal mission and identify the relationships and communities that support your most authentic expression. Remember: there is no single "correct" path through this work. These prompts are invitations, opportunities to *get curious*, *go deeper* and discover what feels aligned for you. Let the insights you have already gained (and those still emerging) guide you toward the version of yourself that feels both true and transformative.

Introspection — What Does Your Ideal Life Look Like?

Spend 10-15 minutes vividly imagining your ideal life, focusing on who is present, what activities you are engaged in and the sensory details of your surroundings. Note how these elements align with your current situation and aspirations.

Reflect on the emotions tied to your ideal life and see if your current life gives you those same feelings. Identify any gaps, and using the tools and practices we have uncovered, consider practical steps to align your daily experiences with the emotional state of your ideal vision.

Compare your current life situation with your ideal vision, examining areas of alignment and discrepancy. Reflect on what changes might help bring your reality closer to your ideal life.

Insights — Ikigai

Ikigai, a profound Japanese concept, represents your "*reason for being*" or the underlying purpose that drives you each day. It is about discovering the "*sweet spot*" where these four key elements converge: what you love to do (passion), what you excel at (vocation), what the world needs (mission) and what gives you a sense of fulfillment (profession). By integrating these elements, Ikigai helps you identify your purpose, guiding you to live a life aligned with your core values and passions. This approach to life emphasizes creating a balanced and fulfilling existence, supporting a deep sense of purpose and satisfaction that impacts both personal and professional aspects of your life. Embracing Ikigai is not merely about achieving success but about creating a meaningful life that resonates deeply with your essence: your authentic self.

Throughout this guidebook, we have explored ideas that naturally tie into the concept of Ikigai, your purpose in life. We have looked closely at what it means to truly understand yourself: your essence, your energy, your belief systems, your values. We have talked about the importance of living consciously and making choices that reflect who you really are. That is the heart of Ikigai. When you connect with this way of life, your decisions, goals and direction begin to align with something deeper, something that resonates with your innermost self. Embodying Ikigai in your daily life is not about having it all figured out. It is about getting clear on what matters most to you and letting that guide how you show up in the world. It helps you make choices with more intention, say yes to what feels right and let go of anything out of alignment. This level of clarity can bring more joy, meaning and fulfillment into your everyday life. Whether you are trying to uncover your purpose or just looking to live with more alignment, Ikigai can help you get there. It starts by tuning into four simple but powerful questions: *What do you love? What are you good at? What does the world need? And what can you be paid for?* When these pieces come together, they point you toward a life that feels deeply meaningful and uniquely yours.

Now, how do we identify our Ikigai? Discovering your Ikigai is a powerful journey of self-exploration, revealing your innermost desires, talents and values to identify what truly brings you joy and fulfillment. By this point, you have experienced numerous moments of introspection, gaining insights into different aspects of your being. These realizations will serve you well as you start to identify your Ikigai.

Here is a simple approach to guide you along this path:

1. Take time for **self-reflection**, contemplating your life experiences and interests. Reflect on past passions and hobbies that have resonated deeply with you and current activities that bring you genuine joy.
2. **Identifying your talents and passions** is a topic we will explore further in the upcoming segment. This process involves pinpointing the activities, topics or hobbies that ignite a flame in your soul and make you feel truly alive. Reflect on the activities that energize you and moments when you experience a true sense of excitement and joy.
3. **Evaluate your skills, strengths and natural talents**, an area we covered in *Chapter 3, Insights and Integration — Self-Empowerment* in the *Harnessing Your Core Power* segment. Reflect on what you excel at effortlessly, your intrinsic power.
4. **Examine your core belief systems and values**, pondering the convictions and principles that hold the most significance to you and the causes that ignite your passion. Consider how these values align with your aspirations and desires. Refer to Chapter 3, *Insights and Integration — Belief Systems and Values* segment to support you with this activity.
5. **Contemplate the impact and contribution you wish to make in the world**, envisioning how you can contribute to the

betterment of society and the lives of others. Think about the positive change you wish to make and the legacy you hope to leave behind.

6. **Engage in experimentation** by trying out different activities, hobbies or projects to discern what resonates most with you. Pay attention to how each endeavor aligns with your talents, values and passions, noting the feelings of fulfillment they evoke.
7. Lastly, **look for patterns and connections** among your passions, skills, values and desired impact. Your Ikigai lies at the intersection of these elements, embodying the essence of who you are and your purpose in life.

Pause now to explore these key elements and guidance for uncovering your Ikigai. Like your vision of an ideal life, discovering your Ikigai is a continually evolving journey, one of self-discovery, growth and deepening awareness. It is a path that invites you to look inward, uncover your unique gifts and consider how your passions, talents and values intersect to create meaning. Approach this exploration with *curiosity* and *openness*, allowing yourself to notice new passions, possibilities and directions as your life's calling unfolds. **There is no fixed destination**; each insight and experience enriches your understanding of what gives your life depth and resonance. Allow yourself to engage with diverse experiences and perspectives, embracing both the familiar and the unknown. Your Ikigai may shift, mature and reveal new dimensions over time, evolving as you grow, learn and deepen your connection to yourself, to others and to the world around you.

Introspection — Ikigai

What activities consistently bring you joy and fulfillment, and how do they align with the principles of Ikigai: your passions, skills, societal needs and potential for compensation? Reflect on how these activities intersect with your more profound sense of purpose and how they contribute to a balanced and meaningful life.

____

____

____

____

____

____

____

____

How do your personal beliefs and values shape your aspirations and goals and how can aligning these with your Ikigai enhance your daily actions and life direction? Assess how your core values influence your sense of purpose and ensure that your pursuits resonate with your Ikigai, leading to greater fulfillment and clarity.

____

____

What specific impact do you want to make in the world that aligns with your Ikigai and how can you start making strides toward this goal? Reflect on the contributions you wish to make and how they connect with your more profound sense of purpose.

Insights and Integration — Identifying Your Talents and Passions

Identifying Your Talents and Passions is a powerful step toward uncovering your Ikigai. It is the foundation for a life rooted in true abundance, deep fulfillment and personal mastery. When you start living in alignment with your natural talents and passions, life feels more purposeful. *You move forward with energy and clarity.* That sense of connection fuels you from the inside out, helping you show up with more joy, kindness and compassion for both yourself and the people around you. Just as discovering your Ikigai requires deep introspection, so too does recognizing the passions and activities that ignite your spirit, make you feel fully alive and place you at the helm of your own journey.

Let us begin a simple introspection exercise now. Set aside some quiet time for self-reflection to consider your life experiences, skills, interests, and, most importantly, what brings you joy. It might be helpful to ask yourself questions like:

What activities do I enjoy doing in my free time?
What tasks or hobbies do I find myself naturally drawn to?
When do I feel most fulfilled and engaged?
What accomplishments am I most proud of?
What am I naturally skilled at?

As you move through this self-reflection, it can be helpful to make a list of activities, hobbies and interests that resonate with you on a deep level or highlight your strengths. These might include creative outlets like writing, singing or making art, physical activities like sports or fitness or even causes you deeply care about like protecting the environment, supporting global health or getting involved in social or community initiatives. Recognizing that we all have blind spots, seeking feedback can be a powerful tool for uncovering hidden talents. Those closest to you, such as your friends, family, teachers, colleagues or mentors, often see your strengths more clearly than you do. Their perspectives can provide invaluable insights into your unique abilities. Additionally, stepping outside your comfort zone to experiment with new activities, career paths or projects can reveal untapped interests and talents you never knew you had. **Embrace the unknown and you may discover passions and skills that transform your life**.

As you explore your talents and passions, take some time to reflect on your successes and remember the moments when you felt truly accomplished or fulfilled in your work. *What skills were you utilizing? Which aspects of the task or project brought you the most satisfaction?* Identifying these recurring themes can lead you to your true passions. Notice the moments when you become so absorbed in an activity that time seems to disappear. These are signs you are in a state of *flow*, demonstrating alignment with your natural gifts and deepest passions. Additionally, look to role models who have transformed their talents and passions into meaningful work or pursuits. Their journeys provide not only inspiration but also practical insight, showing what is possible when purpose and action converge.

As you begin this journey of self-discovery into your talents and passions, remember that they are not fixed; they grow and change over time, and that is completely normal and expected. Identifying what you are truly good at and what lights you up is an ongoing process, not a one-time achievement. Be patient with yourself and trust that, with dedication and honest self-exploration, *clarity will come*. You will begin to see more clearly what brings you real joy and fulfillment. Embrace this process as an exciting adventure, one that brings you closer to your authentic self and the things you value most in life.

Introspection — Identifying Your Talents and Passions

Reflect on key moments when you felt most fulfilled and accomplished, noting the activities and skills involved. Identify recurring themes to reveal your core talents, passions and interests.

For two weeks, track activities where you lose track of time and feel fully engaged. Analyze these moments to pinpoint the skills and passions that induce a state of flow.

____

____

____

____

Ask 3-5 trusted individuals about your greatest strengths and memorable achievements. Use their feedback to uncover talents and passions you may need to fully recognize. What core skills and abilities have you possibly overlooked?

____

____

____

____

____

____

____

____

Insights and Integration — Embodying Your Purpose-Driven Life

Once we have explored our Ikigai, discovered our purpose and identified our talents and passions, the next step is **Embodying Your Purpose-Driven Life**, one that reflects our deepest desires and aligns with what matters most to us. This process calls for fully integrating your core mission, beliefs and values into every aspect of your life with clarity, commitment and intention. It is about directing your actions so they consistently align with a greater purpose, one that resonates deeply with your essence. Next, we will turn our attention to crafting your personal mission statement. This step invites you to embrace your sacred calling, uncover what truly drives and inspires you, and commit to making a meaningful impact. Living a purpose-driven life is not about going through the motions or seeking external validation. It is about dedicating yourself to something greater than yourself and consistently aligning your choices, actions and energy with your deepest values.

Embodying a purpose-driven life is supported by several essential pillars. First is **clarity of purpose**, which calls for deeply knowing what matters most to you and having a clear, purposeful vision for your life. This foundational step helps you answer your calling with confidence and direction. Next is **alignment with values**, ensuring that every action and decision you make aligns with your personal beliefs and principles. This alignment strengthens integrity and authenticity in all areas of your life. Another essential pillar is **making a difference**, which involves actively seeking opportunities to contribute to the well-being of others. Whether through your professional endeavors, personal relationships or community involvement, making a positive impact reflects your commitment to the greater good.

Finally, **resilience** plays a pivotal role in living a purpose-driven life. This cornerstone is about more than simply enduring hardships, it is the ability to find fulfillment, draw strength from your sense of purpose and continue moving forward even when obstacles arise. Life will inevitably present challenges, disappointments and moments of doubt, but resilience allows you to navigate these experiences with grace, determination and clarity. When you embrace resilience, you tap into a well of inner strength that carries you through difficulties and empowers you to act in alignment with your deepest values. It is through this steadfastness that you not only overcome adversity but also uncover a deeper, lasting sense of satisfaction and meaning. *Your mission, your Ikigai, your life's calling,* fuels the energy, courage and conviction needed to keep going, even in the face of setbacks, continually reminding you that **the journey itself is worthwhile**. Resilience transforms challenges into opportunities for growth, sharpening your character, expanding your capacity for self-trust and reinforcing the connection between your actions and your purpose. The more you cultivate it, the more you learn that *fulfillment is not a distant destination but a lived experience, shaped moment by moment through perseverance, conscious choice and unwavering alignment with your core values.*

It is important to note that living a purpose-driven life does not require grand gestures or world-changing efforts. Instead, it involves consistent, meaningful steps that align with your values and enhance your fulfillment and the well-being of yourself and others. A purpose-driven life is about living authentically and intentionally, striving to positively impact the world, regardless of its scale. Once you achieve clarity about your purpose, align it with your core values, and define how you want to influence the world, you will be better prepared to develop a powerful **personal mission statement** and connect with like-minded individuals: your community. We will explore the concept of cultivating your community in our next segment.

Crafting your mission statement will offer a powerful guiding principle, governing blueprint, consistently reminding you of your motivations and what propels you forward. Utilizing the Ikigai framework we have discussed can help you create a precise and focused mission statement that captures your passions, strengths, contributions and sources of fulfillment. Developing a personal mission statement is an enlightening and a profoundly meaningful introspective process. Here is a simplified step-by-step approach to help you create one:

1. **Reflect on your values and passions**: Consider what matters most to you, what brings you joy and fulfillment and what you are deeply passionate about. Reflect on your core beliefs, convictions, principles and the activities that energize you.

2. **Identify your strengths and skills**: Take notice of your strengths, talents and abilities, a topic we covered in *Chapter 3, Insights and Integration — Self-Empowerment* in the *Harnessing Your Core Power* segment. *What are you naturally good at? What do others often commend you for?* Understanding your strengths can help you identify how to best contribute to the world.

3. **Consider your contributions to the world**: Think about how you want to positively impact others and the world around you. *What social issues resonate with you? How do you envision yourself making a difference in this world?*

4. **Define your purpose (goals)**: Using the Ikigai framework or a similar approach, articulate your purpose and goals by identifying the intersection of what you love to do (passion), what you excel at (vocation), what the world needs (mission) and what brings you a sense of fulfillment (profession).

5. **Draft your statement**: Based on your reflections and the insights gained from steps 1-4, begin drafting your mission statement. Keep it succinct, clear and impactful. Aim to capture the essence of who you are, what you stand for and what you aspire to achieve.

6. **Refine and revise**: Review your draft mission statement and fine-tune it as needed. Consider seeking feedback from close

friends, mentors or advisors to ensure that your statement resonates authentically and accurately represents your intentions.

7. **Finalize and commit**: Once you are satisfied with your mission statement, finalize it and commit to living by its principles. Similar to your vision board, display your mission statement prominently where you will see it regularly and use it as a directional guide to align your actions and decisions with your overarching purpose.

Here is a sample personal mission statement: *Through alignment, creativity, awareness and advocacy, my goal is to support collective consciousness and drive positive change by encouraging mindful and intentional living, thereby enhancing the well-being of both current and future generations.* Pause now and reflect deeply on what you wish to incorporate into your personal mission statement. When you feel prepared, go ahead and begin drafting it. It is important to emphasize that creating a mission statement is a highly individualized process without a single prescribed path. It should be an experience that is both enjoyable and enlightening while also reflecting your unique personal journey.

Take the time to reflect deeply on your core values, strengths and aspirations and allow your mission statement to develop and evolve as you grow and gain fresh insights about yourself and the world around you. Embrace the ongoing journey of self-discovery and refinement. As you live authentically in alignment with your purpose and mission, you naturally attract others whose paths and values resonate with your own. This alignment deepens your fulfillment and fosters meaningful connections with those who reflect and amplify your journey.

Introspection — Embodying Your Purpose-Driven Life

What are the core values and deep aspirations that guide your life? How do these principles align with your daily actions and long-term goals? Consider how well your current path reflects these values and aspirations.

____

____

____

____

____

____

____

____

What are your key strengths and natural talents? Reflect on specific examples where these strengths have made a positive impact. How can you apply these abilities to enhance your mission and align with your personal and professional goals?

____

____

____

How do you wish to make a positive difference in the world? Identify how your talents, passions and skills meet the needs of society. How can you translate these insights into concrete actions that support your overall mission and values?

Insights and Integration — Cultivating Your Community

After connecting with our true path through soul-led discovery of passion, purpose and profession, and giving it voice through a mission that reflects our essence, *how do we find others on a similar journey, so our collective efforts can reach further and create a deeper impact?* Building a community of people who share our values and goals opens the door to meaningful collaboration, mutual support and shared growth. When we unite around a common purpose, we strengthen one another, cultivate trust and inspire continuous evolution. A circle grounded in authentic connection can elevate not only our success but also our overall well-being. Creating such a community, however, requires intention, care and consistent effort. It is a conscious act of fostering alignment, nurturing relationships and ensuring that collective energy amplifies the impact of each individual's mission.

You have likely heard the saying, "*Your vibe attracts your tribe*," and its truth is profound. When you radiate a clear energy and frequency through your thoughts, actions and passions, you naturally draw like-minded individuals into your life. This magnetic resonance aligns you with kindred spirits, fostering genuine connections that mirror and amplify your true essence. We will uncover practical approaches for purposefully and mindfully cultivating a community of individuals who resonate with your mindset and state of being and are committed to mutual enrichment while advancing the greater good and collective success.

Humans are inherently social beings, shaped over millennia to thrive within communities. This biological wiring goes beyond survival; it profoundly shapes our mental, emotional, physical and spiritual well-being. From the earliest days of human history, belonging to a community meant greater chances of survival, as individuals worked together to hunt, gather, protect and raise offspring. Yet the human need for connection extends far beyond these primal necessities, influencing how we grow, thrive and find meaning in life today. At a fundamental level, community provides us with a *sense of belonging*, a core human need. This sense of belonging is a stabilizing and powerful force, offering us emotional security and a foundation upon which we can build our identities. Within these social structures, we find acceptance, understanding and appreciation, which are essential for developing self-esteem and resilience. When we connect with others, our brains release oxytocin, often called the "*love hormone*," which lowers stress and boosts feelings of trust and bonding.

Understanding the profound role community plays in human evolution helps us see why its absence can have serious consequences. Just as connection fuels our growth, belonging and purpose, a lack of it can take a significant toll on mind, body and spirit. Loneliness, a pressing public health concern, is closely linked to mental health challenges such as depression and anxiety. Prolonged isolation further undermines physical health, weakening the immune system, increasing inflammation and raising the risk of chronic diseases like heart disease and stroke. These effects occur due to isolation disrupting the body's stress-response system, creating chronic stress that compromises immune function and fuels inflammation. Studies of solitary confinement highlight the extreme consequences of isolation, revealing severe psychological distress, cognitive decline and even shortened life expectancy. Beyond these physiological impacts, loneliness and isolation strip individuals of the joys, support and sense of security that come from meaningful social connections. In contrast, a supportive community serves as a powerful buffer, offering emotional encouragement, practical assistance and a deep sense of belonging and purpose that strengthens resilience and overall well-being.

Given these profound effects, investing intentional energy into cultivating community becomes essential for living a fulfilled and abundant life. This means actively seeking out and nurturing connections, whether through family, friendships, work or shared interests. It involves creating spaces where mutual support, understanding and growth are possible. Fostering and maintaining relationships is not just about being social; it is a vital aspect of holistic health that touches every part of our lives. By fostering community, we are caring for ourselves in the most fundamental way, ensuring that we not only survive but *thrive*, ***together***.

Now, how can we begin to cultivate our community? One highly effective method for **Cultivating Your Community** is to create dedicated platforms for connection, such as online forums or local meetups. These spaces allow you to engage with others, exchange ideas and provide mutual support, fostering a vibrant environment for open dialogue and collaboration. Establishing these platforms creates an accessible and dynamic forum for ongoing interaction and growth. Within these spaces, ensure you engage authentically with your community and be open and transparent about your personal journey, including your successes and challenges. Sharing honestly not only builds trust but also inspires others to embrace the same level of openness. By nurturing **authenticity** and **vulnerability**, you create a supportive and non-judgmental space where individuals feel empowered to connect deeply and contribute to collective success.

Cultivating your community requires deliberate and focused effort to build and deepen connections with others. Do things that genuinely excite you, whether by joining clubs, attending local events or participating in online forums. Take initiative in reaching out, offering support and maintaining consistent communication through phone calls, text messages or face-to-face interactions. Volunteering and contributing to causes you care about are powerful ways to forge meaningful bonds with like-minded individuals. Moreover, creating an open and inclusive atmosphere in your existing relationships fosters deeper connections and a true sense of belonging. By consistently showing up for others and creating spaces where people feel valued, seen and heard, you actively nurture and expand your community.

When fostering your community, it is important to offer meaningful value through a range of resources, knowledge-sharing and dedicated support and mentorship. Show your authentic commitment to each person's well-being and success by being generous with your support and attentive to their growth and achievements. Encourage a spirit of collaboration by creating space for people to come together through shared projects, partnerships or group efforts that strengthen teamwork and connection. At the same time, make it a point to welcome and celebrate diverse backgrounds, perspectives and experiences. When everyone feels seen and included, the community becomes richer, more creative and more united. Yet, it remains essential to prioritize your own needs and respect your limits throughout the process. Taking care of yourself ensures that you can continue to show up fully and sustainably for others. Setting clear limits, asking for support when needed and honoring your own well-being creates a healthy balance that benefits both you and the community you nurture.

To enhance connection and collaboration within your community, consider organizing events and activities such as gatherings, workshops or retreats either in person or virtually. These events create valuable opportunities for networking, learning and strengthening bonds among individuals. As you cultivate your community, lead with integrity, passion and a steadfast commitment to the collective mission whatever that may be. Be a role model who encourages others to adopt authenticity and live out the values and principles that are central to your community. By actively implementing these approaches and fostering a culture of connection, collaboration and support, you can build a thriving community that aligns with a collective vision and drives positive change. Pause now to consider how you can start integrating these approaches to cultivate your community and set the stage for transformative connections and collective growth.

It is important to recognize that building a community extends far beyond the formal settings previously mentioned. The principles of connection, support and shared values can be applied across various contexts, within family dynamics, social groups or professional environments. A strong sense of community can flourish in casual gatherings, informal networks or even within everyday interactions at work, home or in public. By fostering open communication, mutual respect and collaboration in these settings, you can create a supportive, trusting and integrated space that enhances personal and collective growth. Embrace the opportunities in your personal and professional circles to build meaningful connections and strengthen your community, regardless of the setting.

The foundation of cultivating a thriving and impactful community lies in the deliberate and thoughtful integration of connection, shared values and steadfast intentionality. Establishing an environment where people feel deeply connected, supported and motivated is essential for creating a vibrant and resilient community. This approach not only fortifies individual relationships but also magnifies the collective impact, transforming your community into a formidable force for positive change. By adopting these approaches, you create the conditions for your community to grow and thrive, brought together by shared values and a common goal. Through your efforts, a vibrant, purpose-driven network will emerge, one where collaboration and shared vision empower everyone to progress and succeed together.

Introspection — Cultivating Your Community

Identify your top five core values and evaluate how your current relationships and activities measure up to them. Examine any gaps or misalignments and take intentional steps to realign your actions so you not only live authentically but also attract people who embody those same values.

____

____

____

____

____

____

____

____

Close your eyes and visualize your ideal community. Imagine the people, the environment and the interactions that take place. Note the qualities and characteristics of the individuals in this vision. Use these insights to guide your efforts in seeking and nurturing relationships with like-minded individuals.

____

____

Reflect on a recent experience where you felt you made a positive impact within your community. Analyze what elements contributed to this success and how you can replicate these conditions to attract and engage others. Use these reflections to enhance your approach in building and strengthening your community.

Insights and Integration — Transcending the Ego

We have achieved significant milestones on our journey together: redefining wealth and abundance, embracing conscious and intentional living, understanding the power of presence, finding fulfillment in daily experiences, establishing sacred routines and practices and cultivating a simple yet meaningful lifestyle. We have also clarified our vision for an ideal and purpose-driven life through Ikigai and intentional self-discovery, identified our talents and passions and recognized the vital role of community in enriching our lives. With a profound understanding of personal growth and the transformative power of community, we are now ready to shift our focus outward. It is time to embrace a life centered on utility, contribution and connection, focusing on collective consciousness and impact. This will be the central theme of our next segment. With the wisdom, insights and experiences we have gained, we are ready to help advance humanity, support the greater good and build a more connected and compassionate world.

Collective consciousness, the shared awareness and mindset that unites individuals and shapes their experiences, along with living a life of utility, contribution and connection, is a cornerstone of genuine abundance and fulfillment, providing a sense of purpose that transcends personal gain and self-gratification. It is often said that in times of hardship or sorrow, giving back, supporting others and volunteering can be a powerful remedy. This is due to the transformative healing power of true altruism. By dedicating yourself to serving others and making a positive impact, you not only strengthen your community but also cultivate a profound sense of belonging and purpose, elevating your own life in the process. By shifting your focus to what you can give rather than what you lack, moving away from a scarcity mindset, you cultivate gratitude and a state of abundance, leading to greater joy in your life. Collective consciousness and embracing a life of utility, contribution and connection requires a profound shift: **Transcending the Ego**, a transformative process that involves elevating beyond the ego's influence, to align what matters to you with what others may need.

Although we have referenced the ego throughout this guidebook, we have yet to fully explore what it truly is. The ego is a cognitive structure that organizes our *conscious self-identity*. It defines how we understand our uniqueness, interpret our accomplishments and hold our beliefs and values, while also motivating our need for recognition and safety. The ego plays an essential role in shaping our self-image and how we engage with the world, influencing our thoughts, emotions and behaviors. It can motivate us to pursue success and protect us when we feel threatened. Yet, when the ego becomes overactive, it may drive self-centeredness, arrogance and conflict. *To live in alignment with collective consciousness, contribution and genuine connection, we must learn to rise above the ego's need for control and validation.*

Transcending the ego involves dismantling self-centered tendencies that prioritize personal needs, desires and interests above those of others. As we loosen the ego's grip, our attention widens beyond the self, opening us to the well-being of others and a deeper connection to the collective whole. This process allows us to shift our focus from a narrow, self-focused perspective to a broader, more inclusive view that considers the needs and experiences of others. When we transcend the ego, we no longer cling as tightly to our personal identity, desires and past experiences as the primary drivers of our thoughts, beliefs and actions. Instead, we become more attuned to the world around us, which naturally enhances our empathy and compassion.

By loosening the grip of the ego, we become less preoccupied with defending our self-image or fulfilling our immediate desires. This shift in focus creates mental and emotional space to truly listen to others, understand their viewpoints and appreciate the diversity of experiences that shape their lives. As we open ourselves to these varied perspectives, our capacity for empathy deepens, allowing us to connect with others more meaningfully. At the same time, transcending the ego does not mean neglecting our own needs. Instead, it leads to a more balanced approach where we can consider both our well-being and that of others when making decisions. We move beyond the binary of self-interest versus altruism and instead aim for solutions that honor individual and collective needs. This balance is essential for cultivating healthy, sustainable relationships and fostering a sense of fulfillment rooted in mutual respect and shared understanding.

Transcending the ego is a sacred unfolding that breaks down the walls we often build around ourselves, walls that are rooted in fear, pride and the need for self-preservation. These barriers, driven by the ego, can prevent us from experiencing true intimacy with others because they keep us trapped in a cycle of self-centered thoughts and behaviors. When we are overly concerned with protecting our self-image or seeking validation, we may struggle to show our true, "*naked*" selves to others, hindering the formation of authentic connections. By transcending the ego, we allow ourselves to embrace vulnerability, which is the foundation of genuine intimacy.

Vulnerability requires us to be honest, not only with others but with ourselves, about our fears, desires and imperfections. When we let go of the ego's need to appear invulnerable or superior, we create space for honesty, closeness and openness. This transparency fosters mutual respect, as it encourages others to be equally open and genuine in their interactions with us. As these authentic connections take root, our relationships become *deeper*, *more meaningful*, *more real*. We rise above superficial connections and cultivate relationships where each soul is seen, heard and honored in their truth, not for the persona they present, but for the essence they embody. This deeper level of connection not only strengthens our bonds with others but also enriches our own sense of self-worth, as we experience the joy of being accepted and loved for who we truly are. Take a moment now to reflect on how releasing the grip of the ego can transform your relationship with yourself and those around you, guiding your choices toward a more joyful, balanced and fulfilling life.

Once you transcend your ego, you find yourself more in alignment with your ideal, purpose-driven life. This powerful process helps you integrate your intentions and actions with a higher purpose that goes beyond personal desires. By relinquishing ego-driven motivations such as the pursuit of status, notoriety, financial wealth and validation, we redirect our focus toward contributing to something greater than ourselves. This shift leads to a profound sense of fulfillment and purpose. Transcending the ego is crucial in embracing a life of utility, contribution and connection as it allows us to move beyond self-interest, nurture empathy and compassion, foster collaboration, promote authentic connection and align with a higher purpose, greater than ourselves. Through transcending ego-driven behaviors and motivations, we fully acknowledge our bond with others and actively work to enhance the well-being of the wider community and collective consciousness.

The evolutionary journey of transcending the ego demands a comprehensive engagement with the array of practices and tools we have examined throughout our journey together. This pursuit involves finding empowerment in **solitude**, **self-awareness**, **introspection**, **self-reflection**, **mindfulness meditation**, **journaling** and **intentionality**, each of which serves as a powerful resource in this process. To deepen and fortify these practices, spend time going back over the *Integration* sections found throughout this guidebook. These sections offer powerful tools and practices crucial for grounding these transformative insights into your daily life, helping you break free from the ego's hold. By committing to these practices consistently, you solidify your progress and build lasting, meaningful growth over time.

Furthermore, you can deepen your self-awareness and accelerate ego transcendence by embracing practices such as **mindfulness meditation**, **journaling**, **therapy** and intentional **solitude**. These practices help identify and unravel ego-driven thoughts, emotions and behaviors. By observing ego-driven patterns with impartiality, you begin to disassociate from the ego and connect with a more profound sense of self. Additionally, embracing **empathy** and **compassion** shifts the focus from self-interest to understanding and supporting others. **Acts of service** and **volunteering** further transcend the ego by cultivating a sense of purpose and connection beyond personal gain. Moreover, fostering **humility** and embracing **vulnerability** counteract the ego's tendencies toward fear, pride and the need for self-preservation, promoting authentic and meaningful relationships. By consistently incorporating these elements and practices into your lifestyle, you create the foundation for moving beyond the ego and embracing a life that is more purposeful, deeply connected and authentically fulfilling.

Introspection — Transcending the Ego

Spend 10 minutes daily journaling about instances where your ego influenced your thoughts, beliefs or actions. Reflect on how these moments affected your relationships and sense of purpose. Use this practice to identify patterns and adjust your behavior toward a higher purpose.

Dedicate 15 minutes to a mindfulness meditation focused on empathy. Visualize yourself in someone else's position, reflecting on their experiences and needs. Notice ego-driven barriers and set them aside to enhance your compassion and understanding.

After participating in an act of service or volunteering, spend time reflecting on how it influenced your sense of fulfillment and connection with others. Consider how this experience shifted your focus from self-interest to contributing to the greater good.

Insights and Integration — Collective Consciousness

Throughout our journey together, we have frequently engaged with the energy of **Collective Consciousness**, highlighting its pivotal role in achieving true abundance and fulfillment. We explored how embracing your life's purpose, your sacred calling, can profoundly transform your life, emphasizing the power of steadfast dedication and love for your mission. Aligning with your sacred calling grounds you in the collective consciousness, linking your personal purpose with the shared intentions of others. Consider a community leader devoted to environmental conservation: by pursuing their sacred calling, they fulfill their own mission while advancing a larger movement for sustainability. Their work inspires action, fosters unity and amplifies collective commitment. In this way, integrating personal purpose with collective consciousness enriches individual fulfillment while generating meaningful impact for the broader community.

Collective consciousness, as a reminder, embodies the shared mindset and interconnectedness that unify individuals and shape their collective experiences. By pursuing your sacred calling, you contribute to this collective awareness, enhancing your sense of inner wholeness and aligned abundance while fostering deeper connections with others. In the *Insights and Integration — Transcending the Ego* segment, we revisited collective consciousness, highlighting how this collective awareness not only promotes deep connections and a sense of purpose but also transcends personal gain and self-interest. Integrating your sacred calling with collective consciousness means that your personal journey aligns with a broader, shared vision, leading to a more meaningful and impactful life of abundance, fulfillment and contribution.

You can understand collective consciousness as the shared set of beliefs, values, ideas and attitudes within a group or society. It reflects the collective awareness that emerges when people share common perspectives and experiences. This is evident in cultural norms and traditions, such as the widespread celebration of holidays like Christmas, which represents a shared sense of connection and experience. A nation's collective consciousness is also reflected in its history, culture and symbols, such as flags and anthems, which foster unity. Social movements, including civil rights and environmental activism, leverage collective consciousness to unite people around common goals. Popular culture, through trends in fashion, music and art, mirrors societal values and collective identity. Religious communities further embody collective consciousness through shared beliefs and practices that shape their sense of belonging and purpose.

Now, how does collective consciousness intersect with a life of abundance and fulfillment? At its essence, collective consciousness highlights our interconnectedness and shared human experience, emphasizing the importance of mutual support and empathy. By aligning personal goals with our communities' broader needs and values, we can significantly contribute to collective progress and well-being. This awareness enables us to identify where our skills and resources can make a meaningful impact, fostering a profound sense of purpose and fulfillment through acts of service and contribution, a topic we will be discussing next. By embracing collective consciousness, we become more aware of our own emotions and the feelings of others, which strengthens relationships and fosters mutual respect. This awareness promotes collaboration and shared purpose, encouraging collective action toward common goals. In turn, this deepens our sense of abundance and fulfillment, as contributing to the greater good creates meaningful connection and a more compassionate, integrated society.

Collective consciousness is not only expressed through large-scale movements, cultural shifts or collective action. It is also revealed in the smallest, most ordinary moments of daily life. Consider something as simple as offering a genuine smile to someone you pass in a hallway, a grocery store or on the street. You have no way of knowing what that person may be carrying internally: stress, grief, self-doubt or quiet overwhelm. That brief moment of warmth could soften their inner state, interrupt a negative spiral or remind them that they are not alone. Very likely, it could change the emotional and spiritual trajectory of their entire day. What makes this act so powerful is its *simplicity*. It costs you nothing, yet it *gives* to everyone involved. You benefit by opening your own heart and shifting your internal energy. The other person receives a moment of recognition or relief. And beyond the two of you, the shared energetic field subtly changes. The collective space you both inhabit becomes more coherent, more compassionate. This is collective consciousness in motion: *quiet*, *relational* and *deeply impactful.*

At its deepest level, collective consciousness does not rise only through sweeping societal shifts or visible leaders. It evolves through millions of ordinary humans making intentional, embodied choices each day: regulating their nervous systems, healing trauma, ending cycles of harm, speaking truth with clarity and kindness, and choosing to live grounded, present and embodied lives. Every time an individual chooses awareness over reactivity, compassion over harm or presence over dissociation, the collective field subtly shifts. This is how cultural change truly happens: *quietly*, *relationally* and *from the inside out*. Ask yourself: *What kind of world do I want to live in?* That question alone opens the pathway to how you move through the world, how you relate to others and how your inner work becomes collective consciousness in motion.

Another way collective consciousness expresses itself is through the sharing of insights, wisdom or relevant information. Imagine noticing that a colleague is struggling with a process you have already navigated, or realizing that someone is unaware of a resource, opportunity or perspective that could meaningfully support them. Offering that information, when it is helpful, relevant and aligned, can save time, reduce stress or open a new way forward. These moments of conscious sharing flow outward, strengthening trust, collaboration and collective well-being. As you move throughout your days, consider pausing to ask yourself a simple question: *What decision, action or response would create the greatest benefit for the most people at this moment?* When possible, **choose that path**. Over time, these small, intentional choices accumulate, shaping not only your experience of abundance and fulfillment, but the collective reality you are actively participating in and co-creating.

Our exploration of collective consciousness and its role in achieving abundance and fulfillment is deeply connected to the dynamic between individualism and collectivism. Individualistic societies, like those in the United States and Western Europe, emphasize personal autonomy, independence and the pursuit of individual goals. In contrast, collectivist cultures, such as Japan, China and Nordic countries, prioritize communal well-being, cooperation and shared responsibility for the collective good. While individualism promotes self-reliance and personal success, collectivism encourages collective accountability and support for community welfare. Understanding the relationship between these perspectives provides valuable insights into how individuals can effectively balance personal aspirations with contributions to the greater good, enhancing their overall sense of purpose and fulfillment. Pause for a moment and reflect deeply on how the interplay between individualism, collectivism and collective consciousness shapes your approach to abundance and fulfillment.

Embracing a life of collective consciousness, abundance and fulfillment means learning to draw from both individualistic and collectivist principles. It is about pursuing your personal goals and dreams while remaining mindful of collective well-being and the needs of those around you. When you achieve equilibrium, honoring your individuality while contributing to a higher purpose, you not only advance your own vision but also help move society forward in meaningful ways. As you become more aware of these tendencies within yourself, you will begin to see how they influence your relationships, work and engagement with your community. Perhaps entrepreneurship and personal innovation resonate with you, or maybe collective action and community organizing call to you. Understanding how individualism, collectivism and collective consciousness intersect can deepen your impact and help you forge stronger, more authentic connections. This awareness has the power to transform how you live, opening the door to greater fulfillment and a life of genuine abundance.

Introspection — Collective Consciousness

Reflect on how your sacred calling aligns with the broader values and needs of your community or society. Consider how pursuing your calling contributes to a larger, shared vision.

Write a paragraph about how your personal mission resonates with collective consciousness. How does your work or passion enhance the collective good and foster a sense of unity? Share specific examples if possible.

Create two lists. On one list, write down your personal goals and aspirations. On the other, list your community's or society's needs and values. Identify areas where your goals overlap with community needs. How can you balance pursuing personal success while contributing to the collective good?

Insights — Contribution

With a profound understanding of the value of community and collective consciousness, and having transcended the ego, we are now prepared to explore impactful ways to make meaningful **Contributions** to the greater good and fulfill our social responsibilities. *When we show up with intention and create positive change in how we live, connect and contribute, we help shape a stronger, healthier and more joyful world for both those around us today and for future generations.* The energy we put into building a supportive, uplifting world does not just impact our own lives, it spreads outward, creating a ripple effect that can reach far beyond what we see. When we embrace this way of thinking, we open the door to a more aligned, abundant and fulfilling future for ourselves, our communities and generations to come.

Understanding that contributing to the greater good does not always demand grand gestures or sweeping transformations is crucial. Embracing a pragmatic and mindful approach to contribution means thoughtfully evaluating how your daily choices affect others while also ensuring that you do not impose unnecessary stress or exhaustion on yourself. This practice allows for meaningful contributions without overwhelming personal sacrifice. Integrating this mindset into your everyday life can be both simple and impactful. For example, opting to carpool or take public transportation instead of driving alone can help reduce traffic congestion and lower carbon emissions. Similarly, choosing to support local businesses rather than large corporations can strengthen the local economy and foster community growth. These small, intentional actions not only support environmental sustainability and economic health but also enhance community well-being. Through regular mindful practice, you not only cultivate your own growth but also amplify a broader positive impact, supporting change that endures.

In personal interactions, actively listening to a colleague who needs support and offering genuine empathy is a powerful example of meaningful contribution. Similarly, making mindful choices, like supporting ethical and sustainable brands or reducing single-use plastics, reflects a commitment to positive societal and environmental impact. Volunteering at a local shelter in ways that align with your interests and availability can uplift others and strengthen community connections. If possible, contributing financially to charitable organizations also allows you to support causes you care about in practical, valuable ways. Even simple acts such as helping someone move or providing support to a friend during a tough time hold deep meaning. These everyday gestures of care and compassion do not just offer immediate comfort; they set off a chain reaction of positive change that reaches far and wide.

Take Stacy, for example. During a particularly overwhelming week at work, a neighbor noticed her struggle and brought over a homemade meal, even offering to watch her dog so she could rest. That small kindness made all the difference, reminding Stacy she was not alone and inspiring her to find ways to give back to her community. It is these quiet, powerful acts of kindness that truly move the world forward. Take a moment now to reflect on how you can contribute in a way that nourishes both yourself and those around you, creating a cycle of support that uplifts everyone involved.

While contribution and leading a life of utility can be profoundly enriching, it is important to prioritize your well-being and set healthy boundaries. Ensuring that your acts of kindness and service are sustainable and do not come at the expense of your own needs is crucial. True giving should be a source of joy and fulfillment, not something that depletes your resources, drains your energy or consumes your time to the point of exhaustion. It is essential to strike a sustainable balance where your contribution, acts of love, kindness and service uplift both others and yourself, supporting a positive and nurturing cycle of collective growth. By setting boundaries and being mindful of your own needs, you ensure that your contributions remain a source of vitality and inspiration, rather than a burden. This approach enhances your personal well-being and amplifies the impact of your contributions, creating a healthy balance that benefits everyone involved.

Introspection — Contribution

Identify one daily choice you make that impacts others. Reflect on how it aligns with your goal of contributing positively without over-extending yourself. Write down any adjustments needed to enhance its impact while maintaining your well-being.

Look back at recent acts of support or kindness. Evaluate their effects on both others and yourself. Consider if any led to personal strain and think about how to balance future contributions with self-care.

Think back to a recent time when you made a positive difference in someone's life. Picture the moment clearly, how your actions impacted them and how it made you feel. Now, consider how you can continue giving in a way that strengthens that balance, protecting your own energy and resources so you can keep making a meaningful impact without burning out.

Insights — Love and Connection (Recap)

Love and meaningful human connection are often regarded as life's highest achievements, the truest reflection of a successful life. In our final moments, what matters most is not what we acquired, the accolades, possessions or milestones we collected along the way, but the love we shared and the relationships we nurtured. Love is not something we must chase outside ourselves; it is an innate and transformative force already within us, integrated into both our biology and our spirit, shaping not only how we function, but also how we feel, connect and evolve. When we embrace this truth, love becomes our natural guide, infusing every aspect of our lives with greater joy, purpose and meaning.

Self-love is the foundation of all love. Without it, every other form of love becomes fragile and uncertain. When we are disconnected from our own worth, our ability to give and receive love is limited. True self-love arises from knowing who we are at our deepest levels, honoring our values, embracing our truth and aligning with what we believe in. This inner foundation shapes every relationship we form. Just as we take time to truly know a partner before committing, we must first cultivate a secure and unwavering love for ourselves. Only then can we enter relationships that are authentic, nourishing and enduring. *Self-love becomes the standard by which we measure the love we offer and accept, elevating the depth and quality of every connection in our lives.*

Connection, intimately linked with the principle of love, is a profound alignment with your true self and purpose. It is a magnetic and comforting force that transcends logic, reflecting a deep resonance with your core spirit. Whether through relationships with others or devotion to personal missions, meaningful connections enrich life and give it depth. When you live with love and intention, in alignment with your purpose, life unfolds with greater meaning, revealing a sense of unity, belonging and participation in a larger, beautiful story of love.

True connection begins not with what you do or what you have, but with who you *are* at your core. When you lead with your essence, your truth, your values, your soul's presence, you naturally invite deeper, more meaningful relationships into your life. It is not about striving or performing; it is about embodying the most authentic version of yourself. When you devote your energy to *being*, being grounded, compassionate, self-aware and whole, you radiate a frequency that draws in people who recognize, honor and resonate with that energy. This kind of presence does not just attract relationships; it cultivates bonds rooted in mutual respect, emotional safety and spiritual alignment. By shifting your focus from external achievements to internal alignment, you create space for genuine connection, *connections that nourish you, challenge you to grow* and *reflect the highest version of who you are becoming*. In essence, the deepest connections are formed not through effort, but through *embodied truth.*

Insights and Integration — Your Life Partner

One of the most profound connections you will ever establish, and arguably the most defining decision you will make, is **Your Life Partner**. Many people feel that finding the right person is not just luck; it is like discovering a "*life hack*" that makes everything in your world feel lighter, clearer and more meaningful. A life partner does more than provide love and support; they become a powerful driver for accelerating your ambitions and elevating your overall quality of life. With their steady presence, life shifts from a solo journey to a shared adventure, one where challenges are met together and each experience is deepened, strengthened and enriched by partnership.

With this perspective, let us revisit decision-making, now through the lens of choosing a life partner. In *Chapter 2*, we explored the art of decision-making in *Insights — The Art of Manifesting Abundance* in *The Decision: Embodying the State of Abundance* segment. We have highlighted the importance of making conscious choices and following paths that reflect our core values, highest aspirations and vision for a meaningful, fulfilling life. This guidance is particularly vital when it comes to choosing a life partner. When considering a life partner, take a moment to envision your ideal future. Ask yourself: *Does this person align with the life I see for myself?* Reflect on how this choice might shape your future. *Will this relationship support my growth, nurture my well-being and bring lasting joy and fulfillment to the life I am building?*

A powerful indicator that you have made the right decision and chosen the right path is when it resonates deeply with your core beliefs, values and aspirations, creating a profound sense of alignment in your life. Selecting a life partner is among the most significant decisions you will ever make, one that calls for someone who naturally reflects your true essence, shares your beliefs and embodies the values that define who you are. This choice shapes every dimension of your life: your happiness, career, health, financial security, the well-being of your children and your relationships with friends and family. **The weight of this decision influences the entire course of your journey**. Selecting a partner who elevates your highest qualities and fills your life with joy, love and peace is not just important, it is essential for your physical, emotional and spiritual well-being.

Now, how do you go about choosing your life partner? What steps can you take to attract this person into your life? Let us consider a universal principle we have discussed previously: the Law of Attraction. This principle can often reveal itself in surprising ways. Although we consciously seek partners who enhance our lives, we are often irresistibly drawn to those who reflect not only our strengths and virtues but also the deeper, more challenging parts of ourselves. This can mean being attracted to partners who reflect our unresolved emotional experiences, such as inner wounds, past traumas or imbalances. As a result, we might unconsciously recreate familiar patterns from our past within current and future relationships. Often, our choice of partners is influenced not just by our preferences but by a sense of comfort in what is familiar, sometimes rooted in early life experiences. Armed with this knowledge and conscious awareness, we can approach the choice of a partner with greater discernment and clarity, selecting someone who truly aligns with our deepest self.

In selecting a life partner, we must move beyond the challenging patterns of our past, embracing the tools and techniques that foster healing, releasing and liberation. Practices such as **forgiveness**, **acceptance**, **release** and **surrender** help us let go of past pain, attachments and resentments that may hold us back. In addition, **solitude**, **introspection**, **mindfulness meditation**, and, most importantly, **grace and self-compassion** are also beneficial tools in fostering healing and freedom. Releasing these burdens allows us to step into readiness for the partner we have always hoped for, fully open to experiencing love, connection and a deeply fulfilling relationship. To reinforce and integrate these healing and releasing practices, refer to the *Insights and Integration — Healing and Releasing* segment in *Chapter 3*.

Take a moment to gently reflect on your past relationships and explore what might have contributed to their challenges. *Were there elements like control, indifference, jealousy or even pain that felt all too familiar? Did these experiences remind you of patterns from your early years?* These reflections can offer valuable insights, helping you understand whether your current choices are shaped by old wounds or guided by the wisdom of your healed and evolved self.

When choosing a life partner, it is essential to prioritize qualities that go beyond surface-level traits like physical appearance, career success and financial status. While these aspects may hold value for some, they can never replace the importance of emotional maturity, honesty, respect, empathy, sensitivity, integrity and kindness. *The true worth of a person lies in their character and compassion, which should always outweigh material success or outward appearance.* When choosing a life partner, it is important to set personal standards that align with your deepest values, free from the influence of society, past traumas or inner conflicts. Create your own criteria to evaluate the compatibility, strength and alignment of a partnership. Ask yourself key questions as a measure of the relationship's quality, alignment and potential. Examples of questions can include: *Does this partnership bring me real, lasting joy? Is there a consistent flow of unconditional love and support between us? Do we share moments of playfulness and laughter? Do I feel safe and secure in their company?*

Always remember, the richest, most vibrant grass is not found in distant fields; it blooms where you water it with your presence, attention and love. True love is not built in a rush; it evolves and deepens through the experiences you share, the patience, compassion and bravery you show during challenging conversations, the joy you find in each other's successes and the unwavering commitment to each other's growth and evolution. Every moment, every word and every act of kindness and understanding intertwines a bond that grows stronger and more resilient over time. When you put your heart and effort into caring for your relationship, you will see it grow into something strong and beautiful, a bond full of love and connection that is capable of persevering through tough times and thriving in the warmth you both create together.

When choosing a life partner, never underestimate the power of cultivating self-love. It is the foundation of your life, shaping your choices, your relationships and your sense of well-being. Deep self-love allows you to embody the qualities you seek in a partner and supports genuine personal growth. Think of it as a guiding force: the more you care for and honor yourself, the more capable you become of attracting and sustaining meaningful connections. By tending to old wounds and prioritizing your own growth, you lay the groundwork for authentic transformation. This journey of self-acceptance and intentional self-improvement opens doors to new possibilities, aligning you with the abundance and blessings life offers. As your practice of self-love deepens, it enriches your life in unexpected and beautiful ways, propelling you toward your highest potential. In turn, it elevates the quality of your relationships and the overall richness of your life. Embracing this path creates a profound connection to yourself and others, establishing a life grounded in joy, fulfillment and authentic connection.

As we enter a sacred connection with a partner who resonates deeply, it is easy to become swept up in visions of milestones: weddings, anniversaries or shared dreams promising lifelong joy. Yet, as with ambitious goals like training for a marathon or writing a book, the true richness lies not in the destination but in the unfolding journey. When we focus only on the "end," we risk missing the everyday moments that form the foundation of enduring love: the friendship nurtured through honest conversation, the trust grown in shared vulnerability and the bond strengthened by small, consistent acts of care. Embracing this process, the slow, sometimes messy, but profoundly rewarding path, allows us to cultivate a partnership grounded in presence, meaning and a depth of connection far beyond any single event or achievement.

In the pursuit of a life partner, we discover a transformative "*hack*" that goes beyond mere companionship. An aligned partnership fuels the fire that brings our dreams to life as you support and celebrate each other through both challenges and triumphs. Central to this process is moving past old patterns, prioritizing self-love and focusing on the journey, which helps us embody the qualities we desire in a partner, and move with steadiness and mindfulness. Reflecting on past relationships offers valuable insights into recurring patterns and unresolved wounds that affect our current partnership choices, highlighting the importance of valuing qualities such as integrity and kindness over surface-level traits such as material wealth or physical appearance. By nurturing self-love and embracing healing, we naturally draw authentic connections and open ourselves to the limitless abundance life has to offer. Welcoming a life partner who reflects our truest self brings more than companionship; it invites a shared commitment to self-discovery, growth and conscious living. ***This journey is not merely about finding the right partner; it is about becoming the right partner, fully aligned with our own heart, values and potential.***

Introspection — Your Life Partner

Reflect on your past relationships by identifying recurring challenges and patterns and consider how these may have influenced your current choices and personal growth.

____

____

____

____

____

____

____

____

Imagine a day with your ideal partner, paying attention to the way you interact, support each other and nurture joy and peace. Then compare this vision with your current or potential relationships to assess how closely they align with the future you truly desire.

____

____

____

____

Evaluate your self-love and healing practices, noting their impact on your well-being and any unresolved challenges, and create a plan to address these areas to enhance your readiness for a fulfilling life partnership.

Insights — Sustaining Abundance: Co-Creation

Take a moment to recognize and celebrate the beautiful journey of self-discovery, exploration, personal growth and evolution you have undertaken. This inner work requires tremendous courage, dedication and resilience, so pause and **honor how far you have come**. **You have truly earned this celebration**. At this stage, you have attained deep mastery over your mindset (thoughts), essence (self) and energy through conscious, intentional practices, alignment and embodiment. You are now able to channel these insights purposefully, creating a life that fosters community, mindful contribution and a deep connection to collective consciousness. This journey has led you toward a life of lasting abundance and fulfillment. You have now come to realize that each day offers a chance to ***decide, now***, to embrace and integrate abundance into your life.

Abundance has always been available to you, accessible through the beliefs you hold, the way you embody them, the practices you engage in and the profound love you cultivate for yourself. By choosing to align with abundance, you invite conscious action, discipline and dedication, creating a life rich in fulfillment, purpose and possibility. Even amidst challenges and uncertainty, embodying abundance and cultivating gratitude grounds you in awareness, resilience and potential. This state of being supports you in navigating obstacles, achieving your goals and realizing the life you were always meant to live. As you have likely experienced, this journey calls for a consistent and deliberate commitment to nurturing joy, peace, positivity and abundance across every dimension of your life.

As you embrace abundance and embody gratitude in your life, you begin to notice how the Universe mirrors your inner state. It responds by becoming a space of movement and possibility, constantly offering challenges that test your resilience and grace. How you respond to these moments reveals your dedication to growth and your ongoing evolution toward self-mastery. By rising into your highest self and consciously breaking free from unhealthy patterns and cycles, you step into alignment with the person you were always destined to become. Imagine your life journey as a grand quest in a video game, where overcoming each obstacle represents a crucial milestone in our development. Each victory allows us to *level up*, gaining strength, wisdom and resilience, while also sustaining our sense of abundance. Just as a video game protagonist emerges stronger after each challenge, we, too, become better equipped to face the next phase of our journey. Embracing and embodying joy, abundance and gratitude goes beyond mere mindset; it becomes a soul-shifting and life-altering practice that drives us toward self-realization and sustained fulfillment. Every triumph in life reminds us of our strength to overcome setbacks and grow into the fullest version of ourselves on this ever-evolving journey of life.

You are a creator with the innate power to shape your reality according to your deepest desires. Within you lies the tools you need to create the life you have always envisioned. As you move toward a life of abundance and fulfillment, remember you do not have to do it all on your own. Let it be a collaboration between you and the Universe as you take aligned steps toward your dreams, trusting that you are being supported every step of the way. This process involves aligning your thoughts, beliefs, emotions, spoken words, intentions, actions and energy with universal principles such as the Law of Attraction. Visualize your desired outcomes, take inspired action and stay open to guidance, opportunities and blessings from the Universe. By recognizing your role as a creator and engaging in co-creation with the natural flow of the Universe, you can shape your reality and manifest the life you truly desire.

Rather than passively waiting for life to unfold in our favor or relying solely on individual effort, co-creation acknowledges the interconnectedness of all existence and recognizes the role of universal intelligence in guiding and supporting our endeavors. It calls for a posture of openness, receptivity and faith in the Universe's natural abundance and benevolence, allowing a balanced exchange of energy and inspiration to emerge between you and the unfolding forces of life. Co-creation arises when personal intention aligns with the energy of the Universe, where you actively contribute to shaping your reality while surrendering to the divine flow of life. **Trust the Universe**; it is a wise life energy operating for and through you.

Today, and every day, presents a powerful opportunity to ***decide, now*** to commit to abundance as your enduring state of being. Embrace self-love and welcome a life overflowing with joy, prosperity and fulfillment. This choice is profoundly personal and represents one of the most pivotal decisions you will ever make in your life, reinforced by the rich array of practices you already have at your disposal. To turn this commitment into reality, cultivate a positive and resilient mindset that serves as the foundation for every aspect of your life. Dedicate yourself to the insights, introspection and practices presented in this guidebook, recognizing how each is designed to empower and elevate you. Embrace the tools you have acquired on your journey, applying them thoughtfully and consistently, especially when challenges arise. **Remember, this path is not defined by a single decision but by the daily choice to reinforce and embody it**. By fully engaging with these practices and maintaining steadfast dedication to your growth, you lay the foundation for meaningful transformation and lasting well-being.

Imagine a life pulsating with boundless abundance, unbridled joy and profound fulfillment. A gorgeous blend of prosperity, effortless grace and unmatched freedom, where the possibilities are endless, inviting limitless possibilities. Envision a realm where every aspiration and dream feels tantalizingly within grasp. What if this dimension, this exalted state of existence, was not a mere distant mirage but a tangible reality ripe for the taking, *here, now, today*? I challenge you to entertain this idea, to grasp the profound truth that such a life awaits your embrace: *Believe it, feel it, know it*. This is no unattainable fantasy. It is a tangible destiny awaiting your deliberate choice. *The gateway?* A life-changing decision to awaken your transformative power of abundance, integrating a clear, intentional approach that empowers you to master your mind, essence and energy and ultimately align your life with the flow of collective consciousness. All it takes is for you to ***decide, NOW*** to embrace and embody a life overflowing with infinite, and lasting, abundance and fulfillment.

INTROSPECTION — SUSTAINING ABUNDANCE: CO-CREATION

Explore the concept of co-creation with the Universe. How do you actively engage in the process of manifesting your desires, dreams and aspirations in sync with the natural rhythm of the Universe? Reflect on how aligning your thoughts, beliefs, intentions, actions and energy with universal principles has influenced your journey.

Contemplate the interconnectedness of all existence and the role of divine or universal intelligence in guiding and supporting your endeavors. How do you foster openness, receptivity and trust in the inherent abundance and benevolence of the Universe? Reflect on the dynamic exchange of energy and inspiration between yourself and the Universal forces at play.

____

____

____

____

____

____

Reflect on the power of your choices and the transformative potential of embodying a state of abundance. How can you channel this consciousness to master your mind, essence and energy, and ultimately, your life and collective consciousness? Consider the conscious decisions you can make to align with your desired reality and embrace abundance today.

____

____

____

____

____

____

____

____

Chapter Recap: The Abundance Pillars – Mastering Your Life and Collective Consciousness

Chapter 4 explores mastering your life and collective consciousness to achieve abundance and fulfillment in perpetuity.

Redefining the Concept of Wealth and Abundance

Key Insights: True wealth and abundance arises from inner fulfillment, not external possessions. It is a living expression of gratitude, a steady awareness of life's richness and endless possibilities, in alignment with the natural flow of the Universe's intelligence.

Integration: To truly embody abundance, shift your focus from material wealth to inner well-being. Embrace joy, gratitude and love as integral to your sense of richness. Invest in relationships and personal growth to enhance your overall sense of abundance.

Conscious and Intentional Living

Key Insights: Conscious and intentional living involves aligning your daily habits and actions with your core beliefs and values. It requires self-awareness, clarity of intention and a commitment to personal growth. This lifestyle fosters authenticity and purposeful action, guiding you toward a meaningful existence.

Integration: Reflect on how your daily routines align with your inner values and long-term goals. Identify and address any discrepancies that hinder your alignment with your true self. Cultivate mindfulness and establish sacred routines that support your vision for an ideal life.

The Value of Being Present

Key Insights: The present moment is where life unfolds, offering the only space where true awareness and growth occur. By immersing yourself in the now, you connect deeply with your experiences, fostering clarity and appreciation. This presence allows you to live with intention, embracing the richness of life as it happens.

Integration: To cultivate presence, practice fully immersing yourself in each moment and observe when your attention drifts. Regularly return to the present by engaging deeply with your current experiences and surroundings. Make mindfulness and grounding a consistent part of your daily routine to deeply cultivate and maintain a state of presence.

Finding Fulfillment Each Day

Key Insights: True fulfillment lies in embracing the journey, not just the destination. Non-attachment to outcomes allows us to find joy and contentment in daily efforts and experiences.

Integration: Practice mindfulness in your daily activities by focusing on the present moment, which can transform routine tasks into profound sources of joy. Reflect daily on your goals, letting go of attachment to outcomes, and celebrate small victories along the way.

Sacred Routines and Practices

Key Insights: Sacred routines and practices form the foundation of an abundant and fulfilling life, aligning daily habits with your deeper values, long-term goals and vision.

Integration: Identify a daily habit that resonates with your aspirations and elevate it into a sacred routine, infusing it with intention and purpose. Focus on consistency rather than perfection to cultivate a meaningful and balanced life.

Simple Living

Key Insights: Simple living means intentionally focusing on what truly matters, clearing out physical, mental and emotional clutter and valuing quality over quantity. This approach promotes mindfulness, reduces stress and enhances overall well-being, creating a sense of peace, liberation and freedom.

Integration: Assess your living space for alignment and functionality. Make changes to support well-being. Eliminate excess possessions and simplify digital content to create a more balanced and intentional lifestyle.

What Does Your Ideal Life Look Like?

Key Insights: Your vision of an ideal life will change and evolve as you grow and experience life. Regularly reflect on and refine this vision to stay aligned with your current values and goals.

Integration: Spend time imagining your ideal life, focusing on sensory details and emotions to understand how closely your current life aligns with this vision. Identify gaps between your current reality and ideal vision, then take practical steps to bridge these gaps and align daily experiences with your aspirations.

Ikigai

Key Insights: Ikigai represents the intersection of what you love, what you excel at, what the world needs and what you can be rewarded for, guiding you toward a purpose-driven life.

Integration: Reflect on activities that bring you joy and assess how they fit with your passions, skills, societal needs and potential for compensation to ensure they align with your deeper purpose.

Identifying Your Talents and Passions

Key Insights: Aligning with your innate talents and passions is crucial for discovering a life of abundance and fulfillment, thereby fostering a profound sense of purpose and enthusiasm.

Integration: Analyze key moments of accomplishment and joy to identify activities and skills that reveal your core passions and interests. Monitor activities where you lose track of time and feel fully engaged to pinpoint your skills and passions that induce a state of flow.

Embodying Your Purpose-Driven Life

Key Insights: Embodying your purpose-driven life means integrating your core mission, beliefs and values into every aspect of your actions and decisions. It is about aligning with your deepest desires and making a meaningful impact.

Integration: Reflect on your core values, strengths and passions to define what matters most to you and how you want to make a difference in the world. Use the following steps to create and live by a personal mission statement:

- **Reflect**: Identify your core values, strengths and passions.
- **Define**: Clarify what truly matters to you and how you want to contribute to the world.
- **Draft**: Write a personal mission statement that captures the essence of your purpose and aspirations.
- **Refine**: Review and adjust your statement based on feedback, ensuring it aligns with your true self and guiding principles.
- **Commit**: Finalize your mission statement and use it as guidance for your decisions and actions.

Cultivating Your Community

Key Insights: Humans are inherently social, and being part of a community provides essential emotional, psychological and spiritual benefits, including self-esteem, stress reduction and a sense of belonging. The absence of community can lead to adverse health outcomes, emphasizing the importance of fostering meaningful and healthy connections.

Integration: Visualize your ideal community, noting the qualities and interactions that align with your vision. Use these insights to guide your efforts in seeking and nurturing relationships with like-minded individuals.

Transcending the Ego

Key Insights: Shifting from ego-driven desires to focusing on contribution and connection can gently steer you toward a more fulfilling life that aligns with a deeper sense of collective purpose and awareness.

Integration: Regularly engage in mindfulness, self-reflection and service to dismantle ego-driven patterns and foster a more profound sense of purpose and connection with others.

Collective Consciousness

Key Insights: Aligning your mission with collective consciousness amplifies both individual fulfillment and community impact, supporting a sense of unity and common purpose. By pursuing a sacred calling, you enhance collective awareness and contribute to broader societal goals.

Integration: Ensure your personal goals resonate with broader community values, enhancing collective well-being and unity through meaningful contributions. Recognize the intersection of your aspirations with societal needs to effectively pursue individual success while contributing to the collective good.

Contribution

Key Insights: You can achieve meaningful contributions to the greater good through small, intentional actions and mindful choices, such as supporting local businesses or offering genuine empathy in personal interactions. These efforts create a positive ripple effect, enhancing community well-being and leaving a lasting legacy. Sustainable contributions enhance both personal fulfillment and broader impact.

Integration: Integrate mindful practices into your daily life to make impactful contributions without overwhelming personal sacrifice, ensuring your actions support community well-being and personal balance.

Love and Connection (Recap)

Key Insights: Love and meaningful human connections are often seen as the ultimate success and true measure of life's achievements. Fulfillment arises from embracing love as an inherent part of our being, which guides us with joy and purpose. At the foundation of this is self-love, the key to all other forms of love.

Integration: Navigate life with love as your guiding principle, allowing it to infuse your actions with joy and fulfillment. Embrace love as an innate aspect of your being to achieve a more profound sense of joy and accomplishment. Prioritize self-love as the essential foundation for meaningful relationships.

Your Life Partner

Key Insights: Choosing a life partner is a pivotal decision that can profoundly shape your ambitions, quality of life and overall journey. The right partner should not only complement your strengths but also turn your journey into a shared adventure, enriching your life with increased joy and fulfillment.

Integration: Ensure that choosing a life partner aligns with your core values and future vision. Consider how this decision will affect your overall well-being and fulfillment. Address unresolved emotional experiences through healing, releasing, forgiveness and introspection. This process will help you attract and embrace the right partner, free from past patterns.

Sustaining Abundance: Co-Creation

Key Insights: Consistently embody a state of abundance and practice gratitude to navigate challenges and reach your goals. Recognize your power as a creator in shaping your reality. Work in collaboration with the Universe by aligning your thoughts, beliefs, emotions and actions with universal principles like the Law of Attraction.

Integration: Integrate abundance into your daily life through intentional action and a positive perspective. Visualize your goals and stay receptive to guidance and opportunities. Rely on the Universe's support while actively shaping your reality.

Introspection Exercises: Use the introspection exercises from each section to apply these principles to your life. Reflect on how redefining wealth, conscious living, presence and fulfillment align with your personal values and aspirations. Assess the alignment of your daily actions with your core beliefs and identify how integrating joy, love and mindfulness into your routines enhances your overall sense of abundance. Use these reflections to refine your vision. Cultivate a purpose-driven life and contribute meaningfully to your community.

Conclusion: Mastering your life and aligning with collective consciousness involves a continuous journey of personal growth, mindful living and authentic contribution. By embracing a holistic view of abundance that transcends material wealth and focusing on inner fulfillment, you create a more meaningful and impactful existence. Understanding and applying these principles supports individual transformation and enhances your ability to contribute positively to the collective good, ultimately leading to a richer, more fulfilling life.

Conclusion

Take a sacred pause and celebrate the beautiful journey you have created through self-discovery, exploration, growth and evolution. The inner work you have done takes immense courage, devotion and resilience. Pause. Breathe. Acknowledge just how far you have come. You have earned this moment of reflection and celebration. By now, you have created and given birth to a profound mastery of your mindset, your essence and your energy. You have learned how to intentionally use these insights to shape a life grounded in community, contribution and collective consciousness. You are now embracing a life where abundance flows through every choice, every act of self-love and every moment of conscious alignment.

Abundance has always been available to you; it was and is never out of reach. You simply need to tap into it through the beliefs you hold, the way you embody your highest self and the intentional practices you choose each day. Self-love serves as the foundation, nurturing your connection to the limitless possibilities around you. As you align your mind, body and spirit, abundance shifts from being a concept to a living experience, accessible in every thought, choice and interaction. **Remember, abundance is not something to attain, it is something to live, to radiate and to share**. Now that you recognize abundance as an ever-present possibility, it becomes clear that it is not something you chase, but something you *choose*. Each day presents an opportunity to embody abundance through intentional action, discipline and commitment.

In moments of difficulty, rely on your discernment: **choose abundance and gratitude**. You always have the gift of choice which gives you command, presence and empowerment. This way of being becomes your North Star. But let this be clear: you do not achieve abundance and fulfillment through sacred practices alone. You actualize them through embodiment, through healing, through alignment, through becoming. You grow into the version of yourself capable of holding this life. And that version of you is being forged, refined and empowered every single day. *You master abundance and fulfillment not by reaching a final destination, but by waking up to the truth that each day is an opportunity, to be of service, to make meaningful connections, to find joy, to give and receive love.*

Finding abundance and fulfillment means creating balance and wholeness, where every aspect of your life is nurtured and intentionally invested in: your community, your work, your relationships, your passions, your career and your well-being. True fulfillment is holistic. It asks you to show up fully and tend to the garden of your life with care and love. Abundance and fulfillment live on a spectrum. They will not always look or feel the same. But at their core, they have always been the answer. Joy, love, peace and abundance were never missing; we were simply taught to forget them through layers of conditioning and societal expectation. Now, you remember. And in remembering, you rise.

The path to abundance extends far beyond merely accumulating material wealth; it involves a profound exploration of powerful insights, self-discovery and the integration of practices that cultivate lasting joy, gratitude and prosperity. In this guidebook, we have journeyed from the depths of scarcity to the heights of joy, love, connection and gratitude, uncovering the core principles that underpin a truly fulfilling, abundant and meaningful existence. We have revealed the essence of our being, aligned mind, body and soul and explored our profound connection with the Universe. Throughout this journey of mastery, we have navigated the complex landscapes of consciousness, diving into the depths of our thoughts, essence and energy. By leveraging introspection and mindfulness, we reshaped our reality, manifesting abundance through deliberate decision-making, intentional thought and purposeful action. We tapped into our intuition and inner power, embracing the transformative potential of our energetic vibrations and the wisdom of our inner voice.

Our journey has transcended personal mastery, extending into collective consciousness and co-creation with the Universe. We released the constraints of the ego, embraced the flow of life and recognized the interconnectedness of all existence. Through acts of contribution and collaboration, we felt the deep joy that derives from serving others and fostering a sense of community. We learned that abundance is not a solitary pursuit but a dynamic dance between individual effort, collective impact and Universal alignment, a partnership with the Universe where we actively shape our reality while surrendering to the divine flow of existence.

As we conclude this guidebook, let us carry forward the wisdom and insights gained, infusing every moment with gratitude, presence and purpose. Remember that abundance is not a final destination but a continuous state of being, a deliberate decision to ***decide, now*** to align with the inherent richness of life. May you continue to cultivate joy, love and connection in every aspect of your existence, embracing abundance as both your birthright and your destiny. As you enter the next chapter of your life, find comfort in knowing that the Universe is always supporting you and conspiring in your favor, guiding you toward a life of boundless fulfillment and infinite possibilities. And never forget, *you are deeply loved.*

Addendum: Practices, Reflections and Resources

This addendum is designed to support your continued evolution beyond the pages of this guidebook. Within these sections, you will find powerful practices to integrate what you have learned, teachable moments that offer deeper reflection and key terms and phrases that define the language of this work. Use these tools as companions on your ongoing journey and return to them whenever you seek clarity, alignment or renewed inspiration.

Powerful Practices

Introspection

Introspection is the mindful act of turning inward to explore your thoughts, emotions and beliefs with curiosity and without judgment.

How to Practice Introspection:

- Set aside quiet time to reflect daily or weekly.
- Ask open-ended questions: "*What am I feeling right now?*" "*What is driving these thoughts?*" "*Am I living in alignment with my truth?*"
- Journal your reflections, noting patterns, triggers and insights.
- Reframe limiting thoughts with empowering alternatives to align your inner dialogue with your higher self.

Introspection is the gateway to profound self-awareness and a life lived with clarity, purpose and intention. Throughout this guidebook, you will find powerful introspective questions designed to lead you deeper into yourself.

Gratitude

Gratitude is a transformative practice that nurtures alignment within your mind, body and soul. It shifts your focus from scarcity to abundance and cultivates joy, resilience and alignment.

How to Practice Gratitude:

- Keep a gratitude journal daily, weekly or monthly. Record moments, people or experiences you deeply appreciate.
- Express thanks aloud, to yourself or others, as a mindful ritual.
- Engage in a gratitude walk: slow down, breathe deeply and notice what you are grateful for in your surroundings.
- Practice visualization: close your eyes, focus on someone or something you cherish, inhale deeply to absorb the joy it brings, and exhale slowly, letting gratitude radiate throughout your being.
- Use affirmations such as, "*I appreciate the strength of my body*" or "*I am thankful for the love and support in my life.*"

Consistency transforms gratitude into a natural state of being, creating a foundation for authentic abundance and fulfillment.

Reframing

Reframing is a simple yet powerful way to shift your perspective, transform emotional responses and open new possibilities.

How to Practice Reframing:

- When negative self-talk arises, pause and ask: "*How else can I see this situation?*"
- Replace limiting thoughts with empowering alternatives. For example: change "*I wasn't good enough*" to "*This ending is creating space for something that better aligns with who I am becoming.*"
- Observe the emotional charge behind your thoughts and choose perspectives that empower you to move forward with clarity and optimism.

Reframing strengthens your ability to approach challenges with resilience and intention.

Mindfulness Meditation and Breathwork

Mindfulness meditation and breathwork are practices that cultivate presence, calm, clarity and emotional balance.

How to Practice Mindfulness Meditation and Breathwork:

- Set aside time each day for mindfulness meditation or conscious breathing.
- Sit comfortably, close your eyes and bring awareness to your breath.
- Notice thoughts or sensations without judgment and gently return your focus to breathing.
- Simple Breathwork Exercise – Box Breathing: Inhale through your nose for a count of 4, hold your breath for a count of 4, exhale slowly through your mouth for a count of 4, and hold again for a count of 4. Repeat this cycle 4–5 times to calm the nervous system and center your energy.
- Experiment with different breathwork techniques to further align your mind, body and energy.

This daily practice trains the mind to remain present and grounded, enhancing your capacity for intentional living.

Embracing Objective Awareness

Objective awareness is the practice of observing your thoughts without judgment, creating space for clarity and inner peace.

How to Practice Objective Awareness:

- Step into the role of the impartial observer of your mind. Notice thoughts as though you are watching from the outside.
- When self-critical thoughts arise, reframe them with compassion and clarity.
- Practice saying to yourself: "*I notice this thought and I choose not to let it define me.*"
- Use journaling to explore recurring thought patterns and shift perspectives over time.

This practice develops detachment from ego-driven patterns, allowing greater clarity and alignment with your essence.

Affirmations

Affirmations are intentional statements that align your thoughts, words and actions with your highest aspirations. They reshape your inner dialogue and reinforce empowering beliefs.

How to Practice Affirmations:

- Choose affirmations in the present tense, as if they are already true, e.g., "*I am confident and capable*" or "*I attract abundance and joy into my life.*"
- Speak affirmations aloud daily, morning and evening, with *conviction, clarity* and *emotional engagement*. This amplifies their impact by engaging mind, body and soul.
- Pair affirmations with visualization: imagine yourself living fully in the truth of your statement.
- Keep a journal to track shifts in thought patterns and alignment over time.

When practiced consistently, and with full embodied engagement, affirmations anchor your intentions and transform them into lived reality.

Silence and Stillness

Silence and stillness are practices that create space for reflection, clarity and connection to inner wisdom.

How to Practice Silence and Stillness:

- Schedule moments of quiet each day where you are free from distraction.
- Practice mindful pauses in conversation.
- Allow silence to foster deeper listening and understanding.
- Engage in meditative stillness: sit quietly, breathe consciously and observe your thoughts without judgment.
- Spend time in nature to deepen your connection to your inner self and the present moment.

Through silence and stillness, you cultivate clarity, groundedness and a deeper connection to your essence.

Pausing

Pausing is a simple yet powerful practice that interrupts automatic reactions and creates space for conscious choice. In the fast pace of life, we often respond to situations impulsively, driven by habitual thought patterns and emotional reactivity rather than clarity. Pausing allows us to break this cycle. It is the intentional act of stopping before responding to an external stimulus or internal thought.

When you pause, even for just a few seconds, you create a moment of stillness. This stillness is a gateway to perspective: it gives you the ability to observe your thoughts and emotions without immediately identifying with them. It creates mental space where you can choose a response aligned with your values, rather than one driven by impulse or fear.

How to Practice Pausing:

- When you notice a strong emotional reaction, whether in conversation, decision-making or self-talk, pause before responding.
- Take a breath.
- Count to three in silence before speaking or acting.
- Notice sensations in your body: where tension or discomfort arises. This awareness brings you closer to your inner state.
- Use pausing as a daily habit, not only in moments of conflict but also in ordinary life, as a way to bring mindfulness into your flow of experience.

Pausing strengthens your ability to respond rather than react, and over time, it deepens your capacity for emotional regulation and intentional living.

Cultivating Self-Awareness

Self-awareness is the foundation of mental mastery. It is the ongoing practice of observing your inner world, your thoughts, emotions, beliefs and motivations, with curiosity and compassion. Cultivating self-awareness is about noticing the mental patterns that shape your experience without judgment, and understanding how those patterns influence your decisions, relationships and perception of reality.

Self-awareness transforms automatic living into intentional living. By becoming aware of your habitual thought patterns, you gain the ability to consciously choose which beliefs to nurture and which to transform. This practice opens the door to identifying mental blockages and limiting beliefs, allowing you to address them at their root rather than reacting unconsciously to them.

How to Practice Cultivating Self-Awareness:

- **Daily Check-In:** Spend a few moments each day observing your thoughts and emotions without judgment. Ask yourself: "*What am I feeling right now? What thoughts are driving this feeling?*"
- **Journaling:** Use prompts to explore patterns in your thinking, such as "*What recurring beliefs have surfaced today?*" or "*How did I react to challenges, and why?*"
- **Mindful Observation:** During interactions or experiences, notice your internal responses. Observe without immediately acting on them.
- **Track Triggers:** Identify situations, people or thoughts that consistently evoke strong emotional reactions. Understanding these triggers helps you see where limiting beliefs may reside.
- **Body Awareness:** Notice physical sensations, such as tension or tightness, which can reveal subconscious stress or beliefs.

Cultivating self-awareness is not a destination but a continual process. Over time, it builds a deeper sense of clarity, self-mastery and emotional resilience. As self-awareness grows, so does the capacity to consciously align your mind, thoughts and actions with your highest intentions.

Grace and Self-Compassion

Grace and self-compassion are intentional practices that cultivate kindness toward yourself and nurture mental well-being. They invite you to embrace your humanity, acknowledging that imperfection is part of the human experience. Rather than resisting or criticizing yourself for mistakes or shortcomings, these practices encourage a gentler, more supportive inner dialogue. When you practice grace and self-compassion, you create a mental environment that fosters growth, resilience and self-acceptance. This mindset allows you to approach challenges with calmness, learn from setbacks and treat yourself with the same empathy you extend to others.

How to Practice Grace and Self-Compassion:

- When you notice self-critical thoughts, pause and reframe them with kindness. For example: "*It's okay to make mistakes; I can learn from this and improve.*"
- Acknowledge your efforts, even when the outcome is not perfect.
- Practice speaking to yourself as you would to a dear friend, with patience, encouragement and empathy.
- Set aside moments each day for self-reflection, asking: "*How can I show myself more grace today?*"

Grace and self-compassion strengthen your emotional resilience, helping you navigate life's uncertainties with balance and openness.

Creative Imagination

Creative imagination is the intentional use of mental imagery to shape your inner world and influence your outer reality. It is a directed, purposeful practice that invites you to envision scenarios and outcomes in vivid detail, engaging your mind and senses to prepare for success. This practice leverages the mind's power to transform possibilities into reality. When you engage in creative imagination, you build a mental rehearsal that primes your subconscious mind, aligning your thoughts and emotions with your desired goals. This not only reduces stress but also enhances confidence and clarity in approaching life's challenges.

How to Practice Creative Imagination:

- Identify a situation that causes stress or uncertainty.
- Close your eyes and imagine the best possible outcome unfolding with clarity.
- Engage all senses: see, hear, feel and even smell the imagined scenario.
- Notice the emotions that arise and immerse yourself fully in those positive feelings.
- Reflect afterward: "*What did I notice about how this changed my perspective?*"

Creative imagination strengthens your ability to consciously direct your thoughts toward desired outcomes, fostering a deeper sense of possibility and empowerment.

Daydreaming

Daydreaming is a free-flowing, reflective practice that allows your mind to wander with intention. It offers a mental space where desires, visions and possibilities can surface naturally without rigid structure or expectation. This practice nurtures creativity and connects you to deeper layers of self-awareness. When you daydream actively, you invite yourself into a creative process that uncovers hidden aspirations and energizes your vision for the future. This gentle exploration fosters inspiration and opens new pathways for manifestation.

How to Practice Daydreaming:

- Find a quiet moment in your day to let your mind wander. Allow images, ideas and emotions to surface without judgment or control.
- Focus on positive scenarios that align with your desired life.

- Notice any recurring themes or feelings that arise.
- Revisit these moments regularly to deepen connection to your vision.

Daydreaming enhances your ability to access subconscious insights and creates fertile ground for visualization and intentional living.

Visualization

Visualization is the deliberate act of imagining your desired outcomes with clarity, detail and emotional engagement. It is a structured mental rehearsal that bridges the gap between imagination and reality by engaging your mind, body and emotions in the creation of your future. When you visualize intentionally, you strengthen your mental connection to your goals and train your subconscious mind to recognize these scenarios as possible, driving motivation and purposeful action.

How to Practice Visualization:

- Choose a goal or desired outcome.
- Sit quietly in a comfortable position and close your eyes.
- Picture the scene vividly: what you see, hear, smell, feel and experience.
- With *full embodied engagement*, imagine yourself living this reality in the present moment.
- Allow yourself to fully experience the emotions associated with this vision.

Focused visualization deepens clarity, aligns your intentions and transforms the way you engage with your aspirations.

Vision Boarding

Vision boarding is a visual manifestation practice that uses imagery, words and symbols to create a tangible representation of your goals and desires. It transforms abstract dreams into concrete, visible reminders that keep your intentions alive and accessible. When you create a vision board, you actively focus your mind and energy on what matters most to you. This process clarifies your values, strengthens your focus and amplifies your capacity to attract your desired future.

How to Practice Vision Boarding:

- Reflect on your values, desires and long-term goals.
- Gather images, words and symbols that resonate with your vision.
- Arrange them meaningfully on a board or digital space.
- Place the vision board somewhere visible daily.
- Spend time regularly connecting with your vision and noticing how it influences your actions.

Vision boarding is a creative, inspiring way to anchor your intentions and keep them alive in your daily life.

Embodiment

Embodiment is the intentional act of living as though your desired reality already exists. It is the practice of aligning your actions, energy, presence and language with the version of yourself who is already living your aspirations. This transforms manifestation from mental exercise into lived experience. When you embody your future self, you close the gap between who you are today and who you wish to become. This alignment creates authenticity and magnetizes opportunities that match your vision.

How to Practice Embodiment:

- Visualize your ideal self in vivid detail: appearance, behavior, energy and presence.
- Identify qualities, habits and attitudes to adopt.
- Begin integrating these qualities into daily life consciously.
- Speak and act as your ideal self would.
- Reflect on your progress and adjust as needed to maintain alignment.

Embodiment transforms intention into reality, making your highest vision a living, breathing part of your present experience.

Nourishing Your Body

Nourishing your body is a foundational practice for aligning your essence and energy. It is the intentional care of your physical vessel, recognizing that your body is the container for your mind and spirit. The way you fuel, hydrate, move and rest your body directly influences your energy, vitality and capacity to experience abundance. Nourishing your body is not merely about diet; it is about cultivating a lifestyle of mindful care, where every choice supports your health and aligns with your higher purpose.

How to Practice Nourishing Your Body:

- Prioritize a balanced diet rich in nutrient-dense foods such as fresh fruits, vegetables, whole grains, lean proteins and healthy fats.
- Minimize or remove processed foods high in added sugars, artificial ingredients, preservatives and inflammatory oils (such as vegetable, soybean, canola, corn and sunflower oil). Replace

them with nutrient-rich options like extra virgin olive oil, coconut oil or grass-fed butter.

- Plan and prepare meals ahead of time to ensure consistent access to nutritious options.
- Choose clean, purified, mineral-rich water whenever possible and aim to drink enough throughout the day. Consider adding sea salt or trace minerals for optimal hydration.
- Limit alcohol intake to preserve energy, clarity and balance.
- Work with a wellness coach, dietitian or nutritionist to create a personalized nutrition plan aligned with your lifestyle, dietary needs and goals.

Consistent nourishment supports not only your body's vitality but also your mental clarity, emotional balance and spiritual alignment.

Rest

Rest is not a luxury or a weakness, but a vital practice to access your most abundant energy. Adequate rest restores your mind, body and spirit, replenishing energy, supporting clarity and maintaining balance. By intentionally prioritizing rest, you cultivate vitality and resilience, allowing you to show up fully in every aspect of your life.

How to Practice Rest:

- **Mindful Pauses:** Schedule short moments throughout your day to pause and breathe deeply, even for a few minutes. Notice the shift in your energy and focus.
- **Quality Sleep:** Prioritize consistent, restorative sleep. Create an environment that supports deep rest, such as limiting screens before bed and maintaining a calm, dark sleeping space.

- **Restorative Activities:** Engage in practices that recharge your mind and body, such as naps, meditation, gentle yoga or Epsom salt baths. Pay attention to what helps you feel truly replenished.
- **Intentional Boundaries:** Set limits around work and obligations. Give yourself permission to step away without guilt, protecting your energy for what matters most.
- **Reflective Journaling:** Spend a few minutes journaling about how your rest impacts your mood, focus and overall well-being. Identify patterns or practices that help you recharge most effectively.
- **Celebrate Rest:** Shift your mindset to honor rest as a vital and productive practice. Recognize that prioritizing restoration enhances your energy, creativity and capacity for meaningful engagement.

Consistent practice transforms rest into a foundational habit, fostering sustained energy, clarity, resilience and a deeper connection to your overall sense of well-being and fulfillment.

Grounding

Grounding reconnects your mind and body to the present moment, fostering clarity, calm and resilience. It anchors awareness in the here and now, reducing stress and enhancing presence.

How to Practice Grounding:

- **Mindful Breathing:** Pause for a few deep breaths, focusing entirely on the sensations of air entering and leaving your body.
- **5-4-3-2-1 Sensory Check:** Identify five things you can see, four you can touch, three you can hear, two you can smell and one you can taste. This sensory awareness draws your mind into the present.

- **Nature Connection:** Spend time outdoors, intentionally noticing natural sights, sounds, textures and scents around you.
- **Body Scan:** Slowly bring attention to different parts of your body, noticing sensations without judgment.
- **Mindful Pause:** Throughout your day, pause for a moment to notice your surroundings, breath and bodily sensations.

Consistency in grounding practices strengthens your ability to remain present, cultivating emotional stability and enriching your experience of life.

Grounding in Nature

Grounding in nature is a powerful practice for realigning your energy and restoring inner balance. It is the act of consciously connecting your body to the Earth's natural frequency, allowing you to release excess energy, reduce stress and return to a state of calm presence. Walking barefoot on grass, sand or soil, also known as "earthing," helps regulate your nervous system, decrease inflammation and enhance overall well-being. This practice reminds you that you are not separate from nature but an integral part of its rhythm and intelligence. By grounding in nature, you align your energy in the present moment, cultivating stability, clarity and peace within yourself.

How to Practice Grounding in Nature:

- Spend time outdoors daily, ideally in direct contact with natural elements such as grass, sand, soil or stone. Walk barefoot when possible to deepen your connection with the Earth's surface energy.
- Sit or lie down on the ground, close your eyes and take slow, deep breaths. Visualize roots extending from your feet or base of your spine into the Earth, anchoring you in stability and calm.

- Practice mindful observation by noticing the sensations under your feet, the sound of leaves, the rhythm of the wind and the warmth of the sun. Allow your senses to fully immerse in the experience.
- Engage in grounding activities such as gardening, hiking, swimming in natural bodies of water or simply sitting under a tree while journaling or meditating.
- Disconnect from digital devices during your time in nature to allow your mind and body to recalibrate without external stimulation.
- Express gratitude to the Earth for its nourishment and stability, setting an intention to live in greater balance with its cycles.

Consistent grounding in nature strengthens your connection to the present moment, replenishes your life force energy and nurtures a deep sense of peace and belonging to the greater whole.

Mindful Movement

Mindful movement is the practice of intentionally engaging your body in ways that strengthen it, elevate energy and nurture well-being. It integrates physical activity with awareness, turning exercise into a form of self-care and energy alignment rather than mere physical exertion. Movement is a form of honoring your body's wisdom and maintaining the vitality necessary for abundance.

How to Practice Mindful Movement:

- Choose forms of movement you enjoy, whether walking, jogging, running, weightlifting, yoga or stretching.
- Create a balanced fitness routine that incorporates cardiovascular exercise for heart health and endurance and strength training for muscle tone, bone density and long-term vitality.

- Integrate movement into your day beyond formal workouts. Take the stairs instead of elevators, stretch during breaks or walk during calls.
- Pay attention to how movement affects your energy and mood and use that feedback to refine your practice.

Mindful movement strengthens your body, clears your mind and enhances your capacity for living in alignment with your purpose.

Connecting With Your Higher Self

Connecting with your higher self is a transformative practice that deepens self-awareness, grounds your choices and aligns you with your highest potential. The higher self is the wise, intuitive presence within, a guiding force that transcends fear, ego and limiting beliefs. It is your inner guidance, helping you navigate life with clarity, purpose and authenticity.

How to Practice Connecting With Your Higher Self:

- Create quiet time daily to listen inwardly without distraction. This could be through meditation, prayer or simple stillness.
- Notice moments when clarity arises spontaneously; these are signs your higher self is speaking.
- Observe emotions without judgment, allowing your higher self to guide you through challenges with compassion and perspective.
- Reflect regularly on your values and intentions to ensure they align with your deeper truth.

Connecting with your higher self nurtures inner wisdom and empowers you to live from a place of alignment and purpose.

Nurturing Your Inner Child

Nurturing your inner child is a practice of embracing vulnerability, creativity, joy and emotional truth. The inner child holds your earliest experiences of love, safety and wonder, and continues to influence your emotional life. By honoring this part of yourself, you heal wounds, reclaim innocence and reconnect with a deeper sense of aliveness.

How to Practice Nurturing Your Inner Child:

- Spend intentional time engaging in playful activities that spark joy such as art, music, dancing or unstructured creative expression.
- Listen deeply to emotional reactions and explore the unmet needs beneath them without self-criticism.
- Practice self-compassion, offering kindness and reassurance to yourself in moments of difficulty.
- Journal reflections on childhood memories, feelings and patterns that influence your present life.

By nurturing your inner child, you restore emotional vitality and deepen your connection to your authentic self.

Aligning With Your Intuition

Aligning with your intuition is the practice of trusting your inner knowing and letting it guide decisions, actions and creative expression. Intuition is the language of your higher self and inner child, a quiet, felt knowing that goes beyond logic. When cultivated, it becomes a powerful tool for navigating life in alignment with your essence.

How to Practice Aligning With Your Intuition:

- Develop mindfulness practices that quiet the mind, such as mindfulness meditation or conscious breathing, to hear intuitive guidance more clearly.
- Notice subtle physical sensations, emotional cues or creative impulses as signals from your inner self.
- Record intuitive insights in a journal and revisit them to deepen awareness of recurring patterns.
- Honor urges toward creativity, nature or service; they may be invitations from your higher self.

Intuition acts as a sacred guide, leading you toward choices aligned with your true path and purpose.

Solitude

Solitude is a deliberate practice of stepping away from external noise to connect deeply with yourself. Unlike loneliness and isolation, solitude is an empowering space for introspection, healing and communion with your higher self and inner child. It fosters clarity, emotional resilience and a deeper understanding of your essence.

How to Practice Solitude:

- Schedule regular periods of uninterrupted time where you can be alone with your thoughts and feelings.
- Use this time to meditate, journal or simply sit in stillness without distraction.
- Disconnect from digital devices to cultivate deeper inner awareness.

- Reflect on your life, values, desires and alignment with your highest vision.

Through solitude, you create space for profound inner connection and the emergence of intuitive guidance.

Exploring and Refining Your Beliefs

Belief systems are the mental frameworks through which we interpret the world. They are shaped by culture, experiences, values and emotions.

How to Practice Exploring and Refining Your Beliefs:

- Travel or engage with new communities to experience different viewpoints.
- Seek role models whose values and lifestyles inspire you.
- Read widely, explore spiritual traditions, philosophies or cultural practices.
- Reflect regularly on your evolving beliefs, allowing shifts to occur naturally.

These systems evolve over time. Opening yourself to diverse perspectives deepens understanding and strengthens authenticity.

Identifying Your Values

Values are guiding principles that shape your choices, actions and interactions. They reflect what matters most to you, influencing your priorities, relationships and sense of purpose. Shaped by your upbringing, culture, experiences and personal reflections, values can evolve over time.

How to Practice Identifying Your Values:

- **Ask Core Questions:** *What matters most to me?*
- **Categorize Life Areas:** Reflect on health, relationships, career and personal growth.
- **Rate Significance:** Evaluate which areas matter most and how they influence your choices.
- **Reflect on Impact:** For example, consider what a healthy lifestyle means to you or how trust and emotional safety influence your relationships.
- **Write it Down:** Journal your values and revisit them periodically to ensure alignment.

Living in alignment with your values fosters authenticity, clarity and a deeper sense of fulfillment.

Healing and Releasing

Healing and releasing is a transformative process that nurtures balance and clarity within your mind, body and soul. It allows you to let go of what no longer serves you, such as emotional pain, limiting beliefs and past trauma, and creates space for renewal, peace and deeper self-connection.

How to Practice Healing and Releasing:

- **Journaling for Release:** Write about emotional experiences, lingering thoughts or limiting beliefs you wish to transform. Reflect on what you feel and why, allowing emotions to surface without judgment.
- **Mindfulness Meditation:** Dedicate time daily or weekly to observe your thoughts and feelings with compassionate awareness, gently letting go of what arises without attachment.

- **Emotional Acknowledgment Rituals:** Sit quietly with feelings such as grief, anger or fear. Name them, honor them and consciously breathe them out.
- **Movement for Healing:** Use yoga, dancing, breathwork or expressive movement to release tension and stored emotion from your body.
- **Nature Immersion:** Spend mindful time outdoors, noticing sensations, sounds and sights that help you reconnect and release mental clutter.
- **Forgiveness and Surrender Practice:** Reflect on relationships or experiences that hold emotional charge and intentionally release through affirmations, prayer or visualization.
- **Self-Compassion Exercises:** Speak kindly to yourself through affirmations such as "*I am healing with patience and grace*" or "*I release what no longer serves my highest good.*"

Consistency transforms healing and releasing into a conscious way of being, creating a foundation for lasting inner peace, clarity and personal transformation.

Harnessing Your Core Power

Harnessing your core power is a transformative practice that deepens self-awareness, builds resilience and strengthens confidence. It empowers you to leverage your strengths while intentionally growing in areas that support your evolution.

How to Harness Your Core Power:

- **Identify Strengths:** Write down your top five strengths, such as resilience, adaptability, emotional intelligence, empathy or leadership. Reflect on how these empower you.

- **Leverage Strengths:** Strategically apply your strengths to achieve goals, overcome challenges and deepen your sense of empowerment.
- **Identify Areas for Growth:** List your top five developmental areas, such as self-doubt, fear of failure, lack of resilience, emotional intelligence or empathy.
- **Develop Growth Strategies:** For each area, take actionable steps: practice affirmations, reframe challenges, embrace risk, build resilience, develop emotional awareness and cultivate compassion.
- **Set Small Goals:** Break larger aspirations into manageable milestones to maintain momentum and avoid overwhelm.
- **Self-Reflection:** Regularly pause to evaluate your progress, recalibrate your approach and celebrate your growth.
- **Affirmations:** Use affirmations such as "*I trust my strengths to guide me forward*" or "*I am growing stronger every day.*"

Consistency in harnessing your core power transforms self-awareness into sustained empowerment, fostering alignment with your true essence and life purpose.

Awakening Your Inner Voice

Awakening your inner voice is a practice of deep self-connection that strengthens intuition, clarity and authenticity. It helps you align choices with your highest self and live with purpose.

How to Awaken Your Inner Voice:

- **Seek Stillness:** Create quiet space through meditation, solitude or mindful breathing to tune into your inner guidance.

- **Practice Self-Reflection:** Journal or engage in self-dialogue to explore your thoughts, feelings and instincts.
- **Listen and Validate:** Trust your intuition as a source of clarity. Affirm your inner voice with statements such as "*I trust my inner guidance to lead me with clarity.*"
- **Set Boundaries:** Practice saying no when necessary to honor your inner truth and maintain alignment with your values.
- **Engage Creativity:** Use visualization, creative expression or mindful daydreaming to access deeper insights and inspiration.
- **Act With Integrity:** Let your choices reflect your authentic self and align with your inner wisdom.

Consistency in listening to and trusting your inner voice strengthens your connection to your true essence, guiding you toward a life of authenticity, confidence and fulfillment.

Energy Alignment

Energy shapes your reality. Low vibrations, marked by fear, anger, sadness or anxiety, drain your vitality and attract resistance. High vibrations, rooted in joy, gratitude, love and clarity, empower you to align with your purpose and manifest your desires. Conscious energy management transforms your inner state and life experiences.

How to Align Your Energy:

- **Reframe Challenges:** View setbacks as opportunities for growth. Ask yourself, "*What lesson can I learn here?*" to shift your perspective and raise your vibration.
- **Practice Daily Gratitude:** Keep a gratitude journal or verbally express thanks each day to nurture joy and abundance.

- **Use Empowering Affirmations:** Repeat statements aligned with your values, e.g., "*I radiate love and abundance*" or "*I am grounded in my highest purpose.*"
- **Engage in Acts of Kindness:** Offer generosity and compassion; these ripple outward, elevating your energy and that of others.
- **Tune Into Your Body:** Nourish yourself with healthy food, movement, rest and mindful breathing to sustain high vibration.
- **Connect With Your Inner Self:** Spend time in solitude, meditation or creative expression to strengthen intuitive guidance.

Consistency with these practices transforms energy alignment into a way of being, one that fosters resilience, balance and a life deeply aligned with your essence and highest aspirations.

Presence

Being present anchors you in peace, clarity and authenticity. It frees you from the weight of the past and the pull of future anxieties, allowing you to fully engage with life as it unfolds. Presence transforms ordinary moments into opportunities for growth, joy and deeper connection.

How to Practice Presence:

- **Mindful Breathing:** Pause daily to take slow, deep breaths, focusing entirely on the sensations of each inhale and exhale to center yourself in the moment.
- **Single-Task Focus:** Choose one activity, whether working, eating or exercising, and give it your full attention, releasing distractions.
- **Body Awareness:** Notice physical sensations, posture or tension during everyday activities to ground yourself in the here and now.

- **Sensory Engagement:** During a walk, consciously notice sounds, textures, scents and visuals, fully immersing yourself in your surroundings.
- **Creative Immersion:** Engage in activities like writing, art or music with total focus, losing track of time, in *flow*, and immersing completely in the process.
- **Gratitude in the Moment:** Pause periodically during your day to acknowledge something you appreciate in the present, however small.

Presence is a muscle; the more consistently you practice it, the deeper your ability to live fully in each moment, creating a foundation for peace, clarity and intentional living.

Non-Attachment

Non-attachment frees you from being overly consumed by past regrets, future worries or expectations. It creates openness, inner peace and acceptance of the present moment as it is.

How to Practice Non-Attachment:

- **Acceptance Reflection:** Notice when you cling to a particular outcome or idea. Pause, acknowledge it and consciously choose to release the grip without judgment.
- **Letting Go Ritual:** At the end of each day, write down any worries, frustrations or attachments you wish to release, and symbolically set them aside.
- **Mindful Observation:** Watch your thoughts and emotions as if they were clouds passing by, without identifying with or resisting them.

- **Affirmations:** Use phrases such as "*I let go of what I cannot control*" or "*I accept this moment as it is.*"
- **Practice Flexibility:** Consciously adjust your expectations and plans when circumstances shift, welcoming uncertainty as part of life's flow.

Through regular practice of non-attachment, you open the door to deeper presence, greater joy and a sustained sense of freedom.

Journaling

Journaling is a sacred act of stillness that reconnects you to yourself. It offers space to slow down, turn inward and remember who you truly are. This practice cultivates self-awareness, emotional clarity and spiritual alignment, grounding you in the present while connecting you to something greater. Over time, it builds a resilient foundation for navigating life with intention, clarity and grace.

How to Practice Journaling:

- **Daily or Weekly Reflection:** Set aside time each day or week to write freely about your thoughts, feelings and experiences without self-judgment.
- **Sacred Space:** Choose a quiet, comfortable space where you feel safe to write and reflect. Add an element that feels sacred: a candle, a meaningful object or a cup of tea.
- **Guided Prompts:** Use prompts such as, "*What am I grateful for today?*" or "*What lessons is life inviting me to learn right now?*" to deepen your reflection.
- **Intention Setting:** Begin each journaling session by setting an intention for clarity, growth or insight.

- **Release and Integrate:** End by noting any insights, lessons or actions to integrate into your life, then close your journal with gratitude.

Consistency transforms journaling from a task into a sacred ritual, turning your reflections into a powerful practice for self-discovery and spiritual growth.

Identifying Your Ikigai

Identifying your Ikigai is a reflective process that helps you uncover your life's deeper purpose by connecting your passions, strengths, values and contributions. This practice brings clarity, balance and a sense of meaning, grounding your actions in intentional living while connecting you to something greater. Over time, it cultivates deeper self-awareness and empowers you to live in alignment with your truest calling.

How to Practice Identifying Your Ikigai:

- **Regular Reflection:** Set aside time daily or weekly to reflect on your passions, strengths, values and what you feel called to contribute. Write freely without judgment.
- **Sacred Space:** Choose a quiet, comfortable space where you feel safe to explore your inner world. Add an element that inspires you: a candle, soft music or a meaningful object.
- **Guided Prompts:** Use prompts such as:
  - "*What brings me joy and fulfillment?*"
  - "*What am I naturally good at?*"
  - "*How can I use my strengths to serve others?*"
  - "*What does the world need that I can give?*"

- **Map Your Ikigai:** Consider the intersection of your passions, strengths, mission and vocation. This is your Ikigai: the North Star of your purpose.
- **Integration and Intention:** Summarize your reflections into a concise personal mission statement or intention. Place it somewhere visible to guide your daily choices.

Consistency transforms identifying your Ikigai from an occasional reflection into an ongoing ritual, turning self-discovery into a living, evolving practice for purposeful and fulfilling living.

Identifying Your Talents and Passions

Identifying your talents and passions is a vital step toward uncovering your Ikigai. It lays the foundation for a life rooted in abundance, fulfillment and personal mastery. When you align with what energizes you and utilizes your strengths, life gains clarity and purpose. This connection fuels joy, generosity and compassion, guiding you toward living your most authentic life.

How to Practice Identifying Your Talents and Passions:

- **Dedicated Reflection:** Set aside quiet time to explore your skills, interests and the activities that bring you joy. Write freely without judgment.
- **Guided Prompts:** Ask yourself:
    - *"What activities bring me joy in my free time?"*
    - *"Which tasks or hobbies am I naturally drawn to?"*
    - *"When do I feel most fulfilled and engaged?"*
    - *"What am I naturally skilled at?"*
    - *"What accomplishments am I most proud of?"*

- **Create a Talents and Passions List:** Note hobbies, activities or causes that inspire you deeply, whether creative, physical, intellectual or altruistic.
- **Seek Feedback:** Ask 3-5 trusted people for insights into your strengths and notable achievements. We all have blindspots. Others can see talents you may overlook.
- **Experiment:** Step outside your comfort zone to try new projects, hobbies or roles. This expands your awareness of potential passions and strengths.
- **Track Flow Moments:** For two weeks, notice when you lose track of time because you are fully immersed. Reflect on what skills and passions these moments reveal.
- **Draw Inspiration:** For ideas and motivation, study the journeys of role models who have transformed their talents into purpose-driven pursuits.

Consistency transforms this exploration from a one-time reflection into an ongoing practice. Over time, you will gain clarity on what truly lights you up and how to integrate it into your life for deeper meaning and alignment.

Creating Your Mission Statement

A mission statement is a powerful declaration of your purpose: a governing force that reflects your deepest values, strengths, passions and aspirations. It serves as a daily reminder of who you are and what you aim to contribute to the world, helping you live with clarity, alignment and intentionality.

How to Create Your Mission Statement:

- **Reflect on Your Values and Passions:** Spend intentional time exploring what matters most to you. Ask yourself:
    - "*What brings me joy?*"
    - "*What principles guide my life?*"
    - "*What activities energize me most?*"
- **Identify Your Strengths and Skills:** List your natural talents and abilities. Consider:
    - "*What am I most proud of accomplishing?*"
    - "*What comes naturally to me?*"
    - "*What strengths do others notice in me?*"
- **Define Your Contribution:** Clarify how you want to serve others and make a difference. Ask:
    - "*What needs in the world resonate with me?*"
    - "*How can I apply my strengths to meet these needs?*"
- **Articulate Your Purpose:** Combine your insights to define your unique mission. Focus on the intersection of:
    - Passion: what you love to do
    - Vocation: what you excel at
    - Mission: what the world needs
    - Profession: what fulfills you
- **Draft Your Statement:** Write a concise, clear and inspiring statement that expresses your purpose. Example:

"*Through mindful creativity and compassionate action, I inspire others to live intentionally and contribute to the greater good.*"

- **Refine and Commit:** Seek feedback from trusted friends or mentors. Refine your statement until it resonates deeply. Place it somewhere visible and revisit it regularly to ensure your actions align with it.

Consistency transforms mission crafting from a task into a transformative practice, one that deepens self-awareness, strengthens your alignment and anchors you in a life of purpose.

Ego-Transcendence

Transcending the ego is a transformative process that fosters deeper empathy, compassion, authentic connection and a life aligned with greater purpose. It allows you to move beyond self-centered motivations toward a mindset rooted in service, humility and unity.

How to Practice Ego-Transcendence:

- **Daily Ego Awareness:** Spend 10 minutes journaling about moments when ego influenced your thoughts or actions. Reflect on how these moments affected your relationships, decisions and sense of purpose.
- **Mindfulness of Empathy:** Dedicate 10–15 minutes daily to a mindfulness meditation focused on empathy. Visualize yourself in another's position, acknowledge their experience and set aside ego-driven barriers to deepen compassion.
- **Acts of Service:** Engage in regular acts of service or volunteer work. Afterwards, reflect on how the experience shifted your focus from self-interest to contributing to the greater good.
- **Vulnerability Practice:** Share honestly with a trusted person about your fears, desires or imperfections. Notice how openness fosters deeper connection and dissolves ego defenses.

- **Reflective Solitude:** Spend quiet time in introspection or meditation, observing your thoughts without judgment. Notice ego-driven patterns and gently let them go.

Consistency transforms ego transcendence from a conscious act into a natural orientation, cultivating humility, compassion, authentic connection and alignment with a higher purpose.

Contribution

Meaningful contribution is a purposeful act of service that nurtures connection, strengthens community and aligns your life with a greater good. Small, mindful actions, done consistently, create ripples of positive change that extend far beyond what you can see.

How to Practice Contribution:

- **Mindful Daily Choices:** Identify one daily decision that impacts others, such as how you commute, what you consume or how you speak to people, and evaluate its alignment with your values. Adjust it to enhance your positive impact without compromising your own well-being.
- **Acts of Kindness:** Engage in small acts of compassion: help a neighbor, offer a sincere compliment or listen deeply to someone who needs support. Notice how these moments deepen connection.
- **Sustainable Giving:** Choose ways to contribute that balance your energy and resources, whether through volunteering, supporting local businesses or donating to causes aligned with your values.
- **Reflective Journaling:** Spend 10 minutes journaling about a recent act of contribution. Reflect on its effects on both others

and yourself, and consider how you might continue giving in ways that nurture mutual benefit.

- **Boundary Awareness:** Set healthy limits around giving. Reflect regularly on how to sustain your ability to contribute without exhausting yourself, ensuring your acts of kindness remain joyful and meaningful.

Consistent practice transforms contribution into a way of life, fostering empathy, connection, joy and a sense of purpose that enriches both your life and the lives of those around you.

Teachable Moments

Embodying Gratitude

Gratitude is more than words, spoken or written. It is a state of being that can be expressed through actions, presence and awareness. True embodiment of gratitude transforms how we experience life, shaping our thoughts, behaviors and interactions with others. When we move beyond merely saying "*thank you*," we allow gratitude to become a *living practice*: noticing the small joys, offering kindness without expectation and aligning our choices with appreciation. In this way, gratitude shifts from a concept to a way of life, cultivating a deeper sense of abundance, fulfillment and connection.

The Balance Between Adaptability and Authenticity

It is important to understand that adapting to different situations or roles does not mean you are being false. Human beings are naturally fluid and adaptable, and much of this flexibility is healthy and essential for navigating life. You might be more animated and outgoing at work, more playful with your children or more reflective and analytical with a close friend or partner. These shifts in expression are not betrayals of your true self; they are reflections of your versatility.

What remains constant, even as your outward personality adjusts, are your core values, moral compass and inner integrity. The distinction lies in *intention*: when adaptation is rooted in clarity and alignment with your essence, it enhances connection, understanding and personal growth. When adaptation hardens into a mask, suppressing your true feelings, denying your needs or seeking only approval, it drifts into the territory of the false self.

Authenticity is not the absence of adaptability. Rather, it is the awareness of when you are adapting in a way that aligns with your essence, and when you are hiding behind a façade that disconnects you from it. Recognizing this difference is key to living a life of integrity, connection and self-respect.

The Practice of Love

Although love is our birthright, it does not always come easily. Just as we are biologically hardwired to seek companionship and community for survival, we are also deeply driven to pursue love and connection, both with others and within ourselves. This impulse, genetically encoded and fundamental to our existence, can feel challenging, vulnerable or even uncomfortable for many, especially when past wounds, fear or mistrust shape the way we connect.

This too is part of the human journey. Loving, including loving yourself, is not always instinctive; it is a practice that unfolds and deepens over time. Be gentle and patient with yourself if expressing, receiving or believing you are worthy of love feels difficult or unfamiliar.

Like a muscle, the art of loving, both yourself and others, strengthens with consistent care and intention. The more you nurture it, the more effortless it becomes, unfolding into a quiet ease that nourishes your life and the lives of those around you.

When you embody self-love and express love in every facet of your life, you naturally radiate an aura of abundant energy. Moving with love as your guiding force cultivates a profound sense of joy, inner tranquility and wholeness that cannot be matched.

The Power of Speaking Your Affirmations Out Loud

Many people underestimate the impact of speaking affirmations aloud. Often, affirmations are written in a journal or repeated silently in the mind but speaking them audibly creates a deeper energetic shift. Saying your affirmation out loud (not shouting or straining, just mouthing it clearly in your natural voice) engages mind, body and soul, anchoring your intention through the body. This vocal expression acts as a kinetic trigger, aligning your energy with the vibration of your affirmation. When spoken aloud, affirmations do more than exist as thoughts; they become a statement of alignment, syncing you with the flow of universal synchronicity and opening the pathway for manifestation.

Beyond Material Wealth

It is important to recognize that having financial resources or material assets does not preclude someone from experiencing true abundance and fulfillment. Our focus, however, is on challenging the common, oversimplified belief that abundance is defined solely by money, possessions or career achievements. Modern perspectives often encourage this narrow view, leading many to overlook the deeper, more meaningful paths to genuine abundance, paths rooted in connection, purpose, joy and alignment with something greater than oneself. True fulfillment emerges not just from what we have, but from how we live and experience life.

The Value of Sacred Practices

The true power of sacred practices lies not in perfection or rigid daily adherence, but in the intentional integration of these practices into your life through a consistent framework. It is the system, the structure and the alignment you create around your practice that sustains growth, awareness and transformation over time.

Example: Imagine someone who sets aside time each morning for meditation. Some days they meditate for twenty minutes, other days only five and occasionally they skip a day entirely. The focus is not on perfect consistency; it is on having a framework, a dedicated time, a space and a habit of returning to the practice, that ensures meditation remains a meaningful and accessible part of their life. Over weeks and months, the benefits compound, even without perfection.

While the importance of sacred practices is evident, it is equally important to recognize that strict adherence is not required. If you happen to miss a day of yoga, exercise or meditation, grant yourself grace and self-compassion. What truly matters is maintaining consistency over time, cultivating a system you can return to, rather than striving for perfection in every single instance.

Glossary

Abundance

Abundance is the conscious recognition that there is more than enough... of love, resources, opportunities and life itself. It is a state of being and energy where gratitude replaces fear, and openness replaces limitation. Abundance is not only about external wealth but an inner orientation of generosity, trust and alignment with the flow of the Universe.

Alchemist

A person who consciously transforms their inner self, awareness and life experiences through intention, insight and alignment of mind, body and spirit, transmuting challenges into opportunities for growth and personal evolution.

Ascend

To rise, move upward or progress to a higher level, state or position. In spiritual or personal development contexts, it often refers to elevating one's consciousness, awareness or sense of self toward greater clarity, understanding and fulfillment. For example: Through mindfulness meditation and self-reflection, one can ascend to a higher state of inner peace and insight.

Awakening

Awakening is the gradual or sudden shift in awareness where you begin to see reality beyond conditioned beliefs, egoic identity and habitual patterns. It is the opening of consciousness to deeper truth, a recognition of interconnectedness, presence and the essence of who you truly are. Awakening is not a destination but an evolving state of expanded awareness and clarity.

Collective Consciousness

Collective consciousness is the shared field of awareness that connects all minds and beings. It is not about uniform belief or thought, but the recognition of an interconnected mental and emotional web that binds humanity. At its highest form, collective consciousness fosters empathy, unity and compassion, enabling humanity to perceive truth beyond personal ego and judgment, and to act in alignment with the greater whole.

Collectivist

A collectivist perspective values the group over the individual, emphasizing shared identity, interdependence and collective well-being. It reflects the understanding that human life is interconnected through mutual cooperation and shared purpose, without requiring conformity of thought or belief. Collectivism highlights the strength of community and the wisdom found in shared responsibility.

Consciousness

Consciousness is the state of being aware of yourself, your thoughts, emotions and surroundings. It is the living awareness that allows you to experience reality, perceive meaning and make choices. Beyond mere awareness, consciousness is the underlying presence that connects all experience, bridging the personal and the universal, the seen and the unseen. It is both the observer and the experience itself.

Default Mode Network (DMN)

A network of interconnected brain regions that becomes active during rest, introspection or self-referential thought, such as daydreaming, reflecting on the past or imagining the future. The DMN is associated with mind-wandering, internal awareness and the processing of personal memories and emotions.

Duality

Duality is the experience of life in complementary opposites, light and dark, joy and sorrow, abundance and scarcity. It reflects the human condition of perceiving reality through contrast, and the potential for transcending it by recognizing the oneness behind all polarities.

Enlightenment

Enlightenment is a profound state of being in which the illusion of separation dissolves, and the mind rests in unity, peace and absolute clarity. It is the embodiment of truth beyond ego, where knowledge is not intellectual but experiential, a living awareness of oneness, unconditional love and boundless freedom. Enlightenment is both the awakening to and the living of your highest self.

Esoteric

Esoteric describes knowledge, teachings or practices that are intended for or likely to be understood by only a small, specialized group of people with specific interest or expertise. It often implies something hidden, secret or not easily accessible to the general public. For example: The philosopher's writings were highly esoteric, understood only by a handful of scholars.

Fulfillment

Fulfillment is a profound sense of joy and satisfaction that arises from living in alignment with your beliefs, values, purpose and passions. It occurs when your external reality reflects your deepest desires and needs, creating a lasting sense of wholeness, peace and meaning.

Growth Mindset

A growth mindset is the belief that abilities, intelligence and circumstances are not fixed but can evolve through effort, learning and openness. It is the choice to view challenges as opportunities, setbacks as lessons and life itself as an unfolding journey of personal evolution.

High Vibrations

High vibrations are emotional and energetic states rooted in love, joy, gratitude and alignment with your true essence. These states include peace, compassion, creativity and openness. High vibrations expand perception, foster harmony and attract experiences that reflect abundance, growth and wellbeing. They are the energetic frequency that aligns you with your highest potential and the flow of the Universe.

Inherent

Inherent describes something that is inseparable from the essence of another thing, a natural, built-in part of its existence. Change, for example, is inherent to life, not an exception but the foundation of living. To understand what is inherent is to recognize the unalterable truths of existence.

Individualistic

Individualistic describes a perspective that emphasizes personal autonomy, self-expression and independence. It values the unique identity, choices and freedom of the individual over group consensus.

Being individualistic is not about isolation, but about honoring one's distinct path while engaging with the world in authentic and intentional ways. Individualism highlights the power of personal responsibility and the importance of living in alignment with one's own truth.

Introspection

Introspection is the practice of turning inward to reflect deeply on your thoughts, feelings and experiences. It fosters self-awareness by evaluating how insights align with your current life, uncovering your true desires and motivations, and identifying opportunities for growth. Introspection ensures that your actions remain aligned with your essence and purpose.

Low Vibrations

Low vibrations are emotional states grounded in fear, resistance and limitation. These states include anxiety, doubt, anger, resentment and insecurity. They restrict perception and manifest outcomes aligned with lack. Raising your vibration shifts your emotional state toward joy, openness and creative flow.

Metacognition

Metacognition is the art of stepping outside your thoughts to observe them. It is the conscious awareness of how you think, learn and process information. More than self-reflection, it is a skill, a mental lens, that allows you to regulate your thinking, shift perspectives and adapt strategies to align with higher clarity and deeper wisdom.

Non-Attachment

Non-attachment is the ability to fully engage in life without clinging to outcomes, identities or possessions. It is freedom from dependency on external validation or fixed expectations, allowing one to experience life with openness, flow and peace.

Reframing

Reframing is the conscious act of shifting perspective to change the meaning of an experience. It transforms challenges into opportunities, limitations into lessons and fear into growth. Reframing is not denial of reality; it is a skillful re-interpretation that empowers and expands possibility.

Scarcity

Scarcity is the state of perceiving life through lack...of resources, love, time or possibility. It is an energy of limitation, rooted in fear, that shapes decisions and beliefs. Moving beyond scarcity requires shifting perception to one of abundance, where possibility and gratitude replace fear and limitation.

Spiritual Intelligence

Spiritual intelligence is the capacity to access deeper meaning, purpose and connection beyond the material world. It blends awareness, intuition, empathy and wisdom to guide life decisions aligned with higher values and universal truths.

Spirituality

Spirituality is the exploration and experience of connection to something greater than the individual self, whether understood as the Universe, divine presence or the deeper essence within. It emphasizes inner growth, meaning and alignment with truth, love and purpose. Unlike organized religion, spirituality is not confined to dogma or tradition; it is a deeply personal and continuous journey of awakening, self-discovery and integration with the flow of life.

Transcendence

Transcendence is the movement beyond ordinary perception and limitation, rising above egoic thinking to a state of unity, peace and expanded consciousness. It is an awakening to the interconnectedness of all life.

Transcending Ego

Transcending ego is the conscious shift from self-centered identity to a state of unity and openness. It is the practice of releasing the need for control, validation or separation and embracing a perspective rooted in authenticity, compassion and higher awareness.

Unparalleled

Unparalleled describes something without equal, unique in quality, depth or experience. It is the state of being distinctively exceptional, beyond comparison or competition.

Utility

Utility is the practical value or purpose of something, describing how it serves a meaningful function. In language and thought, utility is reflected in the power of words and ideas to bring clarity, inspire action and align intention with desired outcomes.

Phraseology

Abundance is not something you chase; it is something you choose (Epigraph).

The journey toward reclaiming authenticity, abundance and fulfillment often requires confronting vulnerabilities, transcending societal norms and pursuing a transformative path of self-discovery (Preface).

There is no gift more invaluable than strengthening the bond between yourself and your soul (Preface).

May you realize, today and always, that you have everything within you to ***decide, now*** to live a life of unadulterated abundance and fulfillment (Preface).

The pathway to abundance and fulfillment unfolds from a conscious decision, a deliberate choice echoing with immediacy (Introduction).

Abundance lives within you, waiting to be awakened and gracefully infused into your life the moment you decide to align with it (Chapter 1: The Core Principles of Abundance).

When our lives draw to a close, the true measure of success will be the love we have given and received in our lifetime (Insights — Love and Connection).

Falling in love with your life's purpose can be an unparalleled union, especially if you navigate it with love, intentionality and dedication (Insights — Love and Connection).

Think of growth and evolution as a dove, soaring high into the sky, reaching destinations beyond the naked eye, uncaged and liberated (Insights — Growth and Evolution).

Our minds function as conduits for the flow of thoughts rather than authoritative judges of reality (Insights — Achieving Self-Awareness).

A resilient and optimistic mindset establishes the foundation for an abundant and fulfilling life and acts as the driving force behind more deliberate and impactful actions (Integration — Cultivating A Healthy Mind).

The more we connect with our essence, the more naturally we feel moved to create ripples of healing and evolution beyond ourselves (Insights — Your Intuition).

Our value system is a vital filter, connecting us with individuals and circumstances that align with our deepest beliefs (Insights and Integration — Belief Systems and Values).

Personal growth and understanding often emerge through lived experience, reflection and attunement to the deeper currents of life (Insights — Self-Experience (Lived Experience).

Individuals who exhibit consciousness and self-awareness demonstrate a profound capacity for spiritual intelligence, reflecting a deep understanding of their inner truths, beliefs, values and life purpose (Insights — Spirituality and Spiritual Intelligence).

The more regulated your nervous system becomes, the greater your capacity to hold higher frequencies: love, joy, creativity and abundance (Insights and Integration — Healing and Releasing).

True restoration of balance in mind, body and spirit does not come through bypassing pain, but by bravely moving through it (Insights and Integration — Healing and Releasing).

Embrace the journey and find fulfillment in the progress you make, rather than solely focusing on the final outcome or destination. It is not about the tangible achievement itself but rather the transformation you undergo throughout your evolutionary journey. It is about who you become in the process that holds the most value (Insights and Integration — Self-Empowerment | Harnessing Your Core Power).

Gratitude reaches its fullest potential from fully living and breathing it in every moment (Integration — Energy).

Abundance is not a distant aspiration but a conscious decision to embody it now, through the energy you hold, the beliefs you affirm and the way you show up in the world (Chapter 4: The Abundance Pillars – Mastering Your Life and Collective Consciousness).

Through building resilient trust in the innate abundance within you, you come to realize that everything essential for a rich and fulfilling life is already within your reach (Insights — Redefining the Concept of Wealth and Abundance).

As we make presence a central practice in our daily lives, we reveal the transformative potential to navigate each moment with grace and purpose, ultimately enriching our lived experience and deepening our engagement with the essence of our being (Integration – The Value of Being Present).

True fulfillment emerges from the daily efforts and intentional habits nurtured throughout the journey. Finding fulfillment each day means recognizing that joy does not wait at the end but is found in embracing each moment of the process, where real growth and transformation occur (Insights — Finding Fulfillment Each Day).

By carefully curating what enters your life, you can foster a deeper appreciation and gratitude for everything you possess, in all aspects of your life (Insights — Simple Living).

The more you release what no longer supports your growth, the more space you open for what truly resonates with your values, purpose and highest self. Letting go clears the path for the energy needed to welcome what genuinely belongs in your life, physically and spiritually (Insights — Simple Living).

Fulfillment is not a distant destination but a lived experience, shaped moment by moment through perseverance, conscious choice and unwavering alignment with your core values (Insights and Integration — Embody Your Purpose-Driven Life).

Collective consciousness, the shared awareness and mindset that unites individuals and shapes their experiences, along with living a life of utility, contribution and connection, is a cornerstone of genuine abundance and fulfillment, providing a sense of purpose that transcends personal gain and self-gratification (Insights and Integration — Transcending the Ego).

To live in alignment with collective consciousness, contribution and genuine connection, we must learn to rise above the ego's need for control and validation (Insights and Integration — Transcending the Ego).

Once you transcend your ego, you find yourself more in alignment with your ideal, purpose-driven life (Insights and Integration — Transcending the Ego).

When we show up with intention and create positive change in how we live, connect and contribute, we help shape a stronger, healthier and more joyful world for both those around us today and for future generations (Insights — Contribution).

Self-love becomes the standard by which we measure the love we offer and accept, elevating the depth and quality of every connection in our lives (Insights — Love and Connection (Recap).

Always remember, the richest, most vibrant grass is not found in distant fields; it blooms where you water it with your presence, attention and love. True love is not built in a rush; it evolves and deepens through the experiences you share, the patience, compassion and bravery you show during challenging conversations, the joy you find in each other's successes and the unwavering commitment to each other's growth and evolution. Every moment, every word and every act of kindness and understanding intertwines a bond that grows stronger and more resilient over time. When you put your heart and effort into caring for your relationship, you will see it grow into something strong and beautiful, a bond full of love and connection that is capable of persevering through tough times and thriving in the warmth you both create together (Insights and Integration — Your Life Partner).

You are a creator with the innate power to shape your reality according to your deepest desires. Within you lies the tools you need to create the life you have always envisioned (Insights — Sustaining Abundance: Co-Creation).

You master abundance and fulfillment not by reaching a final destination, but by waking up to the truth that each day is an opportunity, to be of service, to make meaningful connections, to find joy, to give and receive love (Conclusion).

References

Covey, Stephen R. *The 7 Habits of Highly Effective People: Powerful Lessons in Personal Change*. New York: Free Press, 1989.

Hawkins, David R. *Letting Go: The Pathway of Surrender*. Carlsbad, CA: Hay House, 2012.

Jung, Carl G. *The Archetypes and the Collective Unconscious*. 2nd ed. Princeton, NJ: Princeton University Press, 1968.

The Holy Bible. English Standard Version. Wheaton, IL: Crossway, 2001. Luke 12:15.

Tolle, Eckhart. *The Power of Now: A Guide to Spiritual Enlightenment*. Novato, CA: New World Library, 1999.

Tolle, Eckhart. "Where Do Our Thoughts Come From?" YouTube video, November 17, 2011. https://youtu.be/rWFVi1cPUZo

About The Author: A Journey to Abundance

In the world of personal development and conscious living, Julia Young Sandrock is a life and wellness coach, author and creator of **The Fulfillment Framework™**, a mind–body–soul methodology for conscious living and abundance. Driven by a deep passion for supporting others in reaching their fullest potential, Julia's work bridges spiritual insight, somatic awareness and practical integration to support lasting transformation.

Guided by an early fascination with the interconnectedness of mind, body and spirit, Julia immersed herself in both ancient spiritual traditions and modern scientific research on consciousness and well-being, bridging intuitive wisdom with evidence-based insight. She is a Certified Wellness Coach and certified in Somatic Reprocessing, an accredited mind–body therapeutic approach that supports trauma healing, nervous system regulation and the resolution of chronic stress and emotional patterns stored in the body. This somatic foundation allows her to guide individuals not only through mindset shifts, but through embodied healing, helping clients reconnect with their innate intelligence, resilience and capacity for restoration.

Grounded in both lived experience and professional training, Julia is on a purpose-driven path to share her intuitive wisdom with others. Through her writing, consciously curated spaces designed to foster presence and safety, and one-on-one coaching, she guides individuals toward abundance and fulfillment, a journey she believes begins with a conscious decision and a powerful act of self-love.

Julia's philosophy centers on the belief that abundance is not a fleeting feeling, but a practice, a lifestyle, and a state of consciousness. She teaches that mindset and nervous system health form the foundation of all other aspects of life, empowering individuals to work skillfully with their thoughts, beliefs, intentions, energy and embodied responses to cultivate joy, safety and fulfillment in everyday life.

Connect with Julia on Instagram **@juliasandrock** or learn more at **juliasandrock.com.**

www.ingramcontent.com/pod-product-compliance
Ingram Content Group UK Ltd.
Pitfield, Milton Keynes, MK11 3LW, UK
UKHW062300290726
14090UKWH00017B/794

9 781960 346902